REDEFINING MOTHERHOOD
CHANGING IDENTITIES AND PATTERNS

D1213786

WOMEN'S ISSUES PUBLISHING PROGRAM
SECOND STORY PRESS

REDEFINING MOTHERHOOD

CHANGING IDENTITIES AND PATTERNS

Edited by

Sharon Abbey

&

Andrea O'Reilly

WOMEN'S ISSUES PUBLISHING PROGRAM
SECOND STORY PRESS

SERIES EDITOR: BETH MCAULEY

For our mothers and foremothers
who have deepened our roots and made a difference.

Beryl
Hannah
Helen
Jean

CANADIAN CATALOGUING IN PUBLICATION DATA

Main entry under title:
Redefining Motherhood : changing identities and patterns

Includes bibliographical references.
ISBN 1-896764-06-1

1. Motherhood. 2. Mothers and daughters.
I. Abbey, Sharon. II. O'Reilly, Andrea, 1961– .

HQ759.R42 1998   306.874'3   C98-930970-3

Edited by Beth McAuley

Copyright © 1998 by Sharon Abbey and Andrea O'Reilly

Front Cover: Original monoprint "The Eternal Round" by Vicki Cowan

Second Story Press gratefully acknowledges the assistance of the Ontario Arts
Council and the Canada Council for the Arts for our publishing program.
We acknowledge the financial support of the Government of Canada
through the Book Publishing Industry Development Program for our publishing activities.
Second Story Press acknowledges the financial support of the Government of Canada
through the Canadian Studies Program, (Department of) Canadian Heritage.

Printed in Canada on acid-free, recycled paper

Published by
SECOND STORY PRESS
720 Bathurst Street, Suite 301
Toronto, Ontario
M5S 2R4

M/Other

Rishma Dunlop

The shattering of difference like an entrance into fiction.
An active bliss of rupture.
— NICOLE BROSSARD, "These Our Mothers"

The f/act of m/other
contains us in differences
yet we are pulled
by the heart's tides
the pulses of our children's veins
the salt of their tears
the radiance of their laughter

we grow up knowing
bittersweet symphonies
body-memories
of blood and milk
the consciousness of
the precarious cadences
in the disordered music of love

and everywhere
mothers write stories
of sons and daughters
this one will be fierce
this one will be tender

and they will sing
terrifying, beautiful prophets
for the world

in the gaps between our words
our children's voices pull us
relentless magnets
anchoring us
to the earth.

CONTENTS

ACKNOWLEDGEMENTS

THE AUTHORS WISH to thank the many people at the Centre for Feminist Research at York University who helped make possible the conference from which the idea of this book emerged, including Brenda Cranney, Jaskiran Dhillon, Cheryl Dobinson, Lara Karaian, Charlene Kish, Lisa Rundle, Lily Gilbert and Marlene Richman. In particular, we are deeply indebted to Dr. Nancy Mandell, director of the Centre for Feminist Research, for her initial vision of the conference as well as her characteristic energy, enthusiasm, encouragement and expertise. We also thank the Social Science and Humanities Research Council of Canada for their financial assistance for the conference. We are grateful to Second Story Press for their interest, vision and belief in this project. Our editor and patient guiding force Beth McAuley was invaluable for her ability to edit for clarity, focus and substance. Most of all, we want to thank the contributors for trusting us enough to take this journey with us, for working so diligently and co-operatively to meet demanding time-lines, for sharing their insights and experiences so honestly with words and poems, and especially for celebrating such a rich diversity of motherhood possibilities.

We also want to acknowledge our families for their unfailing support. We are grateful to our spouses and sons who continually challenge us to reach forward, walk beside us and care about what we do. In so doing, they give far more to us than they ask in return. Above all, we thank our mothers and grandmothers, who have passed along their oral stories and maternal wisdom, and our daughters, to whom we now hand the story, trusting that they will appreciate it, add to it and carry it forward.

Finally, we have appreciated our opportunity to work together on this book, inspiring each other in what has become a truly collaborative, energizing experience. Most importantly, when domestic crises interrupted our work on countless occasions and we mumbled more apologies to each other than we care to remember, we were always able to be supportive and to rely on each other to pick up the load with an unspoken understanding and a smile. A special connection developed as we mutually celebrated the confidence, courage and compassion we continue to acquire from our roles as mothers.

INTRODUCTION

Sharon Abbey & Andrea O'Reilly

IN 1976, ADRIENNE RICH challenged feminist scholars to confront their tendency to avoid discussions of motherhood with her observation that "we know more about the air we breath, the seas we travel, than about the nature and meaning of motherhood."[1] In the twenty years since her ground-breaking book, *Of Woman Born*, the topic of motherhood is beginning to take a more central place in women's studies, and the issues uncovered in recent anthologies[2] have become even more diverse, ambiguous and complex than Rich had inherently understood them to be. By examining a broad range of issues, narratives and standpoints, this collection of essays grows out of the expanding field of maternal inquiry and picks up on Rich's challenge to redefine motherhood. It draws together the collective voices of twenty-three women scholars who participated in the "Mothers and Daughters: Moving into the Next Millennium" conference held in September 1997, sponsored by the Centre for Feminist Research at York University, Toronto, Ontario. An overwhelming response by women from across the country expressed a compelling need to come together and share their experiences, insights and concerns about motherhood in a published work. The essays in this volume represent original ideas and writings drawn from the conference.

As editors of this collection, our intention was to provide an honest, thought-provoking and perhaps even transformational book that appeals to a wide readership. The contributors range from well-known feminist scholars and academics to graduate students documenting their first research studies on motherhood. Some chapters are theoretical and complex, challenging readers to engage in scholarly debate. Others are more informal and conversational, allowing readers a brief glimpse into the private lives of women who mother or are mothered.

These chapters also serve as mirrors for readers to make connections that resonate with their own situations. Still others try to provoke emotional responses in readers through the creative artistry of poetics and linguistics. We hope students and faculty will use this collection of essays in women's studies courses to re-image and reflect on their own lives and that others will also find the book challenging and thought-provoking. Study notes have been provided at the end of the collection that offer structured guidelines for developing thematic research studies, case study methodologies and reflective journal notes.

The contributors, drawing on diverse disciplines and fields of expertise such as sociology, history, anthropology, education, film, humanities, psychology, nursing and women's studies, seek to reject or transcend traditional ideologies of motherhood in order to validate a broader range of maternal options. Their research typically favours qualitative methodologies which are best suited to listen to women's voices, to honour the experiences of every day lives in progress and to identify patterns and commonalties that emerge. Based on personal testimonies and ethnographic studies, these authors recognize the multiplicity of maternal patterns enriched by differences of class, race, sexuality, age, ability, geographical location, culture and religion. They emphatically point out that mothers no longer see themselves as "conduits and perpetuators of the dominant culture" and instead are transforming themselves "into a powerful catalyst for social change."[3]

From a variety of maternal standpoints, such as lesbian mothers, foster mothers, mothers who are disabled, activist mothers, interracial mothers, nonmothers, first-time mothers and single mothers, the book problematizes the fixed notion of the term "mother." In doing so, these authors move beyond the myths and stereotypes of mothering to explore differences among women and within individual women in order to challenge the existence of a universal meaning of motherhood and the notion of a fixed and stable maternal identity. Mothers are never only mothers. Simultaneously, they are lovers, workers, activists, daughters, partners, sisters, neighbours, aunts, friends and so on. Subjectivity shifts synchronically and diachronically. In any given day, a mother will move from one identity to another. At any given moment several selves will be complementary and conflicted. A common argument that runs through the book contends that the concept of "mother" is not a singular practice but is always context bound. Mielle Chandler summarizes this position in Chapter 16 by suggesting that "mother" is best understood as a verb.

The contributors challenge readers to redefine themselves as both emancipated and autonomous agents within nonessentialist frameworks who will seek opportunities to disrupt stereotypical divisions of labour. They also encourage women to recognize their role and moral responsibility for creating change and respect for mothering acts by utilizing their own power, privilege and authority. They challenge mothers to make it clear that they are not expendable and to lobby for economic changes by ending their isolation and by raising their collective voices. These authors emphasize that it is not even necessary to be a biological mother in order to take responsibility for society's children. To be a mother is far more than a repetitive imitation of multifaceted socially constructed ideals, performed in such a way as to be accepted in the social sphere one inhabits. Perhaps Katherine Arnup best summarizes the role of an effective mother in Chapter 2 as someone whose strength of character and struggles to create livable space around herself offer choices, possibilities and freedom to her daughter by encouraging her to confidently believe in herself, to love her body and be comfortable with her femaleness, and to take care of herself.

By foregrounding themes such as matrophopia, abortion, childlessness, mother blame, mother loss and state control of reproduction, the contributors confront issues that are still considered private or "taboo" and, consequently, are seldom discussed, analyzed or even valued in the public milieu of academia. In addition, these chapters confront the unexamined responses that these issues induce, such as grief, anger and resistance. By writing in a multiplicity of genres, the contributors celebrate diversity, disrupt traditional structures of scholarship and open up alternative ways of viewing the world. By honouring and preserving a variety of personal discourses such as narrative, filmmaking, poetry and letter-writing, the writings in this book draw readers into the personal reflections of women and scholars who are struggling to make choices about the maternal dimensions of their lives.

Some of the essays use personal narrative structures, family oral history and autobiographical material. In doing so, these authors willingly open up their personal lives, positioned within multiple and contradictory discourses, to intense dialogical scrutiny. They invite the reader to explore the intimate connections between knowledge, power and the body as well as the complexities of negotiating what it means to be a mother who is expected to respond to the needs of others with no clear line of differentiation from the self. As a result, these contributors create powerful subjective images and disclosures of realities which are normally excluded from traditional academic discourse. In so doing, they grapple with conflicts of the inner self as they struggle to compromise and reconcile their various roles and culturally prescribed scripts as daughters, mothers, grandmothers, wives, partners, scholars, teachers, writers and poets. As feminists, these authors are "committed to increasing women's autonomy and collective power in the world,"[4] and their struggles to define themselves become particularly difficult since "self-definition has come in opposing their mothers' values, viewpoints and voices."[5] In other words, these writers resist defining themselves in oppositional terms; instead, they advocate dismantling rigid boundaries and disrupting commonly accepted categories in order to see their lives as fluid rather than as compartmentalized and to recognize biases and omissions in the maternal discourse.

In other essays, the contributors examine theoretical perspectives in an attempt to reposition mothering and shake up the status quo. They view the category "mother" as a social position shaped by complex socioeconomic, historical and cultural contexts which potentially limits women's lives and their career choices. Their work unravels, displaces and interrogates traditional scripts of motherhood and seeks to separate these unexamined assumptions from their female identity. In doing so, these authors raise important questions about how to understand the complexity of self as a woman, how to live up to the standards of intrepidity set out for us by our foremothers, how to interpret governance of women's prenatal responsibilities for fetal care and how to reconcile autonomous and encumbered positions of subjectivity.

Organizing the chapters of the book proved to be a difficult task because of the complex intertwining of the topics and issues raised. The flow of energy and the pulse of transformation captured by these authors tends to defy boundaries and category restrictions, which should not have surprised us. In the end, after many revisions, the grouping of chapters that finally emerged seemed to evolve and find its own shape, much like a birthing process ... and it took exactly *nine months* from the time of the initial conception of the idea to the publication of this book. The four sections are arranged in a circular pattern, beginning with the broad topics of education and socialization of motherhood, then moving into the more intimate and subjective realm of changing values and personal maternal histories, and finally coming full circle with discussions of far-reaching implications for state policy, rights and choices of mothers. Each section includes both personal biographies as well as more formalized studies, highlighting the voices of mothers, children of mothers, as well as those who stand apart from mothers and observe them. In order to break from a linear reading structure, each chapter stands alone, compliments other chapters in the section, and also connects with those in other parts of the book. Readers are invited to select their own order of readings. Study notes are included at the end of the book that are intended to further engage students in mining the text for deeper meanings.

DISRUPTING MATERNAL PATTERNS AT HOME, SCHOOL AND WORK

For the most part, the authors in this first section are teachers or researchers in the field of education and, as such, are especially attuned to the socializing power of learning in the home and at school. This section explores the hybridity of maternal subjectivities from various perspectives and considers issues dealing with workplace restrictions and the lack of concessions for mothers' multiple roles (for example, taking baby to work, breast-feeding in public, being sleep deprived, working at home, managing child emergencies, caring for sick children or negotiating maternity/paternity leaves). These authors demonstrate how women's lives still are restricted by motherhood even as their career independence increases, and they argue that few women can measure up to the unrealistic demands in both the private and public domains. Several of the chapters examine the conflicting roles of teachers who are also mothers and how such duality becomes blurred, resulting in the creation of new and innovative modes of teaching and learning. These studies also celebrate the transformation of traditional autocratic teacher roles into more caring, child-centred multidimensional experiences. Finally, they provide further evidence to support Madeleine Grumet's claim that as long as primary parenting is left to women, then schools will be charged with leading children from "the women's world to the man's" and female elementary schoolteachers, our daughters, will be responsible for orchestrating this "great escape."[6]

The first two selections offer personal perspectives of daughters and sons on learning from their mothers at home and how they apply this knowledge in broader contexts. In Chapter 1, "Comparing How Mothers Influence the Education of Daughters and Sons," Sharon Abbey, Joyce Castle and Cecilia Reynolds confront the gender stereotyping that they passed on to their own daughters and the conflicting tensions between their feminist critique of patriarchy and the privileges that it affords their own sons. They conclude that their attitudes toward education were interpreted differently by their sons and their daughters and that the schooling their children received reproduced sexist practices often found in the larger community that continues to advance the interests of males. In Chapter 2, "'Does the Word LESBIAN Mean Anything to You?': Lesbians Raising Daughters," Katherine Arnup discusses the dilemmas faced by a lesbian mother raising two daughters with her partner. She addresses the contradictions and tensions brought about by homophobia and how this affects what her children learn in private and public spheres. Arnup concludes that feminism has not provided adequately for lesbian parents as a sexual minority group and argues for a postmodern paradigm shift in the traditional ways of thinking about motherhood, gender and sexuality.

In Chapter 3, "Across the Divide: Contemporary Anglo-American Feminist Theory on the Mother–Daughter Relationship," Andrea O'Reilly shifts the focus to the school setting and describes the course she designed and teaches on "Mothers and Daughters: From Estrangement to Empowerment." The course aims to identify, challenge and dismantle the patriarchal story of mother/daughter estrangement and seeks to construct an alternative narrative, scripted for the empowerment of mothers and daughters alike. In Chapter 4, "Mothers as Teachers — Teachers as Mothers," Alice Collins studies both home and school influences of mothering on the lives of women teachers in Newfoundland and Labrador from 1930 to the present. Her research examines the impact of becoming a mother on the lives of these women and explores how the identities of mother and teacher interface. Finally, in Chapter 5, "Written on the Body," Rishma Dunlop further investigates the fluidity of women's identities as mother/teacher, exploring connections between the maternal body and women's intellectual experiences. In this section, all of the authors agree that the "split subjectivity" of the mother and teacher roles is interconnected, complementary and beneficial.

MATERNAL VALUES AND IDENTITIES IN TRANSITION FROM ADOLESCENCE TO MID-LIFE

In this section, the authors support the view that the critical task of feminism is to examine the social, economic and political structures of women's inequality and systemic oppression while also reclaiming and identifying the positive aspects of women's experiences.[7] These authors discuss the changing values and understandings of choice and equality in relation to identities of motherhood with different age groups. First, teen's images of realistic or imagined maternal roles are considered, then new mothers' expectations of equity and divisions of labour are described, and finally the concepts of ideal mothering practices are explored by mothers of adolescent daughters.

Although the transition to first-time motherhood is emotionally and physically complex, it has seldom been documented in feminist literature.[8] When babies are born it is often said that women *take time off work* or *stop working* to stay at home with children. Undoubtedly, such phrases were inspired by the universal male norms established by those whose lives, careers and even bodies were relatively uninterrupted and unchanged by the arrival of children. In contrast, as some of these chapters demonstrate, women take on far more work by staying at home to assume the countless drudgery tasks and unrecognized obligations of child-rearing and domestic duties. *Biological expertise* of mothers is often used to justify a partner's abdication of sharing fully in childcare responsibilities. In reality, this so-called *expertise* develops as a result of repetitive practice or an unfulfilled need for women to control or take responsibility of some aspects of their lives, namely childcare and domestic work.[9] If these women do return to careers outside the home, they are often surprised to find that divisions of labour are far from equal. Not only have they lost ground or seniority in their job field but they are also burdened with the majority of ongoing care-taking responsibilities for the home and family as well.

The first two studies in this section consider the shaping of young girls' values and concepts of motherhood. In Chapter 6, "Teenage Girls Making Sense of Mothering: What Has (Relational) Equality Got To Do With It?," Arlene Tigar McLaren and Ann Vanderbijl address egalitarian family structures and challenge the double standards and self-serving expectations of patriarchy. They point out that equality exists only if and when mothers are willing and able to successfully negotiate with their husbands or partners. Repeatedly, the burden of changing or disrupting domestic patterns and relationships falls on women. They conclude that this process has been silenced for too long and as a result, adolescent girls continue to view their future maternal roles through an idyllic lens. In Chapter 7, "Mother to Daughter: The Shaping of a Girl's Values in the Context of a Parent with a Chronic Illness," Karen Blackford contends that the lives of mothers with disabilities remain largely invisible in feminist writing and that their struggles to overcome innumerable barriers are seldom addressed. She challenges readers to re-think common assumptions about able-bodiedness and the interactive link between mothers' values and those of their daughters. Blackford concludes that daughters are positively influenced and advantaged by a disabled mothers' flexibility as well as by her ability to cope with transitions and unexpected difficulties in their lives.

The next two essays examine how maternal identities change for more and less experienced mothers. In Chapter 8, "Motherhood, Changing Relationships and the Reproduction of Gender Inequality," Bonnie Fox reports on her study of first-time mothers and the perpetuation of gender inequality, conventional divisions of labour and social isolation. Using social constructivist theory, she points out that new mother's agency is dependent on their partners' willingness to take responsibility for domestic chores. She also notes that when the participants in her study became mothers, they often rekindled closer bonds with their own mothers. In Chapter 9, "Unravelling the Myth of the Perfect Mother with Mothers of Early Adolescent Girls," Elizabeth Diem dispels the myth that all "good" mothers are caring, loving and selfless. She examines mothers' unrealistic expectations of their maternal roles and harmonious relationships with adolescent daughters. She then charts the progress of support group sessions whereby these mothers were able to affirm their own needs, opinions and feelings within a safe, trusting context. These studies emphasize how motherhood abruptly repositions women in a space between self and family where it is a perpetual struggle to find a balance between nurturing others and fulfilling the self.

THE MOTHERLINE:
PERSONAL AND HISTORICAL NARRATIVES

The contributors in this section, for the most part, write as participant observers of their own lives. Their personal narratives document the *everydayness* of life and it is in this everyday space that much of their learning takes place and quietly turns into wisdom and self-understanding. This section of the book begins with Chapter 10, "Between Exile and Home," in which Martha McMahon underscores the complexity of maternal identity by theorizing about the subjectivity of women who are *not* mothers. She questions the identification and binary nature of motherhood as a universal norm for women and the negative consequences of terms such as "nonmothers" or "childless," which are used to describe women who choose not to reproduce or raise children. She points out that patriarchal society classifies women as either mothers or nonmothers and invariably assigns more admirable and valued characteristics to mothers. This classification, McMahon argues, belies the multiplicities of women's lived identities.

In Chapter 11, "Black Women and the Meaning of Motherhood," Nina Lyon Jenkins surveys the scholarship on Black motherhood and observes that "scant attention has been given to examining the *subjective* meaning of motherhood for Black women." She also identifies the salient features of Black motherhood and foregrounds the specificity and complexity of Black maternal subjectivity. By problematizing accepted notions of mothering, Jenkins calls for the reconceptualization of feminist maternal thought to include the divergent experiences of Black motherhood.

A disproportionately large number of women care for others, especially aging parents, in comparison to men. In Chapter 12, "The Experience of Mother Loss: Voices of Adult Daughters and Implications for Feminist Practice," Mary Valentich and Catherine Foote address issues of aging, death and bereavement from their professional perspective as social workers. Through their honest, poignant autobiographical accounts, they confront the impact of losing vital connections to their maternal roots as well as the struggle to reclaim maternal legacies from their personal standpoint as middle-aged daughters. However, maternal legacies are not always sites of empowerment, as Erin Soros points out in Chapter 13, "If You Die It Will Kill Me: Aborting Maternal History." In a chilling account of intergenerational relationships with her mother and grandmother, she shares her powerful, courageous story of rape, abortion and battles to overcome anorexia nervosa. She explores the power of juxtaposing words and using metaphorical images to sanction the right to choose the giving or the taking of life and death as well as to emphasize concepts such as starvation, abortion, conception, delivery and purging.

Unfortunately, women are still reluctant to talk openly about experiences such as rape, "illegitimate" children and abortion. This silence lulls society into a general complacency about the extent of such violent episodes and their repercussions on the lives of victimized women/mothers. As Nancy Mandell points out, "Fear of violence restricts women's behaviour making them unwilling to assert their needs, unsure of their public use of space."[10] Violence against women remains a tremendous social problem which the entire community must take responsibility for. These authors persuade readers that more of these stories need to be encouraged and documented.

In Chapter 14, "African Nova Scotian Women: Mothering Across the Generations," Sylvia Hamilton highlights the maternal role of advocacy by documenting the African Baptist womenline as a powerful guide and role model for whole communities. Through the use of oratories, church prayers and images of everyday life, she uses the medium of film to make rural Black maternal history visible and also to portray the subjects of her documentaries as worthy and valuable activists committed to self-improvement, equality and community betterment. Hamilton's research brings to a close the section of the book that confronts the confining parameters of motherhood and that attempts to open up the overlapping and uncharted domains of women's experiences by collapsing arbitrary boundaries and unnecessary cultural barriers.

MULTIPLE IDENTITIES OF MOTHERHOOD: RIGHTS, CHOICES AND DIVERGENCE

In the last section of the book, authors share their views from various racial, economic and legal standpoints, which prove to be conflicting and complex. In Chapter 15, "The Other Within the Self: Black Daughter, White Mother and the Narrative Construction of Identity," Elizabeth Yeoman destabilizes the view that maternal experience is universal and singular by profiling the complexity of her identity as a white mother of a biracial daughter and her history as a white woman whose ancestors included both intrepid women and slave traders. Yeoman's reflections on her daughter's interracial identity also point to the hybridity and polysomic nature of subjectivity.

This theme of conflicting identities is also taken up by Mielle Chandler in Chapter 16, "Emancipated Subjectivities and the Subjugation of Mothering Practices." She examines her dual identity as both student and lesbian mother and in doing so, challenges the privileging of the emancipated subject, the free and autonomous separate self found in western philosophical tradition and in much of feminist writing. Pointing out that subjects are always defined and encumbered by the many contexts in which they live, she argues instead that the dichotomy of the individual subjectivity (the student self) and the relational subjectivity (the mother self) is a false one. Chandler calls upon the reader to celebrate the multiplicity of identities and the hybridity of subjectivity as rich sources of knowledge and power for women.

This section also addresses the Canadian legal system and how it acts both to impose constraints and facilitate change that advance the interests of mothers in their search for fair treatment in areas such as family law, childcare allowances, social assistance, immigration, abortion rights and women's health issues. In Chapter 17, "Mothering the Well-Born: Choice as a System of Governance," Fiona Alice Miller and Melanie Rock explore fetal rights, women's choices to abort and state control in relation to a pregnant Aboriginal woman who was addicted to sniffing solvents. They argue in defence of reproductive freedom and self-governance by pointing out that women's bodies remain contested terrain. They describe how the fetus has been given subjective meaning through genetic science and narratives of health which tend to out-weigh the subjective rights of a mother and impose duties of care to her unborn child.

The impact of the state on women's lives is also addressed by Baukje Miedema in Chapter 18, "Mothers for 'Hire': Why Do Women Foster?" She contends that although foster mothers are the backbone of the welfare system, they are often devalued and misunderstood. Using personal interviews with foster mothers to construct realistic profiles, she also uncovers their motives and points out that their intentions are often in direct conflict with the needs of the biological mothers. It might be argued that the views of foster mothers are often limited by ideals of liberal feminism and that they fail to appreciate social factors that impede the mothering abilities of the birth mothers. This final sec-tion of the book challenges definitions of maternal identity and respon-sibility that influence policy and lead to new directions for maternal emancipation.

CONCLUSION

This book documents voices of women who are engaged in an ongoing conversation about motherhood. By broadening the maternal narrative, these authors reveal a rich complexity of maternal patterns that may be unsettling as well as liberating and may shake some very deeply rooted assumptions. Their work also draws attention to the absence of the ma-ternal voices of other women who would also contribute greatly to the dialogue. We still need to include the voices of more women who make up the cultural mosaic of our country such as Native, francophone and economically disadvantaged mothers. We also need to listen to the sto-ries of mothers who have lost children, stepmothers and mothers-in-law, and to appreciate the varied perspectives of adoptive mothers, birth mothers and midwives.

By foregrounding social location, the postmodern notion of mother-hood presented in these chapters challenges universalistic and essentialist

representations of family patterns, forms and structures. A dispropor-
tionate number of mothers are placed in the position of caring for children, husbands and aging parents both at home and as paid employees.
Learning to nurture others, to be self-sacrificing, available and self-de-
preciating is often equated with being a "good" mother. This book
challenges these hegemonic positions that separate women from themselves and marginalize them as mothers and daughters. We hope this
collection of essays engages you, inspires your thinking and encourages
you to deepen your understanding of your own maternal experiences.

Notes

1. Adrienne Rich, *Of Woman Born: Motherhood as Experience and Institution* (New York: W. W. Norton and Co., 1986), 11.

2. See, for example, Joyce Trebilcot, ed., *Mothering: Essays in Feminist Theory* (Totowa, NJ: Rowman and Allanheld, 1983); Brenda Daly and Maureen Reddy, *Narrating Mothers: Theorizing Maternal Subjectivities* (Knoxville: University of Tennessee Press, 1991); Donna Bassin, Margaret Honey, and Meryle Mahrer Kaplan, eds., *Representations of Motherhood* (New Haven, CT: Yale University Press, 1994); Eve-lyn Nakano Glenn, Grace Chang, and Linda Rennie Forcey, eds., *Mothering: Ideology, Experience, and Agency* (New York: Routledge, 1994); Maureen Reddy, Martha Roth, and Amy Sheldon, eds., *Mother Journeys: Feminists Write About Mothering* (Minneapolis: Spinsters Ink, 1994); Elizabeth Brown-Guillory, ed., *Woman of Color: Mother-Daughter Relations in Twentieth-Century Literature* (Austin, TX: University of Texas Press, 1996); Rima Apple and Janet Golden, eds., *Mothers and Motherhood: Readings in American History* (Columbus: Ohio State University Press, 1997); and Alexis Jetter, Annelise Orleck, and Diana Taylor, eds., *The Politics of Motherhood: Activist Voices from Left to Right* (Hanover, NH: University Press of New England, 1997).

3. Elizabeth Debold, Marie Wilson, and Idelisse Malavé, *Mother Daughter Revolution* (New York: Bantam Books, 1993), xvii.

4. Alison Prentice, Paula Bourne, Gail Cuthbert Brandt, Beth Light, Wendy Mitchin-son, and Naomi Black, *Canadian Women: A History*, 2d. ed. (Toronto: Harcourt Brace and Company, Canada, 1996), 3.

5. Maureen Reddy, Martha Roth, and Amy Sheldon, eds., *Mother Journeys: Feminists Write about Mothering* (Minneapolis, MN: Spinsters Ink, 1994), 1.

6. Madeleine Grumet, *Bitter Milk: Women and Teaching* (Amherst: The University of Massachusetts Press, 1988), 25.

7. Ruth Roach Pierson and Alison Prentice, "Feminism and the Writing and Teaching of History," *Atlantis* 7, no. 2 (Spring 1982), 38.

8. A notable exception is the research of Amy Rossiter, *From Private to Public: A Feminist Exploration of Early Mothering* (Toronto: The Women's Press, 1988).

9. Sara Ruddick, *Maternal Thinking: Towards a Politics of Peace* (New York: Ballantine Books, 1989), 17.

10. Nancy Mandell, ed., *Feminist Issues: Race, Class and Sexuality*, 2d. ed. (Scarborough, ON: Prentice Hall Allyn and Bacon Canada, 1998), xvi.

Part I

DISRUPTING MATERNAL PATTERNS AT HOME, SCHOOL AND WORK

Chapter 1

COMPARING HOW MOTHERS INFLUENCE THE EDUCATION OF DAUGHTERS AND SONS

Sharon Abbey, Joyce Castle & Cecilia Reynolds

AS THREE PROFESSORS of education who are also mothers of young adult children, we undertook a three-year project to study how our professions influenced their school experiences. This chapter argues that mothers influence their sons differently than their daughters by examining four interrelated themes that emerged from the data: (1) living up to mother's expectations, (2) coping with the limitations of school, (3) using gender-specific linguistic strategies, and (4) developing identities of masculinity and femininity. As a result of our self-reflective study, we also consider a redefinition of ourselves as mothers.

In our initial study[1] we focused only on our daughters until our sons asked why we were not interested in their opinions as well. As a result of their good-humoured taunting, new questions confronted us. Why were we, as enlightened feminists, predominantly interested in experiences with our daughters and, at the same time, willing to set ourselves apart from our own sons? Had we been influenced by the prevalence of mother–daughter literature or was this yet another example of the pervasiveness of hegemony, the ongoing and complex reworkings of dominant interests to win the consent and domination of subordinate groups? Perhaps these questions were an early indication of the control our sons would presume to exert on our research study.

As a result of these new insights, we decided to replicate the research study with our sons in order to: (1) investigate how our interest in gender deconstruction discourse might have served to disrupt power relations for our sons or encouraged them to resist binary theories of the world, and (2) determine how similar our sons' memories of their schooling experiences had been in comparison to their sisters' and their mothers'.

All three of us began our respective careers as teachers, completed doctoral programs years later while raising our families and working at the same time, and used feminist theories in much of our research. At the time of the study our children ranged in age from late teens to middle twenties and they had not met one another previously. Sharon's children, Hilary and Graham, were raised in a single-parent family and after attending universities away from home and graduating with degrees in arts and political science, embarked on professional careers — Hilary as an elementary school teacher and Graham as an actor. Joyce's daughter, Melissa, has begun graduate studies in physics and her son, Jason, works as a police officer. Both of her children attended the local university where she is a faculty member as does Cecilia's son, James, who is completing his undergraduate degree in computer sciences. Cecilia's daughter, Jennifer, has chosen a career in environmental management after completing her degree in biology and economics in the Maritimes. Prior to university, all of our children attended co-educational publicly funded elementary and secondary schools in Ontario.

THEORETICAL PERSPECTIVES

Historically, society has succeeded in assuming some form of control over the attitudes and behaviours of mothers, making conceptualizations of motherhood very contested ground. Ironically, the examination of these maternal issues has largely been avoided in women's studies[2] and even when such issues are addressed, they tend to focus more on the mothering received by women than on the mothering they give.[3] In view of these limitations, it is not surprising that the educational influence that mothers exert on their sons and daughters has been underestimated and seldom documented or that their maternal voices are rarely included in academic conversations.[4] In order to address these shortcomings and open up new forms of dialogue, we undertook this collaborative research project with our own children.

Research on parent–child relations emphasizes four distinct theoretical perspectives: (1) relationality theories[5] that argue that well-adjusted sons separate from mothers while daughters identify with them; (2) different voice studies[6] that suggest alternatives to male universalities; (3) critiques of the patriarchal institution that define "ideal" mothering and offer cultural judgements about "good" and "bad" mothers;[7] and (4) arguments supporting a return to traditional gender roles.[8] However, our search of the literature revealed relatively few comparative studies on the learning connections between mothers and their sons and daughters. It is interesting to note that parent–child studies focus mainly on the social roles of mothers with respect to daughters or the social roles of fathers with respect to sons. There are surprisingly few cross-gender studies of mother–son relationships and the crucial role these play in the socialization of the next generation. The sources for understanding young men's lives address either exclusive male relationships between fathers and sons[9] or the distinct differences between males and females.[10]

Most of the literature offers a limited or mismeasured interpretation of mother–child relationships set within the dominant framework of fathers, husbands and sons.[11] Feminist researchers point out that mothers are typically viewed as subordinate role models of patriarchal conformity and enforcers of costly losses for their daughters' freedom,[12] while father–son relationships are usually set within a masculine hegemonic context that identifies reality according to white middle-class males and legitimates such personal and social positions of power within social structures.[13] As a result, we believe that mothers have internalized limited, androcentric male descriptions of mother–son dyads as subtle interactions between letting go and clinging.[14] In reaction to these interpretations, women writers and researchers began to focus more on their relationships "with" daughters and "as" daughters. However, it is our opinion that the tensions related to such gender politics and the educational role that mothers assume cannot be dichotomized so simply.

Four notable exceptions to same-gender studies that focus on mother–son interactions include the work of Judith Arcana, Ann Caron, Linda Forcey and Babette Smith.[15] However, we believe that their interpretations are also limited by their emphasis on the loss of female identity in motherhood and inferences that the institution of motherhood oppresses women, impedes mother–son identification and fosters both sexism and patriarchal masculinity. Caron concludes that boys need strong mothers and encourages mothers to break out of compliant, submissive patterns in order to raise sons who are safe, strong and masculine as well as emotional, respectful and caring of women. Forcey emphasizes alternative identities for women outside the mother role and challenges not only how women fulfill their responsibility as mothers but also who assigns these responsibilities in the first place. Arcana argues that sons must see their mothers engaged in work other than mothering. Finally, Smith examines nonmaternal identities of mothers and their effect on mother–son relationships and concludes that mothers who work outside the home benefit the mother–son relationship by providing an identity with something understood and valued in their male world. We argue that such liberal feminist interpretations, even though they may broaden the theoretical framework, tend to discount and marginalize the responsibility, authority and power of women as mothers of sons.

METHODOLOGY:
"INTERLOCKING CONVERSATIONS"

Based on Jerome Bruner's[16] notion that personal narratives are the primary way humans deconstruct and make meaning of events in their lives, we developed a phenomenological qualitative study[17] involving autobiographical data collection,[18] feminist research strategies[19] and narrative inquiry.[20] We also agreed that a conversational format would allow us (mothers, daughters and sons) to listen and enter into one another's thinking, to engage in critical self-reflection and to confront and examine deeper levels of self-knowledge.

The data for this research was collected over a three-year time period, from 1994 to 1997. Using a model that we call "interlocking conversations," three rounds of audio-taped interview/conversations addressed specific protocol questions intended to "describe," "inform," "confront" and "reconstruct" (1) memories of elementary, secondary and postsecondary levels of schooling, (2) influences and involvement of mothers at all three levels, (3) positive and negative schooling experiences and (4) lessons learned. The first two sessions kept mothers' and children's conversations separated in order to encourage more uninhibited dialogue and to downplay any sense of power hierarchy, self-consciousness or intimidation. In the first session, mother-pairs and daughter- or son-pairs took part in rotating two-hour interviews in which one member of the pair would serve as the interviewer and the other as the responder. In the next session, all three mothers met as a group to discuss the first set of transcript notes and the daughters or sons did the same. These triad sessions offered participants a chance for further input or clarification as well as for involvement in the interpretive process, thus ensuring internal and external validity and reliability. The third and last session involved a six-way group conversation. Lastly, a graduate student/mother was invited to read all the transcripts in order to provide the mother/researchers with additional unbiased feedback.

A COMPARATIVE ANALYSIS OF EMERGING THEMES

Interpretations of maternal influences on our children's attitudes about education were shaped by the multiple perspectives we imposed on the data as both "educator-insiders" and "mother-outsiders." The latter standpoint involved the additional complexity of various age-related dyads (adult–child, adult–adolescent and adult–adult). We make no attempt to speak for others and fully realize that we write through the lens of middle-class culture and racial whiteness. Rather, our intention is to encourage others to compare maternal influences from their own cultural perspectives, especially with respect to schooling and gender identities. In the next section, we discuss our findings in terms of four major themes that emerged from our research.[21]

LIVING UP TO MOTHER'S EXPECTATIONS

Alison Griffith and Dorothy Smith[22] point out that for most middle-class women in North America, mothering work conforms to the generalized requirements of schooling and the standard norms of school success. As a result, these mothers have been expected to send their children to school "ready" to learn. As young mothers, we had whole-heartedly embraced this image of the "good" mother by providing experiences and resources to advantage our children at home, which included tutors, music lessons, computer camps, library trips, museum tours and visits to art galleries, as well as enrollment in French Immersion and Gifted Programs.

> I was really involved all the way along. I took it on myself to do a lot of overt teaching ... to provide things I felt the school wasn't going to ... I tried to go places and expose her to things ... We spent a lot of time at the library. We did a lot of reading together. (Cecilia, 23/8/95)

As mothers, we took pride in the accomplishments of our children and tried to provide them with positive support in order to foster their self-worth and confidence. We believed we understood their unique personalities better than anyone else and praised them for their curiosity, creativity, sensitivity and adaptability. We were hopeful for their future and had faith in their ability to succeed.

> He seemed to be always very positive and happy with school, never a complainer. He seemed to be involved in everything, very confident, very popular with students as well as teachers ... the type you would like to be yourself. (Joyce, 8/2/97)

> Jamie asks extremely pertinent questions. He has the kind of curiosity and the kind of ability to deal with complex thought ... Jamie has a very active interior life ... there is a lot going on in his emotions and his intellect that a lot of other people don't clue into. (Cecilia, 8/2/97)

> He was very mature ... He was obviously a kid I could trust. I knew he wanted to do well ... I never had any doubts, I just knew he would be fine. He was very outgoing and he could look after himself ... He was very well rounded and balanced ... He was always very creative and he was kind of radical, a risk taker. He put his heart and soul into his work. (Sharon, 8/2/97)

Our children vividly remember our efforts to supplement their learning at home as well as our interest and involvement in their schooling. For the most part, they seemed to appreciate our support and the security we provided from the harsh realities of schools. Although they credit us with encouraging their curiosity and creativity as well as fostering their confidence, motivation and organizational skills, our children also recall our critical scrutiny of their work. They admit feeling a certain pressure and obligation to please us and live up to the expectations and high standards we had set for ourselves. They all knew that their mothers expected them to attend university and they all complied, some more willingly than others.

> She was always making sure that my homework was done or always giving me extra work to do in every subject. (Jason, 8/2/97)

> I had an advantage in that my mom was the kind of mom she was. She read to me and helped me after school. (Hilary, 23/8/95)

> Our mothers didn't try to harness or control our creativity. They weren't restricting. They let us explore our own avenues ... [They] were very hands-on and involved in our schooling. They played a very "iron-fist" role in our school life. (Jason, 23/5/97)

> Her feedback was always critical in a way. If something wasn't up to what I could do, she wouldn't let me get away with it. She would always sort of drive me on. The advice she gave me was to always strive for one level higher than you think you can do and not ever be satisfied or rest on your laurels ... My mom placed a high value on education. I knew she would be disappointed if I didn't achieve well. (Graham, 9/2/97)

When our children were young, all three of us worked as teachers and also returned to graduate school to complete doctoral studies. As a result, it is not surprising that our sons and daughters saw us as powerful and credible figures who modelled themselves as capable, dedicated life-long learners. Our daughters also credit us with breaking down gender barriers, which exposed them to a wider range of opportunities.

> My mom has always been a big promoter of education ... She knows a lot about education so I try and listen to her. (James, 8/2/97)

> My mom was so busy educating herself ... the example of her going to school made me think I'd go to school. (Jennifer, 23/8/95)

> My mother was always studying and researching and so I think she indirectly showed me that I could do whatever I want. It wasn't supposed to be a hindrance to be a girl. (Melissa, 23/8/95)

> She was a single mom and she held down a full-time job and went to school ever since I can remember ... I was brought up with that kind of strength and perseverance. (Hilary, 23/8/95)

> Indirectly, just by observing her, I learned that you can't succeed without putting in a lot of effort and you tackle education whole-heartedly. It's got to be done to its fullest extent. (Jason, 8/2/97)

As our children grew older, we also provided "insider" information about the educational system and advice on how to keep all their options open, organize their time, write APA style essays and select courses and suitable professors. Sometimes we even resorted to insisting that they read certain books, complete certain courses and stay in school.

> When I went to conferences, I consciously checked out the university and got a syllabus and walked around to get a flavour of the place ... we would have long conversations over the phone every time [Jennifer] chose her courses. (Cecilia, 23/8/95)

> I certainly opened [Melissa's] eyes to opportunities like grants, assistantships, money. (Joyce, 23/8/95)

To some degree, our children all relied on our advice about programs and courses, university politics and interactions with professors or scholarship opportunities based on our "insider" information.

> She definitely helped me. She had a professor's point of view and helped me find ways of making things that I found boring more interesting. (Jennifer, 23/8/95)

> She was involved all along in letting me know how things worked at a university and what I have to do to get ahead. (Melissa, 32/8/95)

> My mom was very academically involved in my first year university — clearly laying out angles and approaches you needed when writing a paper or an essay or an exam. (Jason, 8/2/97)

For the most part, it was our daughters who identified with the "perfectionist" characteristics of their mothers and aimed to model our "good girl" behaviours in school. They revealed that they saw us as "having it all" (family, education and careers), something they felt was unattainable for themselves. They disclosed feelings of envy, frustration and disillusionment that time would run out for them and fewer choices and opportunities would be available. We worried that we had set unrealistic, undesirable expectations for our daughters and that they would play out Sadker and Sadker's vision of college women compromising careers, delaying romance and preparing for lesser employment as they took aim at glass ceilings.[23]

> I was always a good student and did really well in school. I always expected a lot of myself and think my parents did too ... Teachers always said good things about me, except that I was too hard on myself and always too disappointed if I didn't do well. (Melissa, 23/8/95)

Unlike feminist mothers who encourage others to take risks,[24] we began to question the degree to which our impact had gone beyond influencing and facilitating to that of overtly controlling. We had advised our children about which university to attend, which courses to take and which options to pursue rather than allowing them to learn from their own mistakes. Although we tried not to interfere or become overly involved in our children's schooling, they often chose to study subjects that their mothers knew very little about in order to escape from their involvement.

In spite of our best efforts, we confessed to one another that we often felt guilty about not being available enough for our children when they were young because we were studying, attending conferences or working on our own career advancement. It is interesting to note that we seemed more concerned about how this affected our sons and had just expected our daughters to cope and to be supportive. Cecilia describes regrets that we could all relate to:

> I was extremely busy. I was just physically not here and when I was here, it was phone calls and lots of things going on ... I was overwhelmed by the start up and trying to fight for tenure and

trying to get all the publications done fast and move myself forward ... The kids used to come in and interrupt me all the time so I made a rule they couldn't. They had to stand at the door until I looked around and noticed them. And one day I looked around and Jamie had fallen asleep in the doorway ... He was quite young and he was just beginning to have all these doubts about himself right at the point that I was defending my thesis ... And he was ambivalent about the amount of time it took. He wanted me there for him and I wasn't ... I was more involved in my own schooling. (Cecilia, 8/2/97)

We now wonder whether we had unwittingly served as perpetuators of the dominant culture by demonstrating to our young children that "good" mothers "do it all" and try to please others at all cost. Not only did we devote ourselves to being available at home but we willingly shouldered additional responsibilities outside the home.

COPING WITH THE LIMITATIONS OF SCHOOL

As we analyzed the transcripts, what surprised us the most was how often our children were critical of their own school experiences and, as educators, how unaware or unresponsive we had been to their plights. They often expressed disappointment that school did not meet their needs or expectations as they searched for self-definition. In the beginning, school was fun and they seemed eager, happy and enthusiastic. But after the elementary years all of that changed and things seemed to go downhill when they faced indifference, closed-mindedness and mediocrity rather than the challenging and inspiring environment they had hoped for. By high school our daughters were struggling with their self-esteem and our sons were finding school to be limited, restricting and impersonal. They talked about being "processed" rather than "motivated," "going nowhere" and "wasting their time." They felt that few teachers really cared about them or their academic success and seldom welcomed their creativity, initiative or critical stance. They resented the fact that teachers did not help them set personal goals or learn to manage their time well. Above all, they look back on school as being largely inapplicable or irrelevant to the real world as they were now experiencing it.

Teachers just put a box around you and then they only concentrated on that box. And there might have been other parts outside that box and those were left untouched. I'm waiting to have control over my own destiny. (James, 23/5/97)

In high school the teachers were not open to different types of teaching styles or assignments. It was the same lesson plans that they had been using for thirty years. They weren't willing to interpret anything they were not familiar with. They weren't willing to explore new avenues. (Jason, 23/5/97)

I guess I had a very romanticized idea about actually learning for the sake of learning and university was at first disappointing in a lot of ways ... anything that was interesting always seemed to be peripheral to the course. (Jennifer, 23/8/95)

I think the system is not very human. It's set up to deal with machines, sort of. Most of the older teachers are not really relating to kids. You should be able to talk to your teacher and there should be mutual respect. (James, 8/2/97)

As mothers, we also voiced our dissatisfaction with the system for being too large, too impersonal and unable (or unwilling) to tap into the unique learning styles and individual interests of our children.

It's disappointing that [Jennifer and James] met so few good teachers ... who were inspiring, creative and caring. (Cecilia, 23/8/95)

I had tried to open up doors for my kids and these teachers were shutting them down and there was nothing you could do about it except teach them to cope ... to get by, do what you have to do and get on with your life. (Sharon, 8/2/97)

We believed that we had been strong advocates and fierce protectors of our children's integrity and self-worth and tried our best to buffer them against unfair criticism and consequences at school. Occasionally we came to their defence and readily blamed schools and teachers for their lack of care, sensitivity or insight.

Once in elementary school he was sent home to write out lines two hundred times and I remember refusing to let him do it and going to the school and having somewhat of a confrontation with the teacher. (Joyce, 8/2/97)

This vice-principal didn't have a clue about my son. She had no idea about his gifted tendencies. All she saw was a belligerent adolescent that they wanted to get rid of. And I was angry ... All you had to do with Jamie was challenge him and yet it wasn't happening ... A lot of people really let him down. (Cecilia, 8/2/97)

However, we were reluctant to interfere with school, avoided school confrontations and refrained from action on behalf of our children. On many occasions, we also recall being silenced by school experts who discounted our intuitive wisdom as mothers and teachers. We had turned our young children over to the schools unquestioningly, even though we did not completely trust the system to offer them all they would need to become confident, inspired and insightful learners. In retrospect, we now regret some of those decisions.

She was a December baby and I just didn't feel she was ready for school ... I went ahead and sent her off ... I should have listened to my gut feeling and kept her home. I think she would have been much better off. (Sharon, 23/8/95)

I had to leave the teachers alone. So I learned not be involved. (Joyce, 8/2/97)

My mom never got involved directly in anything I did. She would never storm down to the school. But she was always interested in what happened and she was completely appalled by stories I would tell her. (Graham, 9/2/97)

We now realize that we failed to appreciate the extent to which our children felt let down by schools and once again sensed that familiar guilt about not being willing to take more action at the time. We were especially troubled when one of our daughters accused us of deliberate betrayal by suggesting that, as mothers, we were well aware of the schools' inadequacies and yet had remained silent and not willing to intervene.

You all [mothers] spoke about seeing injustices in the education
system but you still made us go to school ... I guess I have some
resentment about that. Why didn't you take me out? I wasn't
being fulfilled ... I knew it and you knew it ... you were playing
the game and getting somewhere ... I think it just did me a lot of
harm. (Jennifer, 1/9/95)

Our daughters forced us to confront our own reluctance to speak
out against a school system that inhibited, restricted, diminished and
denied female experiences.[25] Although we were aware of their dissatisfaction and their pain, we chose to do very little about it. As teachers-
insiders, we were well aware of the boundaries between home and
school[26] and how defensive and territorial teachers could be and we
worried about the repercussions that might jeopardize our children's
successes at school. Consequently, we were pressured into silence by a
culture that believed mothers often crossed the line and interfered with
the work of schools. As mother-outsiders as well, we were reluctant to
be labelled as bothersome parents who might create problems that our
children would ultimately be held accountable for.

I probably wanted to be more involved but found that I had already established a pattern of noninvolvement ... I was now dis-
tracted [by my new job] and I had all the other things to spend
my time on. (Cecilia, 23/8/95)

We had broken out of traditional female patterns of conformity
ourselves and our preoccupation with perhaps our own forms of resistance has kept us from attending to our children's struggles. We were
busy with our own postgraduate studies and hoped that our children
would find their own ways to cope. By advocating liberal feminism[27] at
the time, we may have focused more on exercising our freedom to
move beyond our teaching positions into careers in higher education
than we had on how school experiences of our children influenced the
construction of their gendered positions. Perhaps our lack of action was
due to what Lyn Mikel Brown and Carol Gilligan refer to as a need to
"cover up" and "not to know" because no alternatives seem possible.[28]
On the other hand, we may have appropriated silence as an "act of resistance and transformation"[29] and used it to serve our best interests by

reducing conflict and allowing us to get on with our own careers.

Rather than actively intervening, we remember offering our children strategies on how to cope with the inadequacies they faced in schools. However, we had not realized how differently we had advised our sons and daughters. While we encouraged our daughters to carry on and comply with what was expected of them in order to successfully complete their programs, we took pride in our sons' ability to take a stand and actively confront and challenge the system. As mothers, we encouraged our sons to be more assertive, and they seemed to exhibit more self-confidence than our daughters did.

> He always got along well with teachers except for a few times I remember him needing to stand up for himself. He wouldn't back down necessarily. He would speak his mind ... I remember we had long talks about realizing that you couldn't let those teachers hold you down and take away your confidence or dictate the right way to do things. You had to follow your heart and listen to yourself even if it meant risking their anger or their retaliation. (Sharon, 8/2/97)

> Perhaps everything you are getting in school isn't particularly valuable or the way it is being delivered isn't interesting ... but once you started you were expected to finish. (Joyce, 8/2/97)

> In high school I started to confront teachers. I started to ask more questions and didn't get as many answers, I guess. I began to see that teachers don't understand things or don't want to try to ... I always felt I had an "in" on the system — that I knew how it worked, and they [teachers] weren't gods and I wouldn't let them dictate what I felt about myself. In doing that, I developed a pretty strong sense of self-confidence and self-worth. (Graham, 9/2/97)

In contrast, our daughters generally accepted their frustration and disappointment with school and seemed resigned to dutifully following the rules and pleasing others at all cost. In order to cope, they chose to remain silent, to keep their emotions hidden and to wait for improvements at the next level. Their reactions reflected what Carol Gilligan describes as "drifting," a way of avoiding responsibility for decision making.[30] Feeling powerless to change the existing structure, our daughters allowed it to remain unchallenged.

> I just went along and did what I had to so I could get out. Sometimes I got mad at how stupid it all was, but mostly I just kept quiet. (Melissa, 25/8/95)

> I think the school system, the way it was set up, didn't work for me ... I just went along with the flow ... On the outside it might have looked like I was getting along fine, but I know inside I felt horrible. I was desperate to please. (Hilary, 23/8/95)

> Teachers didn't really have any idea who I was ... I was putting up a lot of walls. (Jennifer, 23/8/95)

The boys responded by taking school less seriously than their sisters. They seemed to rely more on their social skills and interrelationships with teachers to bolster their self-worth and to experience success.

> I got along great with my teachers. They liked me and I was able to communicate with them. That is probably the main reason why my marks were more than acceptable. (Jason, 9/2/97)

> I always enjoyed school, not so much for the academic side but for the social aspects as well, I guess. I was always into the playground stuff and was a bit of a class clown. (Graham, 9/2/97)

Our sons seemed to develop an early awareness that school was a game with rules that they could question and change. As their mothers, we fully supported them in their quest to take charge and stay in control of their own destinies. They seemed to see a bigger picture, which helped them to understand what they had to do to succeed and how they could get by even if they slacked off.

> I learned at a very early age from my mom how to play the game. I certainly took school as a game and I certainly was good at it ... A lot of my marks in university were solely based on who I was, not necessarily on the work that I did. (Jason, 21/7/97)

> We wanted to play the game and we got sort of a thrill out of it because you can beat them at the game. I enjoyed the memorizing as a game to play. But if you don't want to play the game, why

should you have to play it? In my opinion education doesn't open doors, it closes them. By the time you're done, you have only one door that you go through. (Graham, 21/7/97)

In most cases, the boys turned to sports or other outside interests to relieve their frustrations, to fulfill their need for attention and to gain a sense of pride as well as the respect of their peers. As a result, they were able to channel their cynicism or resistance to the school system much more overtly than their sisters.

The stuff I remember from high school and university is the athletics, the extracurricular stuff and not particularly stuff within the school system itself ... the stuff I learned most of all I didn't get in the classroom. (Graham, 21/7/97)

I probably put more time into playing sports through high school than I did studying. I always made sure my work was done but it was never done to the fullest extent. (Jason, 8/2/97)

Jamie began to get very interested in his more artistic side — painting and drawing and photography seemed once again to rekindle some of his enthusiasm. (Cecilia, 8/2/97)

DIFFERENTIATED USES OF LINGUISTIC STRATEGIES

From the outset, we noticed immediate differences in the way our daughters and sons responded to their involvement in this research project. Our daughters seemed to take the study far more seriously than their brothers, readily made themselves available and followed our directions without questions. It also seemed obvious that they spent more time reflecting on the written transcripts prior to subsequent meetings, while our sons confessed to skimming the material at the last minute. Our sons seemed to be less committed to this project even though they had suggested we include them in the first place. Unlike our daughters, it was difficult to co-ordinate our sons' busy lives and we were forced to postpone several of our scheduled group sessions. As a result, we found ourselves altering our own plans and even the structure of the research project to suit the needs of our sons.

Our daughters also seemed to be more comfortable sharing their feelings and more willing to confront their thoughts on a deeper emotional level. In contrast, we felt that our sons were holding back. When this observation was voiced, our sons criticized us for not making our intentions more explicit. They insisted that they could have shared their feelings if only we had asked them to, and they expressed their resentment that the rules and expectations had not been clearly explained to them in advance. In spite of this, it appeared that our sons had more to say about the issues raised, including many analytic, theoretical and interpretive comments peppered with references to laws, theories and statistics.

We had not noticed the same use of linguistic tactics to control the conversations when working with our daughters in the initial study but it was readily apparent that our sons were attempting to take charge of the agenda. As Robin Lakoff points out, "both sexes use the same words in the same constructions, but understand them differently."[31] She suggests that gender differences in language constantly cause comparisons and the need to polarize. Related to her findings, we noticed that our sons seemed to engage in more "report" talk and closed statements that focused on the final outcome of the research process itself, while our daughters preferred "rapport" talk and immersion in the research process itself. For example, the girls tried to find common ground right from the beginning and to quickly establish a positive, trusting rapport with one another. We noticed that they seemed content to linger awhile after each session as well, chatting and laughing together about common experiences. Their brothers, however, dispersed immediately.

In our all-female group sessions as mothers and daughters, we found ourselves talking on a more personal level, using expressive adjectives and making an effort to be collaborative and polite by encouraging one another with tagalong questions. The girls remarked privately to their mothers just how much they had enjoyed meeting one another and how easily they seemed to relate and empathize. The girls obviously found these group conversations to be supportive and therapeutic, and they were willing to trust one another with very personal feelings. They seemed to bond readily and shared many similar personality traits and values, especially their quiet reservation, independence and sensitive reflective dispositions.

In contrast, there was the noticeable shift in the tone to the discourse when our sons interacted with one another as opposed to when they were in conversation with their mothers. They seemed to have two distinct conversational modes, one for the "guy circle" and another for the mothers. Among themselves, their comments seemed relatively brief and guarded and their conversations tended to be more superficial. They often made jokes that trivialized the significance of the points they were raising, presumably to keep their conversations on safe ground. They also used theories and objective remarks to keep their personal feelings in check and maintain a position of authority. They seemed to avoid subjective references to emotions that might expose their vulnerabilities. Sometimes they even chose to be silent, ambiguous or indirect.

> I don't let my feelings get in the way because once they get in the way my mind gets all fogged and once it gets fogged I can't think clear ... I don't let a lot of different groups know my feelings or my interpretations on certain aspects because I don't want people to know what I am thinking ... I don't reveal. It's a control game. (Jason, 21/7/97)

With their mothers, however, they raised more topics, their comments became more theoretical, assertive and lengthy, almost to the point of lecturing. They were overtly assertive and confident during our group conversations, offering us advice on how to improve our study, altering our procedures, and even presuming to interpret the data for us. However, we know our sons well and agree that they were all quite eager to impress one another and put on "a show" for their mothers. They were concerned about presenting themselves well and not letting their mothers down. To some degree, they tried to predict our purposes in order to deliver what they thought we wanted to hear or backpedal if necessary to win the approval of the mothers. At times, they even included deliberate "shock" statements just to make us pay attention. Deborah Tannen argues that these kinds of linguistic strategies are predominately used by men in mixed groups to dominate the conversation or show solidarity for one another.[32]

We also observed that our sons had learned to use silence as a form of resistance or rebellion whereas our daughters, modelling their mothers perhaps, had used silence to please, to comply or to avoid confrontation. By refusing to answer certain questions in the interviews or declining to comment during our group discussions, our sons were demonstrating their understanding of the power of silence to guard their privacy, to reveal very little about themselves or to withhold information from us. We suggest that their silence may serve to mask male power relations and structures and agree with Blye Frank that such "masculine hegemony" is a highly rational, if not costly, choice that may result in a loss of freedom of relational experience or a tendency to ignore needs and desires.[33]

> I've said things honestly and I've left things out that I don't want you to know about. There are things you don't know about me and you're probably never going to know. I only gave you a quarter of the package ... certainly it's couched in terms of you [Mother] sitting there. (Jason, 21/7/97)

If the power and style of language is culturally learned and engendered,[34] then we must recognize these factors at work during our group conversations. In other words, our daughters were involved in women-only discourse while our sons took part in a mixed-gender dialogue. For our sons, this would obviously involve not only a code switch from peer (guy) to intergenerational dialogue but also one with women who held power positions as their mothers and also as researchers. The context of our dialogue was academic, professional and purpose oriented rather than familiar and egalitarian. "[U]nlike ordinary conversation, institutional and professional talk, has, until recently, been almost totally a male preserve, so the rules of male discourse are not only seen as the better way to talk but as the only way."[35] This complicates the power balance significantly. It is also important to remember that when we embarked on the study with our sons we had already been strongly influenced by the work with our daughters. Knowing that they were being compared with their sisters in this study would also make our sons more self-conscious and cautious. In fact, among themselves they acknowledged their vulnerability and suspicions and wondered if their mothers were deliberately trying to set them up, or make them look bad as men.

> Do you withhold stuff, knowing your mother would be reading it and you would have to answer for it? (Jason, 21/7/97)

GENDERED STANDPOINTS AT HOME AND SCHOOL

The role played by schools and families in defining sexuality was also discussed in our conversations. Our daughters associated social factors, dances and dates with school much more than their brothers did and felt they had fewer options or alternatives to establish their self-worth during their adolescence. They seemed to be more vulnerable to rejections and exclusions in high school whereas their brothers could more readily turn to sports in order to build positive self-esteem and peer acceptance.

> I went to those stupid little dances and I hated it. It was all a struggle. I think if I had just stopped and said to somebody, "There's something wrong here. This isn't working for me," then maybe something could have been done. (Hilary, 25/8/95)

Although we made conscious efforts to break down gender barriers for our children at home (sons doing laundry, daughters cutting grass), we were forced to admit that we had perpetuated traditional divisions of labour. Even though our children accepted their feminist mothers as a normative state, inevitably, we were aware of the gender barriers that promoted individuation and disconnection or disrupted our best role-modelling efforts.

> I relied more on Jennifer. She would pick up more of the responsibilities ... She resents that Jamie got to do sort of nothing and she got to be in charge and take the responsibility and cook the dinner. (Cecilia, 19/6/97)

> I also relied on Hilary as the little homemaker. When I worked full time, she'd be the one to think to put dinner on. Graham would be parked in front of the TV and if he got hungry, he'd go and make something for himself. But she would think more of everybody or she might bake cookies. (Sharon, 19/6/97)

> When I'm at school I expect Melissa to put something on the table for her father and brother ... And I remember thinking that the tree has to be cut down and Jason can do it. (Joyce, 19/6/97)

Our daughters clearly remember the effect of our absence during the years when we pursued our graduate studies and returned to our teaching careers. They recall their resentment about being expected to prepare meals and take care of their fathers and brothers. However, they seemed more family oriented and "other" focused, identifying readily with their mothers' maternal roles and often mentioning their brothers as part of their significant childhood experiences. In contrast, our sons seemed to be less aware of what their mothers or sisters were doing during this same period and were more focused on themselves and on their own lives. They just accepted that their mothers went to school and studied at night and that this did not involve them in any way.

> I just recall you working and going to school. For me, I knew nothing else. That seemed to be the norm ... My mom would come back from school late at night and she would sit in the computer room all night. (Jason, 21/7/97)

Our sons took for granted that their mothers were providing for their needs and paid little attention to their mothers' activities, unless it affected them directly. In fact, our sons seemed to take more notice of their mothers' careers outside the home. We question the paradox of this viewpoint that recognizes mothers for their professional accomplishments on the one hand while devaluing their work within the maternal domain on the other.[36]

> Your life revolved around us kids. Ultimately you'd go to work ... come home, cook dinner and drive us somewhere. We'd come home, go to bed. (Jason, 21/7/97)

> If she's home then you interact with her. But if she's not, then you kind of don't think about it. (James, 21/7/97)

> In elementary school you just assumed your mother was there to revolve around you but in high school that changed. I do remember fending for myself the odd time. (Graham, 21/7/97)

Both our sons and our daughters definitely agreed that gender inequities were also prevalent throughout their schooling. Our sons felt they had an advantage over girls in primary grades and remember manipulating female teachers by being "cute and charming." It was obvious that on many occasions our sons were able to use gender to their advantage in schools, and we would watch as they charmed their way to special favours with female teachers. They were also able to influence male teachers because of their interest and abilities in sports and computers. They were coachable and they could make the coaches look good. However, they vehemently pointed out that this advantage had reversed by high school and university when it became obvious that male teachers and professors gave preferential treatment to female students.

On the other hand, our daughters resisted flirtation tactics to win approval from male teachers and resented being put in a position where that might be expected. These girls were quiet and shy and when they spoke up they were often ignored. As a result, they spoke less and less. As mothers, we supported their silence by the silence we modelled in our own lives. We expected them to endure teachers they did not respect, to tread water and even paddle upstream rather than stand their ground or climb up on it.

> Although their test scores were very close, Jamie was often given this respect by the teachers for being very intelligent, very quick and Jennifer didn't always get given that by the teachers. She had to keep reminding them she was intelligent ... When Jennifer spoke sometimes she wasn't heard ... she was doing exciting things but you had to notice her first. When Jamie spoke, he was heard ... he was very noisy, vociferous and in your face. (Cecilia, 19/6/97)

> A lot of professors showed immense favouritism towards female students. They let them rewrite their papers. Female teachers were easier on guys. I played the game with them. (Jason, 21/7/97)

> Sure, as guys, we had an advantage for sure! ... I never remember as a young man saying, "Jeez, I wish I was a young girl to get by in the system." But I do remember talking to a lot of girls who said, "Jeez, I wish I was a guy." (Graham, 21/7/97)

The topic of feminism was not consciously addressed with our daughters in this study and we are not sure why. Perhaps we assumed some common understandings with our daughters that we felt we needed to clarify with our sons. Although their views on what constitutes a feminist were somewhat varied (replacing domestic tasks with careers, resenting men or nurturing others), most of our children would not consider themselves to be feminists, with the exception of Graham.

> I see things from a feminist point of view that I don't think maybe other guys my age see. I think that results from growing up with my mother and sister in a single-parent home. (Graham, 21/7/97)

> All of Graham's girlfriends have been feminists — very much like me, I would say. I can really relate to these girls and become friends with them ... Independent women don't threaten him. I guess that is a big part of why I call him a feminist. (Sharon, 19/6/97)

While our daughters might have resisted feminism based on the strong positions we have taken about gender equity, which they tend to view as difficult ground-breaking work, our sons seemed more concerned about stereotypical impressions held by their peer group that might threaten their male identities and set them apart as different. They did not want to appear too closely identified with their mothers or thought of as a "sissy" or "momma's boy." It was obvious that our children all believed that there were painful consequences and penalties associated with being perceived as a feminist.

> Jason certainly has some feminist tendencies. He would be shocked to hear me say that and would not want to admit them ... He would see it as something which separated him from a lot of other males as effeminate, kind of wimpy, derogatory. It would make him too different ... too influenced by his mother. (Joyce, 19/6/97)

> It would be very hard for him in certain groups of friends to even show at all that his mother is a feminist ... James and his father take the corporate line and Jennifer and I take the humanist position. (Cecilia, 19/6/97)

Regardless of how our sons embraced feminism, we agreed that our feminist standpoints had probably affected their relationships with female teachers who were in positions of power. Our sons held high expectations for such women and could give them a tough time if they fell short of their image as strong leaders.

> James has been very hard on incompetent women teachers who can't manage the classes. I think he expects women in authority over him to be somewhat like the model that I think I have been for him. (Cecilia, 19/6/97)

As our conversation about sexuality intensified with our sons, we were even more surprised at how hesitant our sons were to define their own masculinity. There was obviously a lot of emotional baggage attached to the term for them. We noticed a real sense of apprehension involved in defining male identities that might threaten to expose them to ridicule or criticism. They were obviously feeling defensive and embarrassed about being white middle-class males in North America and frustrated with a society that imposed such anxieties and inhibitions on them. It was obvious that they were unsure of what we expected them to say and whether we were deliberately trying to set them up. Their reactions support Judith Arcana's[37] conclusions that most Anglo-American mothers reject traditional definitions of masculinity while their sons assume a conventional gender identity which they feel is expected of them.

> If we say the wrong thing we will have to answer for it! We are not proud to be a male. Men are on the run ... There are a lot of guys that embarrass me by the way they treat others. (Jason, 21/7/97)

> Testosterone ... is seen as a bad thing. (Graham, 21/7/97)

Our sons seemed almost speechless and tongue-tied as well as apologetic about endorsing possible stereotypical interpretations of maleness. Their description of masculinity included very different concepts, exemplifying the multiplicity of the term. For example, Jason associated masculinity with control and physical appearance of heavy muscle-bound jocks who "hit on women" or strong, powerful mythology figures such as Zeus, Hercules or Apollo. For his part, James defined masculinity as the antithesis of all that is considered feminine such as "knowing too much about gourmet cooking or going to the theatre." For Graham, however, masculinity meant "freedom of movement or power" and it brought to mind such images as "cigars, scotch and football games." Their images were also influenced by people they associated with on the police force, in computer studies or at the theatre.

According to Blye Frank the meaning of "masculinity" is in a constant state of flux and conflict.[38] It often resides in the dichotomy between fulfilling internalized needs and meeting standards mostly set by other men and boys as authority and domination are merged into the systemic structuring of personality itself. There is general consensus that there appears to be a gap and often a great deal of tension between the collective public ideal and the actual lived private practice of male students, which may be compounded by the societal schisms pitting subservience against independence

> I loved to act, recite poetry and sing at a young age but I kept it hidden. Your friends don't take kindly to singers ... I remember being in a school play and being just traumatized and mortified because I had to dance around in tights and I didn't want my friends to see me. (Graham, 9/2/97)

Our sons helped us to realize that their gender identities were just as emotionally loaded as their sisters' and that their defensiveness serves to silence them in ways that are perhaps less defined. This made us appreciate that young men need to have their voices heard also and that school must encourage boys to talk about their sexuality and their body image more overtly. Changing images of masculinity and identity consciousness-raising for both girls and boys must become valued priorities for education. As long as we willingly reward oppression, competition and violence in our schools, we are supporting the authorial voice of gender hegemony. As educators, illuminating issues related to mother–child relationships points to the need to develop courses where issues of gender are central and where critical and reflective discussion about gendered realities in school settings and across diverse racial and class populations can occur. In the end, we must also question our own reluctance to speak out against a school system that inhibits, restricts, diminishes or denies diverse gendered needs and experiences.

> I think it is important for men to communicate more than they do. A vision of my masculinity is more openness, more communication, no chauvinism, no competition. I think heterosexual men have a lot to learn about caring. (Graham, 21/7/97)

School didn't teach me a heck of a lot about masculinity. None of the male teachers I had were particularly masculine guys if you think of a muscle-bound jock. Nothing was done directly. It was more subtly done by watching them. (Jason, 21/7/97)

CONCLUSION

We are aware that raising daughters is an extremely political act in which mothers teach daughters to fit into a world shaped by men while at the same time trying to foster in them the self-confidence and courage to determine their own needs, voice their opinions and take a stand on issues affecting their lives.[39] What we model for our daughters as capable, independent professionals is consistent with revised images of women currently accepted by our society. At the same time, we also support the notion that "good" mothering involves raising well-adjusted sons who will resist traditional male values.[40] Realizing how ingrained schools are in patriarchal teachings, we worry that as destabilizors of normative masculine practice we might have confused or upset our sons by encouraging unrealistic expectations that prevented them from fitting into traditional social structures. As well, we fear that the gender equity that we advocate and model as mothers and as feminists may ultimately result in loss of power and privilege for our sons and that they will view us as working against their best interests. Our research has forced us to question whether we indirectly accommodate traditional gender socialization even though we do not initiate or enforce it.

This project has taught us a great deal about how we have influenced our children's education and also about redefining ourselves as mothers. The interview questions brought issues to the surface that we had seldom discussed with our children, giving us all an opportunity to clarify and alter our culturally imposed gender identities and orientations as well as our feelings of resentment and inadequacy. If we had a second chance as mothers, perhaps we would disrupt gender roles more deliberately or advocate more strongly and visibly in schools in order to protect and validate our children's unique qualities and interests. We might even be less controlling and more open to a wider range of learning possibilities for our children and to alternative strategies for attaining these. However, we also realize the control exerted on us by the school system, and in reassessing our maternal relationships with our children, we must avoid being overly harsh on ourselves and falling into the cultural guilt trap of blaming ourselves for falling short of unrealistic expectations.[41] Perhaps we should be pleased with ourselves as role models and take heart in what our children have accomplished as young adults, in where they seem to be headed and, above all, in their willingness to participate in such intense reflective dialogue with their mothers.

Notes

1. Joyce Castle, Sharon Abbey, and Cecilia Reynolds, "Mothers, Daughters, and Education: Struggles between Conformity and Resistance," *Canadian Journal of Education* (in press, 1998).

2. Elizabeth Debold, Marie Wilson, and Idelisse Malavé, *Mother Daughter Revolution: From Good Girls to Great Women* (New York: Bantam Books, 1993), xvii.

3. Ramona Mercer, Elizabeth Nichols, and Glen Caper Doyle, *Transitions in a Woman's Life: Major Life Events in Developmental Context* (New York: Springer Publishing Company, 1989).

4. See, for example, Sandra Acker, *Gendered Education* (Toronto, ON: OISE Press, 1994); Mary Catherine Bateson, *Peripheral Visions: Learning Along the Way* (New York: HarperCollins, 1994); Paula Caplan, *Don't Blame Mother: Mending the Mother–Daughter Relationship* (New York: Harper and Row, 1989); Madelaine Grumet, *Bitter Milk: Women and Teaching* (Amherst, MA: University of Massachusetts Press, 1988); and Carol Heilbrun, *Writing a Woman's Life* (New York: Ballantine Books, 1988).

5. See, for example, Nancy Chodorow, *The Reproduction of Mothering* (Berkeley, CA: University of California Press, 1978), and Michael Gurian, *The Wonder of Boys: What Parents, Mentors and Educators Can Do to Shape Boys into Exceptional Men* (New York: Jeremy P. Tarcher/Putman Inc., 1996).

6. See, for example, M. Belenky, B. Clinchy, N. Goldberger, and J. Tarule, *Women's Ways of Knowing* (New York: Basic Books, Inc., 1986), and Carol Gilligan, *In a Different Voice: Psychological Theory and Women's Development* (Cambridge, MA: Harvard University Press, 1982).

7. See, for example, Katherine Arnup, *Education for Motherhood: Advice for Mothers in Twentieth-Century Canada* (Toronto: University of Toronto Press, 1994); Caplan, *Don't Blame Mother*; Evelyn Glenn, Grace Chang, and Linda Forcey, *Mothering: Ideology, Experience and Agency* (New York: Routledge, 1994); Martha McMahon, *Engendering Motherhood: Identity and Self-Transformation in Women's Lives* (New York: The Guilford Press, 1995); Adrienne Rich, *Of Woman Born: Motherhood as Experience and Institution* (New York: W. W. Norton, 1986); and Sara Ruddick,

Maternal Thinking: Toward a Politic of Peace (New York: Ballantine, 1989).

8. See, for example, Robert Bly, *Iron John* (Reading, MA: Addison-Wesley, 1990). Bly reacts to feminism's critique of contemporary masculinity by advising sons to leave their mothers and find their strong, aggressive selves in the company of men.

9. See, for example, Bly, *Iron John*; Guy Corneau, *Absent Fathers, Lost Sons: The Search for Masculine Identity* (Boston: Shambhala, 1991); Sam Keen, *Fire in the Belly: On Being a Man* (New York: Bantam Books, 1990); Michael Kimmel, *Changing Men: New Directions in Research on Men and Masculinity* (Newbury Park, CA: Sage Publications, 1987); John Lee, *At My Father's Wedding: Reclaiming Our True Masculinity* (New York: Bantam Books, 1991); and Samuel Osherson, *Finding Our Fathers: How a Man's Life is Shaped by His Relationship with His Father* (New York: Ballantine Books, 1986).

10. See, for example, Gilligan, *In a Different Voice* and John Gray, *Men are from Mars, Women are from Venus* (New York: HarperCollins, 1992).

11. Carol Tavris, *The Mismeasure of Women* (New York: Simon and Schuster, 1992).

12. See, for example: Debold, Wilson, and Malavé, *Mother Daughter Revolution*; Rose Glickman, *Daughters of Feminists* (New York: St. Martin's Press, 1993); Marianne Hirsch, *The Mother/Daughter Plot: Narrative, Psychoanalysis, Feminism* (Bloomington: Indiana University Press, 1989); Peggy Orenstein, *Schoolgirls: Young Women, Self-Esteem and the Confidence Gap* (New York: Doubleday, 1994); Mary Pipher, *Reviving Ophelia: Saving the Selves of Adolescent Girls* (New York: Ballantine, 1994); Valerie Walkerdine and Helen Lucey, *Democracy in the Kitchen: Regulating Mothers and Socializing Daughters* (London: Virago Press, 1989); and Marilyn Webb, "Our Daughters, Ourselves: How Feminists Can Raise Feminists," *Ms.* 3, no. 3 (1992), 31–35.

13. See, for example, Harry Brod and Michael Kaufman, *Theorizing Masculinities* (Thousand Oaks, CA: Sage Publications, 1994); Kenneth Clatterbaugh, *Contemporary Perspectives on Masculinity* (Boulder, CO: Westview Press, 1990); Robert Connell, *Masculinities* (Los Angeles: University of California Press, 1995); Michael Kimmel, *Manhood in America: A Cultural History* (Toronto, ON: The Free Press, 1996); Larry May, Robert Strikwerda, and Patrick Hopkins, *Rethinking Masculinity: Philosophical Explorations in Light of Feminism*, 2d. ed. (New York: Rowman and Littlefield, 1996); Michael Messner, *Power at Play: Sports, Men and the Gender Order: Critical Feminist Perspectives* (Champaign, IL: Human Kinetics Books, 1992); Michael Messner and Donald Sabo, eds., *Sports, Men, and the Gender Order* (Champaign, IL: Human Kinetic Books, 1990); and Victor Seidler, *Rediscovering Masculinity* (London: Routledge, 1980).

14. Paul Olsen, *Sons and Mothers* (New York: M. Evans Co., 1981).

15. Judith Arcana, *Every Mother's Son* (New York: Anchor Press/Doubleday, 1983); Ann Caron, *Strong Mothers, Strong Sons: Raising the Next Generation of Men* (New York: HarperCollins, 1994); Linda Forcey, *Mothers and Sons: Toward an Understanding of Responsibility* (New York: Praeger, 1987); Babette Smith, *Mothers and Sons: The Truth about Mother–Son Relationships* (Sydney: Allen and Unwin, 1995).

16. Jerome Bruner, *Acts of Meaning* (Cambridge, MA: Harvard University Press, 1990).

17. Michael Quinn Paton, *Qualitative Evaluation and Research Methods*, 2d. ed. (Newbury Park, CA: Sage Publications, 1990), and Max van Manen, *Researching Lived Experience: Human Science for an Action Sensitive Pedagogy* (London, ON: Althouse Press, 1990).

18. Madelaine Grumet, "Existential and Phenomenological Foundations of Autobiographical Ethnography," in W. Pinar and W. Reynolds, eds., *Understanding Curriculum as Phenomenological and Deconstructed Text* (New York: Teachers College Press, 1992), 101–120.

19. See, for example, Michelle Fine, *Disruptive Voices: The Possibilities of Feminist Research* (Ann Arbour: University of Michigan Press, 1992); Sandra Harding, *Feminism and Methodology: Social Science Issues* (Bloomington: Indiana University Press, 1987); Sandra Hollingsworth, "Feminist Pedagogy in the Research Classroom," *Educational Action Research* 2, no. 1 (1994), 49–70; Patti Lather, *Getting Smart: Feminist Research and Pedagogy with/in the Postmodern* (New York: Routledge Press, 1992); J. Neilsen, ed., *Feminist Research Methods: Exemplary Readings in the Social Sciences* (San Francisco, CA: Westview Press, 1990); and Annie Oakley, "Interviewing Women: A Contradiction of Terms," in H. Roberts, ed., *Doing Feminist Research* (London: Routledge and Kegan Paul, 1981), 30–61.

20. Kathy Carter, "The Place of a Story in the Study of Teaching and Teacher Education," *Educational Researcher* 22, no. 1 (1993), 5-12; Michael Connelly and Jean Clandinin, "Stories of Experience and Narrative Inquiry," *Educational Researcher* 19, no. 5 (1990), 2–14; and Donald Polkinghorne, *Narrative Knowing and the Human Sciences* (Albany, NY: SUNY Press, 1988).

21. Quotations from our transcripted conversations are used to support each of the themes discussed. Those selected seemed to best support the issue at hand. Although no attempt was made to equalize the representation of each person's voice in the chapter, it would appear that those who were more forthcoming with comments are quoted more often. This is particularly evident in excerpts from the sons' dialogue.

22. Alison Griffith and Dorothy E. Smith, "Constructing Cultural Knowledge: Mothering as Discourse," in J. Gaskell and A. McLaren, eds., *Women and Education: A Canadian Perspective* (Calgary, AB: Detselig Enterprises Ltd., 1987), 219–244.

23. David Sadker and Marilyn Sadker, "Sexism in the Classroom: From Grade School to Graduate School," *Phi Delta Kappan* (1986), 67.

24. Webb, "Our Daughters, Ourselves: How Feminists Can Raise Feminists."

25. Orenstein, *School Girls*, xxiii.

26. See, for example, Sharon Abbey, "Systemic Barriers Between Home and School," in J. Epp and A. Watkinson, eds., *Systemic Violence: How Schools Hurt Children* (Washington, DC: Falmer Press, 1996), 68; Lisa Goldstein, *Teaching with Love: A Feminist Approach to Early Childhood Education* (New York: Peter Lang, 1997); Sara Lightfoot, *Worlds Apart* (New York: Basic Books, Inc., 1978), 25–30; and Jane Roland Martin, *The School-Home: Rethinking Schools for Changing Families*

(Cambridge, MA: Harvard University Press), 167.

27. Rosemarie Tong, *Feminist Thought: A Comprehensive Introduction* (Boulder, CO: Westview Press, 1989), 11–31.

28. Lyn Mikel Brown and Carol Gilligan, *Meeting at the Crossroads: Women's Psychology and Girls' Development* (Cambridge, MA: Harvard University Press, 1992), 112.

29. Magda Lewis, *Without a Word: Teaching Beyond Women's Silence* (New York: Routledge, 1993), 49.

30. Gilligan, *In a Different Voice*, 143.

31. Robin Lakoff, *Talking Power: The Politics of Language in Our Lives* (New York: HarperCollins, 1990), 201–202.

32. Deborah Tannen, *Gender and Discourse* (New York: Oxford University Press, 1994), 21–22.

33. Blye Frank, "Masculinities and Schooling: The Making of Men," in Epp and Watkinson, eds., *Systemic Violence: How Schools Hurt Children*, 123–124.

34. See, for example, Lakoff, *Talking Power*; Dale Spender, *Man-made Language* (Boston: Routledge and Kegan Paul, 1985); and Tannen, *Gender and Discourse*.

35. Lakoff, *Talking Power*, 210.

36. Arcana, *Every Mother's Son*.

37. Ibid.

38. Frank, "Masculinities and Schooling," 113–130.

39. See, for example, Debold, Wilson, and Malavé, *Mother Daughter Revolution*, 311–314, and Pipher, *Reviving Ophelia*, 103.

40. Forcey, *Mothers of Sons*.

41. Caplan, *Don't Blame Mother*, 39–67.

Chapter 2

"DOES THE WORD LESBIAN MEAN ANYTHING TO YOU?"

LESBIANS RAISING DAUGHTERS

Katherine Arnup

Jesse and I are walking down the street, chatting and catching up on the week's events. Two women approach us, holding hands, rainbow pins on their jackets. Jesse and I exchange knowing glances. "Does the word LESBIAN mean anything to you?" Jesse jokes, once they have passed, and we laugh at our shared "secret."

FEW PEOPLE WATCHING that exchange would guess that we are a lesbian mother and her daughter. Indeed, many people could not even imagine that such a possibility exists. Yet, it has been suggested that 10 percent of women are lesbians and that between 20 and 30 percent of lesbians are mothers.[1] A recent study estimated that there are "between 3 and 8 million gay and lesbian parents in the United States, raising between 6 and 14 million children."[2] While no figures are available for Canada, we can assume that proportionately the number of lesbian mothers is equally high.[3]

It is, however, virtually impossible to estimate with any accuracy how many lesbian or gay parents there are. Unless they choose to come out, lesbian and gay parents are largely invisible to the world outside their homes. Many lesbian and gay parents conceal their sexual orientation for fear of losing custody of their children. Others, concerned that their children will suffer from discrimination and harassment, choose to hide their sexual identity. Furthermore, official record-generating agencies, including Statistics Canada, do not include sexual orientation in their census questionnaires. As a result, estimates are at best really educated guesses.

It is important to recognize that these estimates tell us nothing about the enormous diversity of the population of lesbian mothers. Lesbian mothers differ on many dimensions: how they became mothers; how they view their lesbianism; and, of course, how they parent. Many lesbians are mothers as a result of bearing children within heterosexual marriages or relationships; some through choice, some by accident. Other lesbians decide, as lesbians, to have children, sometimes with a partner, sometimes alone. Lesbian mothers may be women of colour or white; working class or middle class; able-bodied or disabled; young or old; immigrant or Canadian born; anglophone or francophone. Clearly, lesbian mothers reflect all the differences among women. In addition, the attitudes of the worlds in which lesbian mothers live can range from complete acceptance to total rejection. Ex-husbands, friends, children, work-mates, parents and siblings and daycare centres and schools respond to the revelation of a lesbian mother's sexual orientation in various more-or-less supportive ways, and these responses affect the ways lesbian mothers present themselves and their families. Some lesbian mothers remain "closeted" and live publicly like heterosexual single mothers. Others "come out" to family and friends, or at school and work. Most, perhaps, are "out" in some contexts and not in others. In our research, our writing and our political organizing, it is important to remember the diversity of these experiences.

OUR STORIES

A couple of years ago, my then six-year-old daughter Katie was playing with her doll. She had developed the habit of yanking up her shirt from her jeans and pushing her baby against her chest, an activity I had come to recognize as breast-feeding. As we sat in the study, Katie breast-feeding and me trying to work, she proclaimed:

"You know, Mom, I'm a lesbian mother."

"Oh really," I responded, as casually as possible. "How do you figure that?"

"Well," she explained, "I'm a mother" (she pointed to her dolly), "and I love women" (she pointed to me), "so I'm a lesbian —

and that makes me a lesbian mother," she concluded triumphantly.

I often think about that conversation, and imagine to myself a world that could be that straightforward, that simple. For Katie, born and raised the child of two lesbian mothers, that world, to a great extent, already exists. Homophobia and discrimination are distant forces in her life. Her world of Mom and Sue, sister Jesse and dog Sophie, is a safe place, a home with a family much like her friend Fatima across the street, the child of a mixed-race heterosexual couple, and of her friend Malia, next door, the adopted child of a single mother. As the picture books tell us, families come in many sizes and shapes, colours and genders, and no one family is the right one. Or at least that's how it is in Katie's world right now.

My daughter Jesse is six years older than Katie. Born in 1982, Jesse is one of the first children of the "lesbian baby boom" in Canada. When she was born I was not "out" to my parents, though I had already been with my partner for six and a half years. We trod the line between single parenthood and lesbian family carefully, inventing as we went, challenging when we could. Like Katie, Jesse found acceptance among friends and family, neighbours and schoolmates.

When she was about to enter Grade 6, however, we moved to Ottawa — a much less diverse city than Toronto, a place with far fewer lesbian families and many more Beaver Cleaver households. Jesse bolted back into the closet. She would not bring friends home, answer questions about her family or explain the presence of Sue in our household. Indeed, she pretended Sue did not exist.

She was just finishing Grade 7 when the book I was editing on lesbian parenting was about to be published. Jesse panicked. "Do you *have* to do that book?" she asked, hoping she could somehow talk me out of it. "All my friends will find out, and everyone will make fun of me." We talked about her fears and about the ways I could try to make things better — I agreed not to be interviewed by the local media, and, since many children from her class passed the women's bookstore on their way home from school, I promised to ask the bookstore not to display my book in the window. I suspect it was the first time an author had asked them not to display her book — but they understood, and were generous in accommodating my request.

We have lived in Ottawa for over four years now, and slowly Jesse has begun to bring her friends home. She still tends not to introduce Sue to them, as if somehow not mentioning her could make her disappear. And I often return to my study to find books turned around — lesbian titles of course — and the small rainbow flag that adorns my desk stuffed into a drawer.

What is my daughter afraid of? In essence, it is the fear of being different, and of being ridiculed because of that difference. For preteens and teenagers, both boys and girls, the desire to fit in is enormous. Their clothes, their makeup, their shoes, their backpacks, what they do on the weekend — one dares not deviate from some imagined (and not so imagined) standard of normal. Normal is broadcast into their homes each and every day on the TV shows they are addicted to, in the magazines they devour, on the ads they read in the subway. A certain height, a certain weight, a certain skin colour. A certain family formation.

It *is* hard for children to be different. But it is important to remember that children differ in many, many ways, and that the vast majority of children and their families do not, in fact, fit that model.

Does my being a lesbian make life difficult for my daughters? I doubt that there is a lesbian mother who does not sometimes worry about what effect her sexual orientation will have on her children. The fact of the matter is, however, that, apart from the fear of disclosure that my sexual orientation and, in particular, my work on lesbian parenting engenders, the hardest things about having me for a mother have nothing at all to do with my sexual orientation. They have to do with how I parent: that I won't let her stay alone in the house overnight, that I insist that she do her chores, that she only gets $12 a week allowance, and so on. While I suppose a case could be made that those are somehow connected to my sexual orientation, it's a pretty far stretch! As a twelve-year-old child living with her two mothers in Oakland, California, explained: "The hardest part of my life right now is that both of my moms are vegetarians."[4]

I do not mean to suggest, though, that there are no problems. I do think it is hard for our children when they stand out. But as the countless studies that have been conducted over the past decade and a half have confirmed, our children are learning valuable lessons about justice, about fairness, about discrimination and about diversity. Regardless of whether they end up being heterosexual or gay,[5] our children end up more tolerant and more accepting of a range of different behaviours and kinds of people than children brought up in non–lesbian-headed households.[6]

They end up that way because they are different — as the children of lesbians they have had to struggle with the notion that equates difference with *bad*. As Audre Lorde argued so powerfully in a 1986 speech: "... if there is any lesson we must teach our children, it is that difference is a creative force for change, that survival and struggle for the future is not a theoretical issue. It is the very texture of our lives."[7]

Lorde's argument is echoed in this comment from Mandy, a twenty-four-year-old daughter of a lesbian mother:

> Mum's lesbianism and her strength of character have given me many choices in my life and so much freedom. My Mum brought me up so that I can take care of myself and so I'm confident enough to be myself. She taught me about being female in this society, about loving your body in a positive way, but being aware of the need to protect yourself from abuse by men. She made me aware of racism and other important issues at a very young age.[8]

On days that I worry the challenge is too great for our children, I take heart from the words of poet and essayist Adrienne Rich, whose work has inspired me for almost two decades. In the chapter on mothers and daughters in *Of Woman Born*, Rich writes:

> The quality of the mother's life — however embattled and unprotected — is her primary bequest to her daughter, because a woman who can believe in herself, who is a fighter, and who continues to struggle to create livable space around her, is demonstrating to her daughter that these possibilities exist.[9]

From our example as lesbian mothers, whether in partnership or as single parents, our daughters learn that choices do exist. Our lives, and the ways in which we organize them, challenge prescribed gender roles, something that is especially important for our daughters in a world that still teaches them that survival without a man is next to impossible. Our daughters see us as women, being active agents in the world both outside and inside the home. Like single mothers, lesbian mothers, whether partnered or not, have to manage all the chores required to maintain a home and family, from changing the furnace filter to getting the car fixed, from cooking dinner to knowing whom to call when you can't do something yourself. Although lesbian couples *can* still fall into roles and patterns, the division of labour is not predetermined by gender stereotypes.[10] Furthermore, studies suggest that divisions of household labour tend to be more egalitarian in lesbian households than in heterosexual households.[11] For our daughters, that can provide an invaluable lesson about female resourcefulness, strength and self-reliance — lessons that can, perhaps, combat some of the messages our daughters receive from the outside world about female helplessness and unworthiness.

Regardless of how egalitarian and empowering our homes may be, we do not raise our children in a vacuum. On the contrary, like all women, lesbian mothers are profoundly affected by the political and legal climate within which we live and raise our children. In many places, lesbianism is still considered a "crime against nature," and a revelation of lesbianism can lead to criminal charges and imprisonment. Although the sexual activities in which lesbians might engage are not criminalized in Canada, provided they take place in the privacy of our own homes, nonetheless, lesbians' relationships with each other and with their nonbiological children remain largely "outside the law." Furthermore, in a number of American states, even "private acts" between same-sex partners remain criminalized. The ongoing parade of anti-gay initiatives in the United States and the opposition to sexual orientation protection witnessed in Canada indicates that the battles that the lesbian and gay movements have fought during the past twenty-five years are far from over. It is within this legal and political context, then, that we lesbian mothers are raising our daughters (and sons).[12]

These challenges are particularly great for lesbian mothers who gave birth to their children within the context of a heterosexual marriage — and who face a custodial challenge from their former husband. It is important for us to remember that the vast majority of lesbian mothers are still women who gave birth to children in heterosexual relationships, and the struggles of these women to retain custody of their children continue. Despite an apparent liberalizing in attitudes, despite "lesbian chic," despite *Ellen*,[13] lesbian mothers continue to lose custody of their children to ex-husbands, to child welfare agencies, to their own mothers — solely because of their sexual orientation.[14]

These decisions are rooted in the belief that living with a lesbian or gay parent runs contrary to the "best interests of the child." Where further explanation is provided, it is usually based on the rationale that a child will suffer the ill effects of peer pressure — teasing, derision and harassment — because of his or her parents' sexual orientation. There can be little doubt that peer pressure is a very real factor in our children's lives. But it is important to recognize that "[i]t is prejudice, rather than homosexuality itself, that represents the [real] source of difficulty for the children of lesbians and gay men."[15]

As Lisa Saffron has recently noted:

> Fear of stigma is merely a defence of prejudice, ignorance and hatred, an implicit acceptance that society is, and should be, ruled by bigotry. It cannot be in the best interests of children to teach them to value conformity, to fear difference, to be ashamed and frightened of homosexuality and to live their lives according to the standards of people who hate.[16]

THE CHALLENGE

Here, then, is our challenge. We have to make the world a safe and accepting place for all our children, our sons and our daughters. We cannot afford to let the chance remarks slide, the "fag" this and "lezzie" that. One of the worst things you can call someone is still a "fag" and if you as a parent confront the remark, you're promptly told it's just a joke, that you are out of step, you just don't understand. The fact is that these are not harmless taunts. For the children of lesbians and gay men, and for the children who will grow up to be lesbian and gay, these remarks cut right to the bone. Our children are beaten up because of our sexual orientation. Gay and lesbian youth have staggering rates of suicide and suicide attempts.[17] Regardless of how rosy we may think things are, our children know that things are definitely NOT OK.

It is not just in the school yard that these remarks are made. We hear them in our workplaces, even in the classrooms where we teach and study.

It is not just the overt remarks that hurt our children. It is the absences. The failure to see representations of their families in the books, lessons and pictures in their classrooms. We all need to be there — me and my children, and you and your children — defending programs for lesbian and gay youth, defending the inclusion of diverse materials in the classrooms, fighting the bigots who seek to remove books like *Heather Has Two Mommies* from our libraries and our schools. Because together we can make a difference.

THE FUTURE

In the summer of 1996, our family, for the first time, attended the annual conference of the Gay and Lesbian Parents Coalition International.[18] For my partner and myself, it was a time of workshops and discussions, like many other conferences we have attended. But for Jesse, who attended the parallel conference for teenaged children of lesbian and gay parents,[19] it was an amazing experience. For the first time in her life, she was surrounded by her peers — other teenaged children of lesbian and gay parents — in a setting where our sexual orientation was simply not an issue. They were an amazing group of young people — dynamic, energetic, open and challenging. Jesse was ecstatic. She rose at six a.m., raced off to breakfast with her new friends and returned to our rooms at the end of the day, long after we had fallen asleep. There were teenagers from all kinds of families, and I laughed to myself when Jesse explained to us on the way home in the car, "My situation is really pretty simple." It was certainly the first time she had ever felt like that!

A week after she came home from the conference, she "came out" to her best friend. "My Mom's gay," she explained.

"With Sue?" her friend asked.

"Yes," Jesse replied.

"Does this mean Sue will be moving in with you guys?"

"She already lives with us," Jesse had to admit, glancing quickly over the twenty-one years we've been together.

"If you ever need to talk about it," her friend offered, "just let me know."

How it will turn out for Katie is anyone's guess. She has Jesse as a pathbreaker, and lots and lots of other children of lesbian mothers to fight with her. In the years ahead, we hope she will have many other allies, challenging homophobia when they encounter it, not just for the benefit of my daughters, but for the benefit of all our children.

Notes

Research for this essay was supported in part by a grant from the Social Sciences and Humanities Research Council of Canada.

1. Ellen Herman, "The Romance of Lesbian Motherhood," *Sojourner: The Women's Forum* (March 1988), 12.

2. April Martin, *The Lesbian and Gay Parenting Handbook: Creating and Raising Our Families* (New York: HarperCollins, 1993), 6.

3. In offering similar estimates, Charlotte Patterson explains: "Such estimates are based on extrapolations from what is known or believed to be known about base rates in the population. According to Kinsey, Pomeroy, and Martin (1948) and others ... approximately 10% of the 250 million people in the United States today can be considered gay or lesbian. According to large-scale survey studies ... about 10% of gay men and about 20% of lesbians are parents. Most have children from a heterosexual marriage that ended in divorce; many have more than one child. Calculations using these figures suggest that there are about 3–4 million gay or lesbian parents in the United States today. If, on average, each parent has two children, that would place the number of children of formerly married lesbians and gay men at about 6-8 million." Charlotte J. Patterson, "Children of Lesbian and Gay Parents," *Child Development* 63 (1992), 1026. In addition, experts suggest that an estimated five to ten thousand lesbians and gay men have become parents after coming out. I would suggest that such estimates vastly underestimate the number of "baby boom" parents.

4. Carl E. Cade, "Two Moms, No Hamburgers!," in Louise Rafkin, ed., *Different Mothers: Sons and Daughters of Lesbians Talk about Their Lives* (San Francisco: Cleis Press, 1990), 53.

5. The studies also indicate that the vast majority of our children grow up to be heterosexual. Not surprisingly, this is an issue that has preoccupied the judicial and public minds in relation to lesbian and gay parents, and the statistic is frequently presented in custody cases involving lesbian mothers as evidence of the fact that lesbian mothers pose little danger to their children.

6. In reviewing previous studies that compared lesbian families with heterosexual single-parent families, Maureen Sullivan reported that "there are no marked differences in parenting practices or effects on children's psychological development, except that children in lesbian households are often described as having more positive, tolerant attitudes towards unconventional lifestyles and social differences." Maureen Sullivan, "Rozzie and Harriet? Gender and Family Patterns of Lesbian Coparents," *Gender and Society* 10, no. 6 (December 1996), 750.

    In a review of literature on lesbian families, Charlotte Patterson notes, "Children of lesbian mothers have described an increased tolerance for divergent viewpoints as a benefit of growing up in lesbian mother families (Rafkin, 1990), but systematic research in this area is still needed." "Children of Lesbian and Gay Parents," 1038.

7. Audre Lorde, "Turning the Beat Around: Lesbian Parenting 1986," in Sandra Pollack and Jeanne Vaughn, eds., *Politics of the Heart: A Lesbian Parenting Anthology* (Ithaca, NY: Firebrand, 1987), 314.

8. Mandy, cited in Lisa Saffron, *"What about the Children?" Sons and Daughters of Lesbian and Gay Parents Talk about Their Lives* (London: Cassell, 1996), 192.

9. Adrienne Rich, *Of Woman Born: Motherhood as Experience and Institution* (New York: Bantam Books, 1977), 250–251.

10. The limited research on child-rearing practices of lesbian families suggests that "lesbian couples who have chosen to bear children are likely to share household and child care duties to a somewhat greater degree than do heterosexual couples." Two separate studies conducted by D.A. Osterweil and by S.I. Hand, cited in Charlotte J. Patterson, "Lesbian and Gay Parents and their Children," in Ritch C. Savin-Williams and Kenneth M. Cohen, eds., *The Lives of Lesbians, Gays, and Bisexuals* (Orlando: Harcourt, Brace and Company, 1996), 284.

11. Maureen Sullivan reports in her study of thirty-four lesbian couples that "[s]imilar to the egalitarian divisions of housework among lesbian couples without children in other studies, the parenting practices combined with paid and unpaid domestic work of these lesbian coparents reflect explicit, self-conscious commitments to equity." Sullivan, "Rozzie and Harriet?," 764.

12. For a discussion of lesbian parents and the law, see Katherine Arnup, "Living in the Margins: Lesbian Families and the Law," in Katherine Arnup, ed., *Lesbian Parenting: Living with Pride and Prejudice* (Charlottetown, PEI: gynergy, 1997).

13. In April 1997, sitcom star Ellen DeGeneres revealed the long-anticipated news that she is a lesbian on her widely syndicated television show, *Ellen*. While many television programs now include gay or lesbian characters, Ellen is the first actor in a leading role to come out.

14. For a discussion of child custody cases involving lesbian mothers, see Katherine Arnup, "'Mothers Just Like Others': Lesbians, Divorce, and Child Custody in Canada," *Canadian Journal of Women and the Law* 3 (1989), 18–32.

15. Saffron, *"What about the Children?,"* 169.

16. Ibid., 167.

17. Gay teens are fourteen times more at risk of making a serious suicide attempt, according to a 1986 University of Calgary study. Earlier American studies corroborate these findings. See, Paul Gibson, "Gay Male and Lesbian Youth Suicide," in M.R. Feinleib, ed., *Report of the Secretary's Task Force on Youth Suicide*, Vol. 3, *Preventions and Interventions in Youth Suicide* (United States Department of Health and Human Services, 1989).

18. Gay and Lesbian Parents Coalition International (GLPCI) can be reached at glpcinat@ix.netcom.com.

19. The youth conference is organized by Children of Lesbians and Gays Everywhere (COLAGE). They can be reached at 2300 Market St., #165, San Francisco, CA 94114. Their e-mail address is colage@colage.org.

Chapter 3

ACROSS THE DIVIDE:
CONTEMPORARY ANGLO-AMERICAN FEMINIST THEORY ON THE MOTHER-DAUGHTER RELATIONSHIP

Andrea O'Reilly

Sometimes it seemed as if we were engaged in an Olympic competition to decide whose mother was absolutely the worst. We
ground them up in our long conversations and spit them out.
— Anne Rophie, *Fruitful: A Real Mother in the Modern World*

I cannot forget my mother. Though not as sturdy as others, she is
my bridge. When I needed to get across, she steadied herself long
enough for me to run across safely.
— Renita Weems, "Hush Mama's Gotta Go Bye-Bye"

"THE CATHEXIS BETWEEN mother and daughter, essential, distorted,
misused," wrote Adrienne Rich in 1976, "is the great unwritten story."[1]
I am a daughter and I am a mother of daughters. My feminism as it is
lived and as it is practised in my scholarship and teaching is decidedly
mother-centred; its aim is to recover, narrate and theorize the unwritten
stories of mothers and daughters. What I discovered close to ten years
ago when I began my work on motherhood and the mother–daughter
relationship was that our stories as mothers and daughters had in fact
already been written, narrated by the larger patriarchal culture that
scripted the roles mothers and daughters were expected to play. The

received view of mothers and daughters, or what author Toni Morrison calls in another context, the master narrative, is that this relationship, particularly in the daughter's adolescent years is one of antagonism and animosity. The daughter must distance and differentiate herself from the mother if she is to assume an autonomous identity as an adult. The mother, in turn, is perceived and understood only in terms of her maternal role, viewed either as devouring shrew or devoted madonna, bitch or victim, her own subjectivity as woman is eclipsed by her maternal identity. The mother represents for the daughter, according to the received narrative, the epitome of patriarchal oppression that she seeks to transcend as she comes to womanhood, and yet the daughter's failings, as interpreted by herself and the culture at large, are said to be the fault of the mother. This is the patriarchal narrative of the mother–daughter relationship.

The lives of mothers and daughters as they are lived are shaped by these larger cultural narratives even as mothers and daughters live lives different from, and in resistance to, these assigned roles. The aim of my research and teaching is to deconstruct this patriarchal narrative by first exposing this narration as precisely that: a narrative, an ideology, which, by definition, is a construction not a reflection of the actual lived reality of mothers and daughters, hence neither natural nor inevitable. Second, my work is concerned with how daughters and mothers may unravel the patriarchal script to write their own stories of motherhood and daughterhood. As part of this larger project, I designed a first year course on mothers and daughters that I have taught at York University for the last four years.[2] The objective of this course, entitled "Mothers and Daughters: From Estrangement to Empowerment," is to situate the mother–daughter relationship as a *cultural* construction. Students are taught to think critically and consciously about the cultural meanings assigned to the mother–daughter relationship; they are taught to explore how their own experiences of being mothered and their perceptions of motherhood in general, and of their own mother in particular, are shaped by the larger patriarchal narrative of motherhood and daughterhood. The course aims to identify, challenge and dismantle the patriarchal narrative of mother–daughter estrangement; in particular, it asks students to uncover the historical/psychological origins of this narrative. Students track the manifestations of patriarchal narrative in various cultural practices as diverse as media, education, government policy, psychological theory; analyze its workings in their own personal relationships; imagine ways it may be deconstructed; and finally construct an alternative mother–daughter narrative scripted for empowerment as opposed to estrangement.

An in-class writing assignment at the beginning of the course asks students to reflect upon their relationship with their mother. They are asked to describe this relationship at three points in their lives and are given a series of instructions and questions to help them do this: Describe your mother both inside and outside her role as mother. What do you want/need from your mother? What does she want/need from you? Are you like your mother? Do you want to be like your mother? Describe how your mother has helped or hindered you in achieving your life goals. This assignment serves as the first entry in the students' course journals: weekly written reflections on course readings, discussions and so forth. One student, reflecting upon this assignment at the close of the course, commented:

> When I look back to the beginning of the course only eight months ago I realize how different I was — how naive I was. To gain some perspective as to how my attitudes have changed concerning my own mother, I reread my first journal entry. I still agree with most of what I wrote, however after looking at the questions you asked us to answer, I realized that I had overlooked the most crucial of all the questions posed. I neglected the questions, "Do you know your mother as a person other than your mother? Who is your mother?" I think at the time I didn't really understand the significance of these questions nor could I have answered them for I didn't know my mother as a person. I didn't even know that I didn't know.[3]

This student's reflections, and in particular her comment "I didn't even know that I didn't know," serve as an appropriate epigraph for our positioning as daughters in the patriarchal narrative of mother–daughter estrangement. So thoroughly do we identify with this script that its cultural staging has been rendered invisible to us and we see it as merely "the way things are" — hence natural and inevitable. African-American essayist and poet Audre Lorde once said we must "name the nameless so that it can be thought."[4] The aim of this course, for daughters and mothers alike, is to render visible the "invisible hand of patriarchy" so as to see how thoroughly our lives are produced and shaped by patriarchal ideologies that are not of our own making.

MATROPHOPIA, MOTHER-BLAME AND DAUGHTER-CENTRICITY

I begin the course with Nancy Chodorow's classic essay, "Family Structure and Feminine Personality"[5] and a lecture on her "reproduction of mothering" thesis as it is developed in her book of the same name.[6] Nancy Chodorow, as Penelope Dixon noted in her feminist annotated bibliography on mothers and mothering, "was one of the first to write on the subject [of mothering] and subsequently has authored more books and articles on this subject than any other feminist writer."[7] Indeed, Chodorow's writings, particularly her now classic *The Reproduction of Mothering* has influenced the way a whole generation of scholars views motherhood. What is less acknowledged, however, is how this influential writer, who is identified as a feminist, reinscribes the patriarchal narrative of mother–daughter estrangement even as she seeks to dismantle it.

Chodorow contends that female mothering constructs gendered identities that are both differentiated and hierarchical. The pre-Oedipal mother–daughter attachment, she argues, is more prolonged and intense than the mother–son relationship. Because the daughter and the mother are the same gender, the mother perceives and treats her daughter as identical to and continuous with her self. The sameness and continuity of the pre-Oedipal mother–daughter symbiosis engenders a feminine psychic structure that is less individuated and differentiated. The daughter's sense of self is relational; she experiences herself as connected to others. The relational sense of self that women inherit from their mothers and bring to their own mothering, Chodorow goes on to argue, exacerbates female self-effacement and frustrates women's achievement of an authentic autonomous identity. Relationality, Chodorow concludes, is problematic for women because it hinders autonomy, psychological and otherwise, and since daughter–mother identification is the cause of this relationality in women, it is, in her words, "bad for mother and [daughter] alike."[8]

Chodorow has been criticized heavily in the twenty years since the publication of *The Reproduction of Mothering*. What concerns critics most is Chodorow's bracketing of the "real" world in her psychoanalytic abstractions of family patterns and gender formations. Critics have pointed out that Chodorow's mother-involved, father-absent family is quite specifically a white, urban, middle-class family structure of the first world. The gendered personalities that this specific family structure might create should not be used, as Chodorow does, to account for universal male dominance and gender difference. Moreover, Chodorow's theory of mother–daughter mutual psychological over-identification, used to explain women's subordination, far too readily glosses over women's lived powerlessness in a patriarchal world. While I argue wholeheartedly with the above criticisms, I am nonetheless disturbed by the fact that among the hundreds of articles written about Chodorow's theory only a handful assume as their focus of critique what I find to be the most troubling premise of Chodorow's reproduction thesis, namely, the pathologizing of mother–daughter identification/intimacy, particularly in positioning it as the cause of women's inadequacy, psychological and otherwise. One early critic of Chodorow, Marcia Westkott, for example, faulted Chodorow for failing to understand that women's relationality and dependency result not from psychology but from culture: "The need of mothers to remain close to their daughters arises because mothers are given few other choices, not just because of an infantile personality structure."[9] Here, as with Chodorow, mother–daughter identification is construed as a liability.

In *Don't Blame Mother*, Paula Caplan writes, "women love connection. But in a society that is phobic about intimacy and extols the virtues of independence, we mistakenly regard connection and closeness as dependency, fusion and merging."[10] The aim of the introductory section is to expose the pervasiveness of the pathology of mother–daughter intimacy and identification in contemporary culture. As one student commented, "It greatly disturbs me when women, such as Chodorow, write powerful stuff which influences a lot of people. I expect it from Freud but not from someone who calls herself a feminist." The sanction against mother–daughter intimacy observed in Chodorow is one of the many cultural practices that render mother–daughter estrangement natural and inevitable. It also originates from and reinscribes another central tenet of mother–daughter estrangement — mother-blame and the devaluation of motherhood.

In *Of Woman Born*, Adrienne Rich distinguishes between two meanings of motherhood: "the *potential relationship* of any woman to her powers of reproduction and to children; and the *institution*, which aims at ensuring that that potential — and all women — shall remain under male control."[11] I use the term motherhood to refer to the institution of motherhood, which is male-defined and controlled, and mothering to refer to experiences of mothering, which are female-defined and centred. According to Rich, the reality of patriarchal motherhood contradicts the possibility of gynocentric mothering. Across cultures and throughout history most women mother in the institution of motherhood; that is, women's mothering is defined and controlled by the larger patriarchal society in which they live. Mothers do not make the rules, Rich emphasizes, they simply enforce them. Whether it is in the form of parenting books, a physician's advice or the father's rules, a mother raises her children in accordance with the values and expectations of the dominant patriarchal culture. Mothers are policed by what theorist Sara Ruddick calls the "gaze of others." Under the gaze of others, mothers "relinquish authority to others, [and] lose confidence in their own values." Ruddick calls this an abdication of maternal authority. "Fear of the gaze of the others," she continues, "can be expressed intellectually as inauthenticity, a repudiation of one's own perceptions and values."[12] The institution of motherhood is predicated upon inauthentic mothering and the abdication of maternal authority.

A daughter, Ruddick emphasizes, perceives this inauthenticity and understands the powerlessness which underpins her mother's compliance and complicity. In *Of Woman Born*, Rich speaks of the rage and resentment daughters feel toward this powerlessness of their mothers. However, at the same time the daughter feels rage toward her mother, she is expected to identify with her because the daughter is also a woman who, it is assumed, will some day become a mother/wife as her mother did. The daughter resists this identification because she does not want a life like her mother's, nor does she wish to be aligned with someone who is oppressed and whose work is so devalued. "Thousands of daughters," writes Rich, "see their mothers as having taught a compromise and self-hatred they are struggling to win free of, the one through whom the restrictions and degradations of a female existence were ... transmitted."[13] Rich calls this distancing between mothers and daughters matrophobia: "the fear not of one's mother or of motherhood but of *becoming one's mother*."[14] Matrophobia, she writes,

> can be seen as a womanly splitting of the self in the desire to become purged once and for all of our mothers' bondage, to become individuated and free. The mother stands for the victim in ourselves, the unfree woman, the martyr. Our personalities seem dangerously to blur and overlap with our mothers, and in a desperate attempt to know where mother ends and daughter begins, we perform radical surgery.[15]

When daughters perform this radical surgery they sever themselves from their attachment with their mother.

The institution of motherhood and the cultural devaluation/subordination of mothers, and the practice of inauthentic mothering on which it is predicated, give rise to mother-blame. Paula Caplan argues that mother-blame is rampant in contemporary culture, among both professionals and the population at large. "The biggest reason daughters are upset and angry with their mothers," writes Caplan, "is that they have been *taught* to do so."[16] Similar to the feeling of matrophobia identified by Rich, mother-blame distances daughters from mothers because mothers come to be seen not as sources of empowerment but as the cause of all and any problems that may ail the daughter.

Marianne Hirsch in her highly acclaimed book, *The Mother/Daughter Plot: Narrative, Psychoanalysis, Feminism*, argues that the feminist theory written in the 1970s is characterized by a daughterly perspective or subjectivity that Maureen Reddy and Brenda Daly call "daughter-centricity."[17] "It is the woman as daughter," Hirsch writes, "who occupies the center of the global reconstruction of subjectivity and subject-object relation. The woman as mother remains in the position of other, and the emergence of feminine daughterly subjectivity rests and depends on that continued and repeated process of othering the mother."[18] She goes on to say, "The adult woman who is mother continues to exist only in relation to her child, never as a subject in her own right. And in her maternal function, she remains an object, always distanced, always idealized or denigrated, always mystified, always represented through the small child's point of view."[19] Hirsch argues that such ambivalence expresses itself in the rhetoric and politics of the 1970s movement:

> Throughout the 1970s, the metaphor of sisterhood, of friendship or of surrogate motherhood has been the dominant model for female and feminist relationships. To say that "sisterhood is powerful," however, is to isolate feminist discourse within one generation and to banish feminists who are mothers to the "mother-closet." In the 1970s, the prototypical feminist voice was, to a large degree, the voice of the daughter attempting to separate from an overly connected or rejecting mother, in order to bond with her sisters in a relationship of mutual nurturance and support among women. With its possibilities of mutuality and its desire to avoid power, the paradigm of sisterhood has the advantage of freeing women from the biological function of giving birth, even while offering a specifically feminine relational model. "Sisters" can be "maternal" to one another without allowing their bodies to be invaded by men and the physical acts of pregnancy, birth, and lactation. In this feminist family romance, sisters are better mothers, providing more nurturance and greater encouragement of autonomy. In functioning as mutual surrogate mothers, sisters can replace mothers.[20]

Thus, while mothering as nurturance was celebrated amongst 1970s feminists, real mothers and the biological processes of mothering were displaced and disparaged.

Hirsch identifies four reasons for the 1970s "avoidance and discomfort" with the maternal. First, motherhood represented, for daughters, a compliance with patriarchy of which they wanted no part. Second, feminists feared the lack of control associated with motherhood. Third, feminists suffered from what critic Elizabeth Spelman has identified as "somatophophia" — the fear and discomfort with the body.[21] And nothing, as Hirsch has observed, "entangles women more firmly in their bodies than pregnancy, birth, lactation, miscarriage, or the inability to conceive."[22] Fourth, and characteristic of much feminist theorizing in the 1970s, was an ambivalence about power, authority and anger — all of which are part of mothering and associated with the maternal. "Feminist theoretical writing in the U.S.," writes Hirsch, "is permeated with fears of maternal power and with anger at maternal powerlessness."[23] Caplan argues that men fear maternal power. It would seem that women, too, fear it. The sisterhood metaphor of the 1970s thus may be read as a gesture of displacement or containment. The maternal power that is feared is rendered safe by transforming it into mothering between sisters — no power imbalance — and by objectifying and "otherizing" the person who seems to wield this power, the mother.

To a young child, the powers of the mother appear limitless. Our own individual flesh-and-blood mother is also connected to the primordial Great Mother, who held very real life and death powers over mortal men. In our individual and collective unconscious we remember that time when we lived under the mother's power in the pre-Oedipal and prepatriarchal world. In *The Mermaid and the Minotaur*, Dorothy Dinnerstein argues that the fear of maternal power and the hatred of women generally originate from infant experiences which, in turn, come to structure adult consciousness.[24] The mother, Dinnerstein reasons, cannot satisfy all of the child's needs and desires. The inevitable dissatisfaction, discomfort, frustration and anger felt by the child directs itself at the person whose responsibility it was to meet those needs. In contrast to Dinnerstein's view, I would suggest that the experiences of infancy, given that they include both pain and pleasure, engender not misogyny but a deep ambivalence that becomes organized around polarized constructions of the mother. What is created is the Good Mother and the Bad Mother; all that we find desirable about mothers is signified by the former and all that we fear and hate is marked by the latter. This delineation is, I would suggest, mapped along an already established historical topography of separation and specialization. I refer here to what we speculate occurred at the dawn of patriarchy when the many diverse qualities of the original Great Goddess were separated and used to create several distinct goddesses. That which mortal men feared in the original Goddess — particularly her powers over life and death — was displaced upon a terrible mother goddess, like the Hinud goddess Kali, who represented death and destruction while that which was desired was retained and assigned to a beneficent power. In Catholicism, for example, Mary, the mother of Jesus, is such a woman. The polarization and specialization of the maternal self continue to structure our ambivalence.

The fear of maternal power is at the heart of such disparagement and idealization. However, as Ruddick reminds us: "All power lies at least partly in the eye of the beholder. To a child, a mother is huge — a judge, trainer, audience, and provider whose will must be placated ... A mother, in contrast to the perception her children have of her, will mostly experience herself as relatively powerless."[25] However, as we speak to and about the very real powerlessness of mothers, we must not forget the power a mother does possess. Ruddick writes:

> There are many external constraints on [a mother's] capacity to name, feel, and act. But in the daily conflict of wills, at least with her children, a mother has the upper hand. Even the most powerless woman knows that she is physically stronger than her young children. This along with undeniable psychological power gives her the resources to control her children's behavior and influence their perceptions. If a mother didn't have this control, her life would be unbearable.[26]

Mothering is profoundly an experience of both powerlessness and power and it is this paradox of motherhood that helps explain women's ambivalence about motherhood. This ambivalence about maternal power, along with fear of the maternal, mother-blame, cultural devaluation of motherhood and matrophopia, distance daughters from their mothers and scripts the relationship of mother and daughters as one of disconnection and estrangement.

MOTHER-DAUGHTER CONNECTION AND EMPOWERMENT: THEORIES AND NARRATIVE

Once students have identified these cultural practices that distance daughters from the mothers, they explore ways in which these practices can be resisted. The sanction against mother–daughter identification, with which I began this chapter, is challenged by Elizabeth Debold, Marie Wilson and Idelisse Malavé in their important work *Mother*

Daughter Revolution. They argue that psychological theories of development are organized around the assumption that adolescence is a "time of separation when daughters are struggling to be independent, particularly from their mothers; and daughters in adolescence don't want to listen to their mothers or be like them in any way."[27] Separation from parents is mandated in developmental theory to enable the emerging adult to achieve an autonomous sense of self. *Mother Daughter Revolution* calls into question this "sacred cow" of developmental theory — the equivalency of separation and autonomy — and argues that it constitutes a betrayal of both mothers and daughters:

> Separation and autonomy are not equivalent: a person need not separate from mothers emotionally to be autonomous. Under the dominion of experts, mothers are urged to create a separation and disconnection from daughters that their daughters do not want. Early childhood and adolescence are the two stages of life where separation has been decreed as imperative to the independence and autonomy of children. To mother "right," women disconnect from their daughters and begin to see them as society will. Rather than strengthen girls this breach of trust leaves girls weakened and adrift.[28]

Mothers want to "do right" by their daughters so, as dictated by developmental theory, they distance themselves from their daughters when the daughters reach adolescence. At the same time, they propel the daughters out of the maternal space of childhood and into the heterosexual realm of adulthood.

What is most disturbing about this pattern of separation and betrayal is its timing. "In childhood, girls have confidence in what they know, think, and feel."[29] With the onset of adolescence, girls between the ages of nine and twelve come up against what Debold, Wilson and Malavé call the wall. "The wall is our patriarchal culture that values women less than men ... To get through the wall, girls have to give up parts of themselves to be safe and accepted within society."[30] Before adolescence, girls are, in their words, "fully themselves," but at the crossroads between childhood and adolescence, girls

come to label their vitality, desires, and thoughts as "selfish," "bad," or "wrong." They lose the ability to hold on to the truth of their experience ... They begin to see themselves as others see them, and they orient their thinking and themselves towards others ... [They] have to give up their relationship with the world of girls and women, the world that they have lived and loved in, and also give up relationship with parts of themselves that are too dangerous to keep in the adult world of male desire. Girls give up these relationships for the sake of the relationships that have been prescribed for them in male-led societies. The wall of patriarchy expects girls to separate from what they know, from each other, and from the women who care for them.[31]

Daughters are abandoned by their mothers when they need them the most.

Central to *Mother Daughter Revolution* is the belief that mothers can help their daughters resist being influenced by the wall. With her mother beside her, the daughter is empowered and can learn to compromise less of herself. The key to the mother's ability to do this is the reclamation of her own girl self. The authors write:

If mothers decide to join with daughters who are coming of age as women, mothers must first reclaim what they themselves have lost. Reclaiming is the first step in women's joining girls' resistance to their own dis-integration. Reclaiming is simply the process of discovering, describing, and reappropriating the memories and feelings of our preadolescent selves ... The goal is not to become a preadolescent girl. That wouldn't be desirable even if it were possible ... But women can reclaim and, thus, reintegrate the vital parts of themselves that they discarded or drove underground.[32]

This reclamation empowers the mother and enables her to help her daughter in her resistance. As *Mother Daughter Revolution* suggests, if mothers reclaim their driven-underground prepatriarchal selves, their reclaimed selves can join their daughters and empower them to withstand the loss or compromise of their own female selfhood. Mothers and daughters together "can claim the power of connection, community, and choice. And this power just might bring down the wall."[33]

Another contemporary theorist read in the course champions

mother–daughter connectedness as a mode of resistance. Miriam Johnson, the author of *Strong Mothers, Weak Wives*, emphasizes how daughters may connect with their mothers to withstand what may be called the heterosexualizing behaviour of the father. In Chodorow's psychoanalytical account, the differential treatment of sons and daughters by their mothers is said to be the cause of both gender difference and male dominance. Johnson challenges this argument. She writes: "It is the wife role and not the mother role that organizes women's secondary status."[34] Women's secondary status, she maintains, originates not from the maternal core of women's subjectivity (Chodorow's relational self) but from their heterosexual identity as wives of men. In contrast to Chodorow, Johnson maintains that male dominance originates not from the mother–child attachment, but from the father–daughter relationship.

The relationship of father and daughter, Johnson asserts, "trains daughters to be wives who are expected to be secondary to their husbands."[35] She argues that fathers often romanticize the father–daughter relationship and interact with their daughters as a lover would. Fathers feminize their daughters: daddies teach their girls to be passive, pleasing and pretty for men. In Johnson's words, the father–daughter relationship "reproduce[s] in daughters a disposition to please men in a relationship in which the male dominates." In other words, "daddy's girls are in training to be wives."[36] Because daddy's girls are trained and rewarded for pleasing and playing up to men, they grow up to be male-defined and male-orientated women. In most so-called normal (male-dominant) families what is experienced is psychological incest. "The incest ... is psychological, not overtly sexual. The father takes his daughter over. She looks up to him because he is her father. He is the king and she is the princess. It is all OK because the male is dominant in 'normal' adult heterosexual relations."[37]

Johnson argues that these princesses are in need of rescue and the rescuer is the mother: "If daddy's girls are to gain their independence they need to construct an identity as the daughters of strong mothers as well."[38] In *The Reproduction of Mothering*, Chodorow attributes women's lack of autonomy to the feminine-related sense of self which the mother–daughter relationship engendered. In contrast, Johnson argues that women's lack of autonomy originates from the daughter's psychological dependency on her father as a male-orientated daddy's girl. According to Johnson, a daughter's identification with her mother, far from prohibiting authentic female autonomy, produces and promotes that authenticity and autonomy. Chodorow suggested in her earlier sociological work that daughters are empowered by identification with their mothers in matrifocal cultures. Johnson believes that an empowering mother–daughter identification is also possible under patriarchy if the daughter relates to her mother as a mother and friend and not as the father's wife. Johnson contends that the mother–daughter relationship is the key to overcoming women's psychological inauthenticity as daddy's girl and, by implication, women's social oppression in patriarchy. Thus the daughter achieves authentic autonomy not through greater involvement with the father, but through a heightened identification with the mother.

For Johnson, the daughter must identify with the maternal part of her mother's identity rather than the heterosexual one. This identification empowers the daughter in two ways: first it allows her to step outside her oppressive daddy's girl role; and second, it allows her to identify with an adult woman's strength rather than her weakness. In Johnson's view, women are strong as mothers but made weak as wives. In identifying with her mother as mother, the daughter may construct a strong female identity outside of the passive heterosexual one patterned for her by her father and by society at large. In *Mother Daughter Revolution* the emphasis is on the mother joining the daughter while the focus of *Strong Mother, Weak Wives* is the daughter connecting to the mother. Though different, both positions are mapped along what feminist writer Naomi Ruth Lowinsky calls the motherline.

In her splendid work, *Stories from the Motherline: Reclaiming the Mother–Daughter Bond, Finding Our Souls*, Naomi Ruth Lowinsky explores "a worldview that is as old as humankind, a wisdom we have forgotten that we know: the ancient lore of women — the Motherline." She goes on to say:

> Whenever women gather in circles or in pairs, in olden times around the village well, or at the quilting bee, in modern times in support groups, over lunch, or at the children's party, they tell one another stories from the Motherline. These are stories of female

experience: physical, psychological, and historical. They are stories about the dramatic changes of woman's body: developing breasts and pubic hair, bleeding, being sexual, giving birth, suckling, menopause, and of growing old. They are stories of the life cycles that link generations of women: Mothers who are also daughters, daughters who have become mothers; grandmothers who also remain granddaughters.[39]

Most women today, Lowinsky contends, are cut off from their motherline; they suffer from what she calls "the feminist ambivalence about the feminine."[40] "Women," she writes, "seemed to want to live their father's lives. Mother was rejected, looked down upon ... In the headlong race to liberate those aspects of ourselves that had been so long denied, we left behind all that women had been ... Many of us," she continues, "who joyfully accepted the challenge of new opportunities discovered in retrospect that we had cut ourselves off from much of what was meaningful to us as women: our mothers, our collective past, our passion for affiliation and for richness in our personal lives. We felt split between our past and our future."[41] Lowinsky asks that women integrate their feminine and feminist selves: women "must connect the historical self that was freed by feminism to live in the 'real' world, with the feminine self that binds us to our mothers and grandmothers."[42]

Daughters of the so-called baby boom are the first generation of women, at least among the middle classes, whose lives are radically different from those of their mothers. These daughters, Lowinsky argues, have "paid a terrible price for cutting [them]selves off from [their] feminine roots."[43] By disconnecting themselves from their motherline, these daughters have lost the authenticity and authority of their womanhood. Women may reclaim that authority and authenticity by reconnecting to the motherline:

> When a woman today comes to understand her life story as a story from the Motherline, she gains female authority in a number of ways. First, her Motherline grounds her in her feminine nature as she struggles with the many options now open to women. Second, she reclaims carnal knowledge of her own body, its blood mysteries and their power. Third, as she makes the journey back to her female roots, she will encounter ancestors who struggled

with similar difficulties in different historical times. This provides her with a life-cycle perspective that softens her immediate situation ... Fourth, she uncovers her connection to the archetypal mother and to the wisdom of the ancient worldview, which holds that body and soul are open and all life is interconnected. And, finally, she reclaims her female perspective, from which to consider how men are similar and how they are different.[44]

Virginia Woolf wrote in *A Room of One's Own*: "[W]e think back through our mothers if we are women."[45] Writing about Lowinsky's motherline in her book *Motherless Daughters: The Legacy of Loss*, Hope Edelman emphasizes that "motherline stories ground a ... daughter in a gender, a family, and a feminine history. They transform the experience of her female ancestors into maps she can refer to for warning or encouragement."[46]

These stories are made available to daughters through the female oral tradition or what we call gossip and old wives' tales. These feminine discourses, however, have been trivialized, marginalized and discredited; they are, to borrow French theorist Michel Foucault's term, "subjugated knowledge[s]" that circulate outside the master narrative. Moreover, the language of the motherline is rendered in a specifically feminine discourse or dialect that has been discursively and culturally marginalized by patriarchal culture.

In her valuable book *Motherless Daughters*, Edelman studies daughters who lost their mothers between infancy and their early thirties and considers the impact this loss had on the daughters' lives.[47] The daughters' narratives speak of feelings of incompleteness and fragmentation. "Our mothers," Edelman explains, "are our most direct connection to our history and our gender. Regardless of how well we think they did their job, the void their absence creates in our lives is never completely filled again."[48] When the mother dies daughters lose their connection to the motherline. "Without a mother or mother-figure to guide her," writes Edelman, "a daughter has to piece together a female self-image on her own."[49] A girl who loses her mother

> has little readily available, concrete evidence of the adult feminine to draw from. She has neither a direct guide for sex-typed behavior nor an immediate connection to her own gender. Left to piece

together her own feminine identity, she looks to other females for signs that she's developing along an appropriate gendered path.[50]

Motherless daughters long to know and to be connected to, what Lowinsky calls, the deep feminine, or in Edelman's words "that subtle unconscious source of feminine authority and power we mistakenly believe is expressed in scarf knots and thank-you notes but instead originates from a more abstract gendered core."[51] "Without knowledge of her own experiences, and the relationship to her mother's," Edelman continues, "a daughter is snipped from the female cord that connects the generations of women in her family, the feminine line of descent ... the motherline."[52]

Adrienne Rich writes in *Of Woman Born*, "The loss of the daughter to the mother, the mother to the daughter, is the essential female tragedy."[53] In Edelman's work, this loss refers to the daughter losing her mother through death, abandonment or neglect. In these instances separation occurs as a result of the mother's leaving the daughter. More frequent, in patriarchal culture, is the loss of the daughter to the mother: daughters become disconnected from their motherline through specific cultural practices, notably the devaluation of motherhood and the reinforcement of maternal powerlessness, fear of the maternal, mother-blame and matrophobia.

Journalist Marni Jackson calls maternal space "the mother zone; [the] hole in culture where mothers [go]."[54] Motherhood, she writes, "is an unexplored frontier of thought and emotion that we've tried to tame with rules, myth, and knowledge. But the geography remains unmapped."[55] She emphasizes that "[m]otherhood may have become an issue but it's not yet a narrative."[56] Maternal stories are forgotten and lost before they are spoken because "[m]others in the thick of it have not the time or brain cells to write it down, to give it life. [When they] have the time, amnesia moves in ... all the raw extremes of emotion are smoothed over and left behind ... Culture," she continues, "encourages this amnesia, by excluding mothers from its most conspicuous rewards — money, power, social status."[57] Because our mothers' stories remain unspoken, she argues, "the true drama of mother and child is replaced by the idealization of motherhood."[58] Julia Kristeva identifies the maternal with the unspeakable. The maternal is found outside and beyond language, "spoken" only in the extralinguistic, nonverbal discourse of the semiotic.[59] Perhaps the maternal is, as Hirsch speculates in *The Mother/Daughter Plot*, "unnarratable."[60] Or, as Ruddick writes, maternal voices

> have been drowned by professional theory, ideologies of motherhood, sexist arrogance, and childhood fantasy. Voices that have been distorted and censored can only be developing voices. Alternatively silenced and edging toward speech, mothers' voices are not voices of mothers as they are, but as they are becoming.[61]

Much of current feminist writing and activism is concerned with the recovery of the maternal voice. While recognizing how difficult it is to speak that which has been silenced, disguised and marginalized, writers today seek to make the maternal story narratable. In earlier times the ancient lore of the motherline was told around the village well or at the quilting bee; today, the oral tradition of old wives' tales is shared through written narratives.

In *Writing a Woman's Life*, Carolyn Heilbrun observes, "Lives do not serve as models, only stories do that. And it is a hard thing to make up stories to live by. We can only retell and live by stories we have heard ... Stories have formed us all: they are what we must use to make new fictions and new narratives."[62] Recent writings on the mother–daughter relationship call upon the mother to speak and the daughter to listen. Debold, Wilson and Malavé argue in *Mother Daughter Revolution* that the compromise of the female self in adolescence may be resisted or, at the very least, negotiated, when the mother connects with the daughter through stories. The mother, in recalling and sharing with her daughter her own narrative of adolescence, gives the daughter strategies of resistance and, hence, an alternative script for coming into womanhood. Caplan in *Don't Blame Mother* emphasizes that only by speaking and hearing the mother's story can women move beyond mother-blame.[63] In turn, Lowinsky and Edelman argue that a daughter's very identity as a woman is acquired through connection to, and knowledge of, her mother and the motherline of which she is a part. Rich writes, "mothers and daughters have always exchanged with each other — beyond the verbally transmitted lore of female survival — a knowledge that is subliminal, subversive, pre-verbal: the knowledge flowing between two alike bodies, one of which has spent nine months inside the other."[64] The lore Rich refers to here is, of course, the lore of the motherline that constructs female experience outside the phallologocentric narrative of patriarchy.

CONCLUSION

The theories and narratives read by the students in this course expose the cultural practices that underpin the patriarchal narrative of mother–daughter estrangement — sanction against mother–daughter intimacy, mother-blame, daughter-centricity, matrophobia and fear of maternal power — and offer various strategies by which mothers and daughters may deconstruct the patriarchal narrative so as to write their own stories of motherhood and daughterhood, ones scripted from relations of empowerment as opposed to estrangement. As another student remarked in her journal at the conclusion of the course:

> I want to tell you how much your course has meant to me and how much my life has changed because of it. I feel almost as if I am a different person now. You helped me break the cycle instilled in me by a patriarchal society that I was doomed to repeat. Most significantly, you provided me with the means to eliminate mother–blame from my life, and for that I am eternally grateful.

Through this course, I hope to create a dialogue between mothers and daughters that in turn will help them build a bridge over which they can cross the patriarchal divide that separates them. By doing so, mothers and daughters can construct a truly lasting politics of empowerment.

Notes

1. Adrienne Rich, *Of Woman Born: Motherhood as Experience and Institution* (New York: W. W. Norton, 1986), 225.

2. The course described in this chapter was designed and taught from 1993 to 1997 at York University as part of the College Course Programme. In the first two years the course examined the mother–daughter relationship from a cross-cultural perspective: students read selected novels and poetry by Anglo-American, Anglo-Canadian, Caribbean, African, Native, Chinese, Jewish, African-American and African-Canadian women writers. In 1995 the focus of the course became an in-depth and detailed study of the representation of the mother–daughter relationship in the dominant Anglo-American feminist tradition. In the second term of this course, students were introduced to theory and literature on mothers and daughters by African-American and Caribbean women writers in order to problematize the received feminist tradition. This chapter explores only the first part of the course. My research on the mother–daughter in African-American women's theory and literature may be found in "'Ain't that Love?': Anti-racism and Racial Constructions of Motherhood," in Maureen Reddy, ed., *Everyday Acts Against Racism: Raising Children in a Multiracial World* (Washington: Seal Press, 1996); "'In Search of My Mother's Garden, I Found My Own': Motherlove, Healing and Identity in Toni Morrison's *Jazz*," *African American Review* 30, no. 3 (1996); "Talking Back in Mother Tongue: A Feminist Course on Mothering and Motherhood," in Paula Bourne et al., eds., *Feminism and Education* (Toronto: CWSE Press, 1994). This topic is also explored in my article in progress, "'I Come From a Long Line of Uppity Irate Black Women': African-American Feminist Theory on Motherhood, the Motherline and the Mother–Daughter Relation." See also my *Toni Morrison on Motherhood* (Columbus: Ohio State University Press, forthcoming). In this volume Black motherhood is examined by Nina Lyon Jenkins in Chapter 11, "Black Women and the Meaning of Motherhood," and by Sylvia Hamilton in Chapter 14, "African Nova Scotian Women: Mothering Across the Generations."

   Regrettably in 1996 York administration made the decision to cancel the College Course Programme as part of its cost-cutting and restructuring initiative. This was a great loss to the students and faculty at York. I am currently designing, for the School of Women's Studies, a half-year course on mothers and daughters entitled "Anglo-American and African-American Feminist Theory on the Mother–Daughter Relationship: A Dialogue." This course will be taught alongside the half course "Mothers and Sons in Feminist Theory."

3. Journal entry from a student in my "Mothers and Daughters" class, York Univeristy, April 1995. All other student writings used in this chapter are taken from journal entries in this class.

4. Audre Lorde, "Poetry is Not a Luxury," *Sister Outsider* (New York: Quality Paper Back Club, Triangle Classics, 1993), 37.

5. In Nancy Chodorow, *Feminism and Psychoanalytic Theory* (New Haven: Yale University Press, 1989), 44–65.

6. Nancy Chodorow, *The Reproduction of Mothering: Psychoanalysis and the Sociology of Gender* (Berkeley: University of California Press, 1978).

7. Penelope Dixon, *Mothers and Mothering: An Annotated Bibliography* (New York: Garland Publishing, 1991), 4.

8. Chodorow, *The Reproduction of Mothering*, 217.

9. Marcia Westkott, "Mothers and Daughters in the World of the Father," *Frontiers* 3, no. 2 (1978), 9.

10. Paula Caplan, *Don't Blame Mother: Mending the Mother-Daughter Relationship* (New York: Harper and Row, 1989).

11. Rich, *Of Woman Born*, 13. Emphasis in original. Adrienne Rich emphasizes that motherhood is a cultural construction that varies with time and place. Ann Dally in *Inventing Motherhood: The Consequences of an Ideal* (London: The Hutchinson Publishing Group, 1982), argues that there have always been mothers but motherhood was invented. Her book convincingly shows how the ideology/occupation of motherhood as woman's natural calling was constructed in response to the socioeconomical transformation in the late eighteenth century from an agricultural to an industrialized based economy. With the rise of industrialization, middle-class women lost their jobs as active producers/contributors in the agriculturally based family economy, so a new profession was designed for them — motherhood. The 1950s witnessed a similar occurrence. After World War II, women were expected to give up their wartime jobs for the returning soldiers. To facilitate this change a new ideology/occupation of motherhood emerged, that of the full-time mother and housewife. For further information on the historical constructions of motherhood, see Elizabeth Badinter, *Mother Love: Myth and Reality* (New York: MacMillan Publishing Co., Inc., 1980), and Shari L. Thurer, *The Myths of Motherhood: How Culture Reinvents the Good Mother* (New York: Penguin Books, 1994). For an interesting comparative reading of Rich's and Badinter's works, see Liesbeth Woertman, "Mothering in Context: Female Subjectives and Intervening Practices," in Janneke van Mens-Verhulst, Karlein Schreurs, and Liesbeth Woertman, eds., *Daughtering and Mothering* (New York: Routledge, 1993), 57–61.

12. "Teachers, grandparents, mates, friends, employers, even an anonymous passerby," writes Ruddick, "can judge a mother by her child's behavior and find her wanting." Sara Ruddick, *Maternal Thinking: Toward a Politic of Peace* (New York: Ballantine Books, 1989), 111–112.

13. Rich, *Of Woman Born*, 235.

14. Ibid., 236. Emphasis in original.

15. Ibid.

16. Caplan, *Don't Blame Mother*, 2. Emphasis in original.

17. Brenda Daly and Maureen Reddy, *Narrating Mothers: Theorizing Maternal Subjectivities* (Knoxville: The University of Tennessee Press, 1991), 2. "In psychoanalytic studies," write Daly and Reddy, "we frequently learn less about what it is like to mother than what it is like to be mothered, even when the author has both experiences." *Narrating Mothers*, 2.

18. Marianne Hirsch, *The Mother/Daughter Plot: Narrative, Psychoanalysis, Feminism* (Bloomington: Indiana University Press, 1989), 136.

19. Ibid., 167.

20. Ibid., 164.

21. As quoted in Hirsch, *The Mother/Daughter Plot*, 166.

22. Hirsch, *The Mother/Daughter Plot*, 166.

23. Ibid., 167.

24. Dorothy Dinnerstein, *The Mermaid and the Minotaur: Sexual Arrangements and the Human Malaise* (New York: Harper Colophon, 1976).

25. Ruddick, *Maternal Thinking*, 34. Many, many works have examined women's feelings of powerlessness in the institution of motherhood. See, for example, Meg Luxton, *More Than A Labour of Love* (Toronto: The Women's Press, 1980).

26. Ruddick, *Maternal Thinking*, 35.

27. Elizabeth Debold, Marie Wilson, and Idelisse Malavé, *Mother Daughter Revolution: From Good Girls to Great Women* (New York: Bantam Books, 1994), 36.

28. Ibid., 22.

29. Ibid., 11.

30. Ibid., 12. Several feminist scholars have written on the loss of the female self in adolescence. See, for example, Lyn Mikel Brown and Carol Gilligan, *Meeting at the Crossroads: Women's Psychology and Girls' Development* (Cambridge, MA: Harvard University Press, 1992); Shere Hite, *The Hite Report on the Family* (New York: Grove Press, 1994); Judy Mann, *The Difference: Growing Up Female in America* (New York: Time Warner, 1994): Mary Pipher, *Reviving Ophelia: Saving the Selves of Adolescent Girls* (New York: Grosset/Putnam, 1994); Mieke de Waal, "Teenage Daughters on Their Mothers," in van Mens-Verhulst, Schreurs, and Woertman, eds., *Daughtering and Mothering*, 35–43.

31. Debold, Wilson, and Malavé, *Mother Daughter Revolution*, 15.

32. Ibid., 101.

33. Ibid., 38.

34. Miriam Johnson, *Strong Mothers, Weak Wives: The Search for Gender Equality* (Berkeley: University of California Press, 1989), 6.

35. Ibid., 8.

36. Ibid., 184.

37. Ibid., 173.

38. Ibid., 184.

39. Naomi Ruth Lowinsky, *Stories From the Motherline: Reclaiming the Mother-Daughter Bond, Finding Our Female Souls* (Los Angles: Jeremy P. Tarcher, 1992), 1–2.

40. Ibid., 30.

41. Ibid., 29.

42. Ibid., 32. It is important to emphasize that Lowinsky does not advocate "turning

back the clock" and pushing women once again out of historical time.

43. Ibid., 31.

44. Ibid., 13.

45. Virginia Woolf, *A Room of One's Own* (1929; reprint, New York: Granada, 1977), 72.

46. Hope Edelman, *Motherless Daughters: The Legacy of Loss* (New York: Delta, 1994), 201.

47. In Edelman's work, motherless includes several types of absences — "premature death, physical separation, mental illness, emotional abandonment, and neglect." Ibid., xxv.

48. Ibid., 61.

49. Ibid., xxv. One woman, whose mother died when she was eight, spoke about the longing for guidance of a mature, experienced woman who would teach her "how to be."

50. Ibid., 178.

51. Ibid., 179.

52. Ibid., 200.

53. Rich, *Of Woman Born*, 237.

54. Marni Jackson, *The Mother Zone: Love, Sex, Laundry in the Modern Family* (Toronto: Macfarlane Walter and Ross, 1992), 13.

55. Ibid., 9.

56. Ibid., 3.

57. Ibid., 4, 9.

58. Ibid.

59. Julia Kristeva, *Revolution in Poetic Language,* trans. Margaret Walker (New York: Columbia University Press, 1984).

60. Hirsch, *The Mother/Daughter Plot,* 179.

61. Ruddick, *Maternal Thinking,* 40. Emphasis in original.

62. Carolyn Heilbrun, *Writing a Woman's Life* (New York: Ballantine, 1988), 32.

63. Caplan writes: "[Women] must humanize [their] image of [their] mother ... [in order] to see the real woman behind the mother-myths." *Don't Blame Mother,* 147. Significantly, Caplan argues that such may be achieved through listening to the mother's story and writing a biography of her life.

64. Rich, *Of Woman Born*, 220.

Chapter 4

MOTHERS AS TEACHERS — TEACHERS AS MOTHERS

Alice Collins

THE LINES BETWEEN mothering and teaching are blurred. Women teachers' professional and personal lives have been limited and shaped by cultural constructions of gender, and this is magnified for teachers who are mothers. In this chapter, I explore the influence of mothering on the personal and professional lives of women teachers who taught for various periods of time from the 1930s to the 1990s in Newfoundland and Labrador.

There are a number of frameworks that have defined the study of women teachers, the most significant ones being the gendered division of labour and a "domestically oriented ideology of teaching."[1] The gendered division of labour refers to the work traditionally assigned women, most notably unpaid domestic labour that includes prime responsibility for children.[2] The domestically oriented ideology of teaching emanates from the belief in women's nurturing tendencies and holds that women are best suited for caring for children. Teaching is seen for women as "motherhood-in-waiting"[3] and as "teacher-in-training-for-motherhood."[4] These ideologies have shaped and limited women teachers' lives and career paths. Their delayed entry into administration,[5] the low proportion of women in educational administration, interrupted and "flat" careers, relegation of women teachers to young children in preschool and primary school[6] are results of gendered constructions in education. Research has explored the daily lives of women teachers and has demonstrated that in assuming primary responsibility for home and duties for their paid work, women experience the double day of work.[7] This leads to juggling the demands of the two workplaces in a "simultaneous" rather than "sequential" manner.[8] Beth Young uses the term "competing urgencies"[9] to describe the dual commitment to paid and family work.

In this "back and forth" world, women lead fluid lives. They flow from mothering to teaching and from teaching to mothering with no clear demarcation within and between the roles. Feminist literature identifies this as a source of stress and limitation for women. Madeleine Grumet suggests that women do not draw lines between their homes and their classrooms; they mother at home and they mother other mothers' children at school. She argues that women who teach "go back and forth between the experience of domesticity and the experience of teaching, between being with one's own children and being with the children of others, between being the child of one's own mother and the teacher of another mother's children."[10] Similarly, Heather-jane Robertson in *Progress Revisited* suggests that women tend not to have discrete "work lives" and "personal lives," but lives that flow through competing as well as complementary spheres of thought, feeling and responsibility.[11]

The narratives for this chapter are drawn from a larger study that has been ongoing since 1990, during which time twenty-five women in Newfoundland and Labrador have been interviewed. These women have been teachers and administrators in the Newfoundland school system and some have served in leadership positions at other levels in teachers' associations and in the government.

The study uses qualitative research methods that are best suited to understanding the lived experiences of women. Feminist theorists promote qualitative methodologies such as women's personal narratives and biographies because they allow us to listen to women's voices, to learn from the details of their everyday lives (however seemingly insignificant) and, therefore, to reconstruct our understanding of the world.[12] Biography, as a feminist method, allows us to identify the commonalities in women's experiences. The use of narrative allows a full disclosure of the reality of women's lives and work by collapsing the traditional dissociation between women's "private" and "public" lives.[13]

Many and varied themes have emerged from the women's personal narratives. In this chapter, two of these themes are explored because they take us beneath the surface into a fuller exploration of mothering and teaching. The first is an exploration of motherhood as a defining moment and how becoming a mother changed and shaped these women's lives. The second is an examination of the fluidity between mothering and teaching, teaching and mothering, and how these two extremely responsible roles can blend together in one person.

MOTHERHOOD AS A DEFINING MOMENT

The women who taught school in the 1930s and the1940s had to terminate their careers upon marriage. By the 1950s, women were able to teach upon marriage but were expected to resign their teaching positions when they had children: "that was the norm at that point ... if you were expecting a baby you left teaching and spent some time at home with the child."[14] Most of the women experienced interrupted careers, taking time from teaching that spanned periods from six weeks to one year. These women recalled that becoming mothers changed their lives and careers significantly. Lucille recounts:

> Before being a mother you could give more of your time and effort to your job and to your relationship. And when you became a mother you were juggling those. I felt good about being a mother and I gave a lot of my energy to being a good mother. My socialization in terms of being a good mother was strong and there were really distinct expectations of what a good mother should do, and I tried to measure up to all those.[15]

Jennifer's was the quintessential double day of work and her breast-feeding a metaphor for the fluid life she was leading. Jennifer had her third child the last of September and returned to school in mid-November. She arranged her whole life around breast-feeding her baby.

> I breast-fed the baby. Tina never had a mouthful of formula. I had a friend who did every one of my dinner duties at my school, and I would leave school everyday and drive home to nurse my baby at lunch time. I'd jump out of the clothes that I had on and wash my hands, arms and face and pull on a clean gown, and I'd prepare what I had to do and I would just sit down comfortably,

put my feet up and take my baby in my arms and nurse her. I would have my own lunch and go back and teach my Kindergarten class for the afternoon. I had energy plus, I had energy galore.[16]

Claire considered not going back to work, feeling unsure as "a first-time parent and, you know, a lot of it was the influence of my mother ... my mother thought I was the neglectful mother to be doing this ... but in the end I decided to go [back]. I knew if I stayed home I would have rotted."[17]

Being a new mother was replaced with responding to the continuing growing needs of children. Motherhood continued to define these women's choices, especially not to seek professional advancement. Sarah decided not to assume a leadership position with her professional association because she would have to leave her home community and her young son.

That's a big decision and in the formative years of [my] child, when he was four to seven years old, it would have an incredible impact on his life and I wasn't prepared to take that risk. I think he needed his mother at that time, whereas if I chose the other career track, I could not be with him when he got home from school.[18]

Sarah "was unwilling to sacrifice her family." She felt she needed to "keep a balance."[19] Ruth taught at night because she "wanted to be with the children during the day."[20] As a result, she lost her pensionable teaching years.

Women who are now in leadership positions, such as Lucille and Eileen, and whose children are grown up recall delaying their decision in favour of balancing home and teaching. Lucille did not consider administration until later in her career. "I think I was socialized to think that women are teachers."[21] When they began to give thought to improving their professional qualifications, the women made choices that demanded a great deal of time, energy and commitment. Eileen undertook courses at night, in the summer and by correspondence, "arranging my schedule around the children."[22] What began to unfold was a triple day of work where these women tried to study when their children did not need them.

Motherhood defined and shaped these women's lives. They made career decisions, for example not to advance their careers or when best to undertake further studies, based on the needs of their children. They lived out the gendered division of labour by assuming prime responsibility for their children and their work. They performed unpaid work and determined how their paid work of teaching could fit into a schedule that was balanced and did not sacrifice their families. Motherhood as a defining moment started with the birth of their children and continued throughout the careers of these women.

THE INFLUENCES OF MOTHERING ON TEACHING

Having made these career choices, some of the women continued as classroom teachers for the duration of their careers while others made changes when the timing was right for their families. Despite drawing these career lines, the lines between mothering and teaching merged. These women brought their mothering to school, and they acknowledged that many aspects of their teaching lives were influenced because they were mothers.

Margaret had a better understanding of her students because of her own children. "I had a good rapport with my students because of my own children. So I found that some things that teachers would expect of them I didn't expect, because I knew this was happening to my own children, they were doing the same things. And I found it was a great help."[23]

Jeanette and Kathleen mothered in the classroom. For Jeanette, "being a mother and having teenagers ... [means] you can relate more so to teenagers in the classroom. And then to parents who have teenagers as well." And in the classroom, she "used a different approach, maybe more motherly or whatever, which is maybe what they need. They don't need physical or stronger force but a milder, gentler approach especially to some of the troubled students."[24]

For Kathleen, nurturing was evident: "You have to be caring ... [to] them." She also felt she related better to parents because she was a parent herself. Before becoming a parent, she didn't appreciate all the commitments and responsibilities parents have: "I wasn't aware of all that before."[25]

It worked two ways for Catherine. She gained perspective on teaching because she had her own children, and her children benefited from her being a teacher.

> I think, at least I found, that after I had my own children that some of the work that I was doing in education became more meaningful. And also I could see the other perspective better. I could see things from the child's point of view and also from the parents' point of view better than I had before ... I think the whole interactive effect worked. But certainly I think it made me a better teacher, yes. It's good to see the perspective.[26]

Lucille also had a better understanding of parents because she was a parent.

> I had a real empathy for the difficult job [it is] to be a good parent, and I rejected the unrealistic expectations that schools often have of mothers, you know, the whole blame the victim mentality that permeates the school system. I always took active steps to step outside that kind of approach and to recognize that most parents really want the best for their children. I had difficulty finding a bad mother or a bad parent when I really got to know them.[27]

For Elizabeth and Eileen, teaching was a continuation of the mothering they had done at home. Being the oldest in their families, they had always had responsibilities for siblings. As the eldest of a large family whose mother was sick most of the time, Elizabeth had "a lot of the responsibility of taking care of [her] brothers and sisters."[28] When she came back to her home community at age seventeen, after one summer at school, she started a teaching position in which she was responsible for sixty-three children. The children, in Grades 1 to 5, were all in one room that had no indoor plumbing, no electricity and a wood stove. "So that's what I was doing at seventeen. It was just a continuation of what I had been doing at home."[29] Eileen comments, "I was given positions of responsibility in the house quite young and, you know, I had to care for younger siblings ... I remember my brother in so many words saying I was a mother figure."[30]

Elizabeth is a Native woman who views every aspect of her life as fluid and intertwined. "My life revolves around my profession. And I'm very lucky in that the religious aspect of my life and my family life and my community life ties into my professional life." For Elizabeth, there are no borders from home to school. Taking care of children at school is "like a family, except it's bigger."[31] As principal of her school, Elizabeth promotes the philosophy that to come into the school is like coming home.

> This is our home from the time we're here, from nine [in the morning] to five o'clock in the evening ... I want to have it nice and warm and clean. And it's the same way with the kids. And for some of these kids, school is sanctuary. This is the place where they leave all their stresses outside; this is one place where it's calm, it's quiet. It's probably the most peaceful time of their day, so we try to make it like a home.[32]

> For Maureen, mothering and nurturing affects pedagogy.

> Women tend to see education more holistically rather than divided up into little sections, and they tend to teach more on a theme approach, you know. They tend to make connections from one curriculum area to another ... I find that comes very naturally to them.[33]

As administrators, Maureen and Lucille observed differences between women and men that reflected their family responsibilities and attitudes. Maureen described women teachers, including women administrators, as "seeing things differently ... the boundaries ... are more fluid. Even the boundaries between home and school."[34] Maureen sees her male colleagues as separating home and professional lives. Like Maureen, Lucille discovered that male administrators had different concerns.

> It was a culture shock. When I became an administrator, I remember sitting around the school board meetings and the principal's meetings and there would be primarily male administrators. And one of the first things I remember noticing is the different priorities that many of these male administrators and school board administrators had compared with my own. For example, some of my major concerns ... were poverty, the lack of nutritious lunches [for] children, the absence of any good quality daycare

programs that would allow parents to get off welfare, go back to school and improve their quality of life ... And I was practically scoffed at around these principal's meetings when I brought these issues to the table. I remember that the superintendent regularly reminded me to make sure that my staff knew who was boss. He was concerned about my caring, supportive, nurturing model and was afraid that I wouldn't be able to control the teachers if the need arose. In fact, when I took the job he remarked to me that, in his opinion, I would either go ashore on the seas of collegiality or I would do a really good job.[35]

Maureen also noticed differences between male and female administrators.

Men administrators very rarely ever talk about their families you know; they see it as being really separate and they have somebody at home who's doing the family responsibilities, who's doing the homecare responsibilities, so that's not really their concern. And that's why you find that men tend to go into administration a lot easier than women because they don't have as many responsibilities at home as women do ... It's not tying them down ... if they have to be at a meeting until 5:00 or 5:30, they don't have to worry about who's taking the kids to skating, who's taking the kids to brownies and scouts because some mother, or whoever, is there.[36]

However, Maureen contends that homecare responsibilities alone do not explain why women choose not to become administrators. She believes it is more than extra meetings, longer hours and travelling.

Women are not socialized to believe that they have leadership skills. Men are much more empowered than women because women don't feel confident; they've never been taught to feel confident and I think that's why some of them don't go into administration, and they say, "Well, I don't want it; I don't want the headaches." But I think there's a lot more to it than that. I believe it starts when we put a pink blanket on a girl and a blue blanket on a boy, and it never stops.[37]

Lucille recognizes that women's nurturing tendencies have relegated them to primary and elementary schools. This, in turn, says to children that looking after children is "women's work."[38] The effect that childcare and home responsibilities have on women and women teachers is that:

> Women learn to be flexible because of their life styles and the fact that they do juggle so many different roles. As a principal, I noticed that female teachers were much more open in terms of being flexible and being more responsive to the changing needs of students, whereas the male teachers were more resistant to suggestions regarding more flexible classroom settings, more variety in teaching methods, more co-operative learning, more activity-centred sites in the classroom. I found the men that I worked with wanted more control than that. They were reluctant to give over that kind of control to students and parents.[39]

The influence of mothering on teaching and administrative work can be understood in the framework of a domestically oriented ideology of teaching. Women bring their mother-selves to school, into their classrooms and into their administrative positions. They think as mothers in running their classrooms, relating to parents and providing leadership as principals in schools. There is no facet of their professional lives that is untouched by a mothering framework. This is a natural extension of the defining moment of motherhood when every consideration after that event was shaped by their being mothers.

•

The mothering aspect of teaching is strong and entrenched. It begins with the birth of children and continues and grows throughout women teachers' careers and lives. There is need for further research on the mother dimension of teaching, especially thicker, richer descriptions of the day-to-day lives of teachers who are mothers, and a need for deeper understandings of the pedagogy of leadership styles of mothers. The generally negative critique of gender studies, while helpful in discerning the missed opportunities for women, ought to be complemented with a critique that advances mothering experiences and qualities as desirable and appropriate pedagogy and leadership.

Notes

I gratefully acknowledge the financial support of the Newfoundland and Labrador Teachers' Association, Women's Program and Secretary of State, and the Women's Policy Office, Government of Newfoundland and Labrador.

1. Marta Danylewycz, Beth Light, and Alison Prentice, "The Evolution of the Sexual Division of Labour in Teaching: A Nineteenth-Century Ontario and Quebec Case Study," *Histoire Sociale/Social History* 16, no. 3 (May 1983), 82.

2. Alice Collins and Patricia Langlois, "'I Knew I Would Have to Make a Choice': Voices of Women Teachers from Newfoundland and Labrador," *Newfoundland Studies* 11, no. 2 (Fall 1995), 309; Meg Luxton, "Two Hands for the Clock," in Meg Luxton, Harriet Rosenberg, and Sedef Arat Koc, eds., *Through the Kitchen Window: The Politics of Home and Family* (Toronto: Garamond Press, 1990), 39–55.

3. Collins and Langlois, "'I Knew I Would Have to Make a Choice,'" 309.

4. Danylewycz, Light, and Prentice, "The Evolution," 82.

5. Beth Young, "On Careers: Themes from the Lives of Four Western Canadian Women Educators," *Canadian Journal of Education* 17, no. 2 (Spring 1992), 148.

6. Dan C. Lortie, *School-Teacher: A Sociological Study* (Chicago: University of Chicago Press, 1975), 99.

7. See Heather-jane Robertson, *Progress Revisited* (Ottawa: Canadian Teachers' Federation, 1993), 26–27; Laurie Larwood and Barbara A. Gutek, "Working Towards a Theory of Women's Career Development," in Laurie Larwood and Barbara A. Gutek, eds., *Women's Career Development* (Newbury Park, CA: Sage, 1987), 158; Carol Reich and Helen La Fountaine, "The Effect of Sex on Careers within Education: Implications for a Plan of Action," *Canadian Journal of Education* 7, no. 2 (1982), 71.

8. Larwood and Gutek, "Working Towards a Theory of Women's Career Development," 158.

9. Young, "On Careers," 150.

10. Madeleine R. Grumet, *Bitter Milk: Women and Teaching* (Amherst: University of Massachusetts Press, 1988), xv.

11. Roberston, *Progress Revisited,* 2–3.

12. The Personal Narrative Group, eds., *Interpreting Women's Lives: Feminist Theory and Personal Narratives* (Bloomington: Indiana University Press, 1989). See also, Dorothy E. Smith, *Everyday World as Problematic: A Feminist Sociology* (Boston: Northeastern University Press, 1987).

13. In my research, I use biographical interpretations of women's personal narratives as the primary methodology. Multiple, in-depth interviews were conducted and were designed to explore those aspects of women's teaching lives most strongly defined and shaped by their gender. The first set of interviews took place between 1990 and 1992. The second set took place in the fall of 1995 and spring of 1996. From

the first interviews, I identified themes that provided starting points for a second, more focused, set of interviews. Four of the thirteen women had been previously interviewed and, in preparation for the second interview, they read transcripts of their first interview. The interviews were conducted by Alice Collins in 1990 and 1992, and by Patricia Langlois in 1995 and 1996.

14. Interview with Catherine, 31 October 1995.

15. Interview with Lucille, 10 May 1996.

16. Interview with Jennifer, 3 July 1996.

17. Interview with Claire, 27 June 1996.

18. Interview with Sarah, 23 August 1996.

19. Ibid.

20. Interview with Ruth, 21 June 1996.

21. Interview with Lucille, 10 May 1996.

22. Interview with Eileen, 14 November 1995.

23. Interview with Margaret, 5 October 1995.

24. Interview with Jeanette, 15 November 1995.

25. Interview with Kathleen, 13 June 1996.

26. Interview with Catherine, 31 October 1995.

27. Interview with Lucille, 10 May 1996.

28. Interview with Elizabeth, 13 October 1995.

29. Ibid.

30. Interview with Eileen, 14 November 1995.

31. Interview with Elizabeth, 13 October 1995.

32. Ibid.

33. Interview with Maureen, 19 May 1996.

34. Ibid.

35. Interview with Lucille, 10 May 1996.

36. Interview with Maureen, 19 May 1996.

37. Ibid.

38. Interview with Lucille, 10 May 1996.

39. Ibid.

Chapter 5

WRITTEN ON THE BODY

Rishma Dunlop

Bone of my bone. Flesh of my flesh. To remember you its my own body I touch. Thus she was, here and here. The physical memory blunders through the doors the mind has tried to seal ... Wisdom says forget, the body howls. The bolts of your collarbone undo me. Thus she was, here and here.

— Jeanette Winterson, *Written on the Body*

If we ask women who teach to talk about their work in the language that dominates the discourse of schooling, we invite language that celebrates system and denies doubt, that touts objectives and denies ambivalence, that confesses frustration but withholds love.

— Madeleine Grumet, *Bitter Milk*

IN THIS CHAPTER, I envision the development of a critical, feminist and transformative pedagogy that acknowledges sites of positioning from which to negotiate our lives as mothers and as women within the contexts of academic, institutional lives. My writing explores the relational aspects of narratives of women's bodies, of connections between maternal experiences and women's intellectual experiences as teachers and academic scholars. This work is based in feminist autobiography, phenomenology, semiotics and poststructuralism, and experiments with a variety of discursive forms including poetry, journal entries and more traditional scholarly prose. By utilizing diverse forms of writing, I attempt to evoke textually the often disjunctive and paradoxical nature of human experiences. The central focus is on the importance of the body and of our bodily experiences as powerful influences that inform teaching and learning.

BODY AS SITE OF LEARNING

As I contemplate the cycles of creation, the experiences of sexual, sensual life, birth and death, it is the text of the body, with its multiple discourses, that emerges as our most expressive and powerful canon as it reflects lived experience. As I acknowledge the multiple "truths" that are embodied in the commonalities and differences of human experience, I am reminded of Maurice Merleau-Ponty's concept of the body-subject.[1] According to Merleau-Ponty, all the elements of historical, social and political influences are brought together into the body, which represents a country or place where we live in felt experience. In this sense, I am concerned with writing and teaching, with the use of language to reconceptualize educational experience in a way that becomes an act of reforming the world, a return to the body as life-text and source of knowledge.

THE MATERNAL BODY AND THE SPLITTING OF SELF

Aubade to a Newborn

I hold you close,
trying to inhale the pink gleam of dawn
in your sweet flesh.

You are tender-grasped, yet bruised
by my intensity.
I strain to absorb you.

Where is the link
of the twist of sheets,
mouth-kissed skin,
to this glimmer of genes?
Through chasms of pain
the unseeing eye has laboured

to whole sight.

You are sensuous, strange,
cradled in the shining
golden embrace of new morning.[2]

"Aubade to a Newborn" was written about the birth of my first-born
daughter Cara. The play on the traditional form of the aubade, the
morning song to a lover, provides the framework for the contradictions
of maternal experiences: the sense of bittersweet mystery; the paradoxes
of childbirth juxtaposed against the experiences of sexual, sensual life
and conception; tenderness, yet fierceness. Motherhood. Child of
mine. Separate and strange. Separated in the beginning by childbirth,
yet inseparable from my flesh. The recognition of the abyss between
mother and child. A multiplicity of tensions and voices. *Bittermilk,
fluid of our contradictions.*[3]

These notions of the contradictory tensions of maternal experience
expressed in poetic language are echoed in the work of Julia Kristeva. In
the *l'ecriture feminine* of "Stabat Mater; The Paradox: Mother or Primary Narcissism," Kristeva writes in a maternal voice and of maternal
experience, the birth of her son. Her text acknowledges the experience
of the mother through a discursive analysis of the conjunction between
maternity and virginity in Christian theology, allowing the bold-faced
maternal narrative to disrupt and confront the more traditional prose.
This doubling of voice, this visual representation and discursive practice reflects maternal identity as containing doubleness, multiplicity,
mediation and alteration and the discursive technique becomes necessary to Kristeva's representation of birth and maternity. Kristeva reflects
the continuing exploration with forms and representations of language
in text, exposing new kinds of discourse and possibilities for articulation of the women's experiences. Kristeva writes her text in columns,
with personal, associative writing in bold face on one side, and more
traditional academic discourse on the other, creating an interplay of
texts that accepts the paradoxes of the mother's felt experiences: "form-
less, unnamable embryo. Epiphanies ... Words that are always too distant, too abstract for this underground swarming of seconds, folding in
unimaginable spaces. Writing them down is an ordeal of discourse, like
love. What is loving for a woman, the same thing as writing."[4]

Child

In my baby's eyes,
I am locked
in self-extension.

I do not know
where I finish
and she begins;
she is my pact
with life and death
and I must dance for her,
so she will know the uncommon
steps.[5]

"Child" is a representation of Jacques Lacan's notion, in the rewriting of Freud's psychoanalytic discourses, of identity established in the mirror of the other.[6] Recent strands in psychoanalytic feminism, one grounded in a Lacanian and the other in an object-relations theoretical framework, have attempted to challenge the gap between theoretical feminism and maternal experience by emphasizing the maternal. This process of theorizing, brings feminism closer to a position in which maternal voices may be heard and voiced; it also gives rise to difficulties and contradictory elements of these revisionary attempts in discourse. As Kristeva's text in "Stabat Mater" suggests and as I suggest in my own texts, the perception of the gap between mother and child, the permanent separation of the mother and the permanent division of the flesh and the word, are invaluable perspectives to the feminist analysis of culture; the ability to acknowledge otherness becomes an ability which dismantles and challenges symbolic and philosophical power.

In my poem "Child," the child is mirrored in the gaze of the mother, from whom she begins to form her identity. As mother, I am locked in the prisms of my daughter's eyes, inextricable from her gaze. The teaching of the dance, of the uncommon steps, becomes analogous with my teaching self, my writing self, my academic self, extending to my romantic idealizations and desires in the teaching of my students. I want them to step in new directions, estranging the familiar in order to dance toward knowledge and richness of experience in their lives. This notion of estrangement calls to mind Kristeva's idea of the link between exile and intellectual work: "Writing is impossible without some kind of exile." Exile, in this sense, represents a *dépaysement* enabling "a ruthless and irreverent dismantling of the workings of discourse, thought, and existence ..."[7] In this way, exile becomes a means to open up possibilities and challenges, "coming to terms with difference and the other — not destroying them."[8]

Kristeva's expression, *étrangers à nous mêmes* (strangers to ourselves), becomes synonymous with foreignness, the notion of "other," of the unconscious, of difference, of the feminine, the maternal body distancing itself from cultural constructions in order to interweave our texts into dynamic forms of intellectual thought.[9] However, for women engaged in intellectual endeavours and in quests for tenured positions in academic institutions, this estrangement often becomes a splitting or fragmenting of self that is difficult to navigate.

As Adrienne Rich states in her explorations of the bonds of women to their mothers and their daughters, it becomes necessary to understand a type of "double vision or we shall never understand ourselves."[10] In our roles as women in academic institutions, where success is mandated by publication records and research capabilities, the texts of our bodies, of maternal, intuitive, passionate, familial, private selves are necessarily suppressed. We have learned to hide those rich sites of learning and teaching. Rich speaks of the cathexis between mother and daughter as essential, misused and distorted — "the great unwritten story."[11] This flow of energy that she speaks of is one of deep mutuality, holding within it as well, the possibility of intense estrangement from the texts of our bodies.

The notion of incompatibility of writing and motherhood is central to our roles as mothers, writers and academics. Susan Sulieman, in her essay "Writing and Motherhood," explores and then interrogates the psychoanalytic assumption that motherhood and the role of the author are inherently antithetical. In her considerations of mothers who write she uses a psychoanalytic framework for textual analyses in order to discuss the injunctions that inform the authors' writings. When Sulieman departs from this analytical framework, she begins to challenge and question the framework she began with, revealing ultimately that, as well as being written, mothers do write as mothers, in maternal voices, and that their writing can be furthered and enriched rather than hindered by their motherhood.[12]

BODIES OF KNOWLEDGE:
TEACHING AND LEARNING

Phenomenological reflection leads me continually back to the notion of the body as ideological construction, as reflected and constrained by our schooling and by our curricula, yet, I am constantly struck by the body's irrevocable presence that cannot be denied in our teaching worlds. Our carefully ordered classrooms, logical plans and systems collapse with the inevitably human "eruptions of the body, intimacy into public space."[13] I am reminded of Grumet's reflections on the autobiographical text of a teacher in a first-grade classroom undergoing a formal observation by an evaluator. The teacher is at first pleased with herself — "The lessons were going well." Her place behind the new half-round table establishes the separateness between teacher and children. Grumet writes that the children are seen only as expectant faces "sans bodies, sans belches, sans sound, sans everything." This false vision comes to a sudden end when Paul vomits all over and his false teeth land at the teacher's feet. The space between them is closed as she cleans his shoes and she finds shelter in using the euphemism "special child." The evaluator leaves: "her exit was graceful." However, the teacher cannot remain distanced by the language of the governing paradigms of her teaching world. She cannot name Paul as "other"; they are linked, her slacks damp, reeking of sickness. In the acknowledgement of the body, of human truth, she is comfortable with teaching for the first time.

ENTRY FROM MY JOURNAL, NOVEMBER 23, 1994

These reminders of the body surface in our recent doctoral seminar, a course in curriculum theory. We have been engaged in discussions about theory and philosophical stances in relation to curriculum — Rousseau, Tyler, Dewey, Grumet. Students were engaged in a heated debate over the notions of class and privilege and oppression. We bandied terms about as has been our intellectual habit. Suddenly, we are brought back into the realities of lived experience as one of the students interrupts the light-hearted banter with an emotional outburst. She states that in this room sits much privilege and class. She speaks about how she lives and what "her people" live with everyday. She speaks of oppression and of lives battered by violence. She speaks of language that obliterates meaning in its theoretical, political correctness. Racism is, afterall, racism. The pain and anger of her body fills the air of the classroom; her body is palpable, touching us. We cannot avoid it and we cannot fill the silence with words and constructions of language. Where is our curriculum now, if it fails to acknowledge the reality and the depth of this woman's experience, of our experiences? Where is wisdom? The body howls. It is impossible to move or to speak. We are held in place, held inside our bodies. We are salted by the bitterness of her tears. Finally, one woman moves across the room to hold the other's hand. The only language possible, eloquent enough, is that of the flesh. Bittermilk, fluid of our contradictions. Thus she was, here and here.

Route 97

Early morning.
Driving
the winding twists
of Highway 97,
the daily journey.

Echoes
the voices of children,
clatter of breakfast dishes,
chaotic disorders
of family.

I sip on my coffee
mind soothed
by the melodic voice,

the silver brain of radio.
I am lulled
by the blue-green
of Lake Okanagan, glass-smooth,
my bones infused
with warmth through
the sun-glossed
curve
of windshield.

I prepare my lecture,
conversing
with imaginary students,
expounding
on the virtues
of post-structural critical
approaches
in the close reading
of poetry.
Foot on the accelerator,
my route is embraceable,
knowable.

Reaching campus,
the air chills
as gold sky
fades
into gray
concrete hallways, classrooms and offices.
Stuffed under my office door,
notes, crumpled missives,
inarticulate scribblings,
multiple excuses
for late term papers.

My body is estranged
from my tailored flesh;
the skin freezes,

icy bumps rising on the surface.
As I enter the classroom, I am crisp,
my voice staccato
against the walls.

I focus on my students,
listening to the rustling and shuffling
of papers.
The Basketball Boys sprawl,
endless limbs spilling out
of their desks,
their giant sneakers
constantly fidgeting.

There is an audible groan
when I mention poetry.
The woman in the second row says
*I can't **do** poetry.*
I take a long drag
of my coffee,
feel it flow warm,
deep into my throat,
filling the hollows of my body.
And I begin.

Teaching, I am calm,
my voice soothed into lyric hum
as I speak of the slants of language,
passion, sorrow, love,
moments keenly remembered
and recorded.
I search for the breathing tissue,
embedding hooks into
their flesh.

I rivet them with my eyes,
wrap them in my voice,
imagine them in
violet evenings,

smoky dusks filled with
twilight scents of green,
ripe foliage,
poets' voices floating
a slow music of sorcery,
flutes and lyres at the gates,
echoing through the groves
of olive trees
and almond blossoms.

I will them
to peel back their skins,
with fingers streaming light
into the river
of rhythms and meters
of transcribed heartbeats.
Pour yourselves skinless,
liquid through the glass of language
into the irises of eyes.

My body thaws
and in its heat
the Basketball Boys are still,
their restless noises hushed
in the infinite pleats of skin.
And we begin,
my students and I,
the route of mystery,

unfolding in the
cadence of breath,
iridescent poems
housed beneath the flesh.[14]

I move from the place of the familiar, from my familial and my maternal contexts, to the oppression of the institution and to the notion of curriculum as something to be delivered in the classroom, back to a reclamation of the body in the desire to encourage students to find the poetic and the aesthetically beautiful in their own worlds of experience, under their own human skins and in their hearts. I envision a reclamation of what teaching needs to be, found within a recovery of the world through poetic text. From this perspective, teaching and learning decentre fixed conceptions of knowledge, reclaiming what we seem to have unlearned about sensory experiences — forgetting how to see, taste, hear and feel.

Like Madeleine Grumet, I consider what teaching means to women. In *Bitter Milk*, Grumet discusses the bonds of women, first to their own mothers, then to their children and to other women's children, underscoring the contradictions inherent between our experiences of childhood, mothering and the curriculum we offer as teachers. Grumet writes of the ingrained notions that we are too emotional, too sensitive, that our work as mothers is valued only by our immediate families and that we hide our maternal knowledge, keeping it to ourselves, as we dispense the curriculum to the children of other women.[15]

Grumet claims that we must interpret our reproductive experience (procreation and nurturance) and our productive experience (curriculum and teaching) each through the other's terms, not by negating the differences between them but by naming and accepting their contradictions. It is necessary here to acknowledge that not all women will necessarily relate to or embrace Grumet's "reproductive" metaphor, nor is the maternal necessarily embodied in all women's experiences or desires. However, Grumet points us towards a negotiation of differences that might allow us to reconceive our commitment to education. In searching to find the words and language to express my experiences as a woman, seeking to acknowledge the texts of my embodied experiences as sites of teaching and learning, I realize that in the classroom and in the home, I encounter others in ways that move back and forth in the multiple tensions and contradictions inherent to life: between public and private self, familial life, sensual and sexual life, and between social, political and pedagogic discourses. As Adrienne Rich states: "In the interstices of language lie powerful secrets of the culture."[16]

BODIES OF INTELLECT:
SEEKING THE "EDUCATED" WOMAN

Adrienne Rich writes of the split that women encounter in themselves when faced with aligning their biological and social realities with their quests for intellectual and creative goals:

> Many women have been caught — have split themselves — be-tween two mothers: one, usually the biological one, who repre-sents the culture of domesticity, of male-centeredness, of conventional expectations, and another, perhaps a woman artist or teacher, who becomes the countervailing figure ... This split-ting may allow the young woman to fantasize alternately living as one or the other "mother," to test out two identifications. But it can also lead to a life in which she never consciously resolves choices, in which she alternately tries to play hostess and please her husband as her mother did, and to write her novel or doctoral thesis. She has tried to break through the existing models, but she has not gone far enough, usually because nobody has told her how far there is to go.[17]

More recently, contemporary feminist theory has attempted to break down existing models of women's lives in a wide variety of argu-ments that explore issues of difference and discursive representation. French feminist poststructuralists like Luce Irigaray[18] and Hélène Cixous[19] have focused on language as the foundation of woman's op-pression, developing *l'écriture féminine* to challenge linguistic conven-tions. *L'écriture féminine* may in itself be perceived as essentialist, however, poststructuralist feminists have strengthened discursive prac-tices that consider women's bodies as sources of "metaphor for multiplic-ity and difference." Rebecca Martusewicz poses a question that is central to women's explorations of academic life through autobiography and the reconstruction of self: What does it mean to be an educated woman? "To live as feminist educators is to live a tension between a critical theo-retical space and an affirmative political space. It is within this in-be-tween, this 'elsewhere,' that we must seek the educated woman."[20]

It is time to expand the term "the educated woman" to give way to more inclusive perceptions that reflect the diversity and plurality and nonessentialness of those who occupy any particular social location. The roles of intellectual women have an uneasy history, played out against prescribed social relations. For women committed to intellectual work, achieving coherence with their social lives is difficult and contradictory. If we adopt practices required by mandates of academic work, we are labelled as "aggressive," "pushy," "less feminine," ultimately "inadequate" women. Recently, I listened to a student teacher recount the story of surviving in the competitive, marks-conscious arena of a teacher education program at a major university. As she continuously asked her instructor for clarification on evaluation and her grades for her course, she encountered a rather alarming response from a married, tenured, female professor. The professor told the student that she was very "pushy" and too aggressive. The professor also observed aloud that the student-teacher was not wearing a wedding ring and proceeded to tell her that if she refrained from such aggressive behaviour, acting more feminine, she might find it easier to find a man.

This example, ludicrous in its occurrence in 1996 in a faculty of education at a Canadian postsecondary institution, is nevertheless indicative of the pervasive nature of social relations and constructions that are replicated in all spheres of women's lives. On the other hand, in most academic endeavours, if we adhere to roles of wives and mothers that have been historically and socially circumscribed, we may be perceived as unable to produce rigorous scholarly work. Magda Gere Lewis describes this struggle:

> Regardless of how — or even whether or not — women take up the practices of mother/wife, the contradictory social coding maintains. The power of patriarchy to universalize the principles of heterosexuality, femininity, and the nuclear family, whether or not one participates in these social forms, means that engagement in intellectual work, by any woman, is, by social–historical contingency, named questionable.[21]

THE DISPLACED BODY: SHIFTING GEOGRAPHY

Life has obliged me to ask myself this question in painful form: how writing is experienced as a third party in all dual relationships.

For me it is not a third party — I am not separate from writing, I only began to become myself through writing. But it has a separating function. Which reaches very far, in my opinion. I will begin with the relationship of love, of friendship, the familial relationships. There is a third party. I do not see it but I see that others see it … It repairs the author. But it does not repair the relationship.
— Hélène Cixous, *Rootprints: Memory and Lifewriting* [22]

While my two daughters were very young, I seemed to manage the demands, the frustrations and the joys of childrearing with jobs, writing, teaching and graduate work. These roles were played out as they accommodated the career path of my husband, the moves to new locations for his promotions and the societal dictates of the nuclear family model we were both raised in. I spent much of this time supporting his career, and his public and professional image, entertaining clients and contributing to what I perceived to be "our" successes. As my children grew older and my husband achieved considerable financial success and professional advancement, I maintained a teaching position at the local college. As the college gained status as a full university, instructors were required to have PhDs for full time employment. My husband and I decided that it was the right time for me to pursue doctoral studies and I plunged from completion of my master's degree into doctoral research. The ground began to shift and split.

Although my husband had outwardly supported my intellectual work and expressed a willingness to care for our daughters in order for me to complete my university residency requirements and my teaching obligations, the demands of this negotiation took a devastating toll. My "seduction" by academic life, my increasing successes with publications of poetry and scholarly articles distanced me from my husband, who did not share my love of reading and writing. My husband had been raised in a home devoid of literature and my pursuits became puzzling to him. When I accused him of not understanding my need for an intellectual life, he extended this lack of understanding as the general opinion of society at large in our community and in our families. "No one understands why you are doing a PhD," he told me, after months of silence and increasing discomfort. Although I perceived the PhD and my writing as necessary to my career, he perceived me to be neglecting my roles as a woman and as a wife, corrupted by other writers and academic colleagues. He felt that I no longer "needed" him and that my priorities were skewed, that I had abandoned him and our daughters for impractical and meaningless goals. The demands of parenting alone during the week became an embarrassment to my husband, seen through the lenses of community, diminishing his self-perception in his role as a male and as my partner. He had never spoken of these concerns during my eighteen-month residency so these difficulties and fears involved with negotiating family relationships were contained in silence, under the surface of language. He felt that I was located in "places where he could not reach me."

On my part, it seemed to take immense effort to drive the five hours to the university from our small town residence, to return on weekends, to take care of family needs, to work, to teach and to provide emotional support for all, including my students, other women's children. In order to remain in my marriage, I would have to remain in that nuclear organization that recognized me as a woman and a mother only in the social relations constructed by conventional notions of community. None of the complex dynamics we were wrestling with seemed to have affected us during the years in which I supported my husband emotionally, intellectually and financially throughout his career endeavours, because, as my mother-in-law and my mother both reminded me, he was the "head of the household," the financial backbone of the family, the father of my children, therefore deserving of unequivocal support. Academia did not quite provide "home" either, as it could not embrace all the complexities of the roles I seemed destined to play. The university residency requirement for doctoral candidacy was antiquated and did not meet the needs of professional women, mothers and wives. The long drives home from university became agonizing journeys during which I wept as I approached home and subsequently as I departed from home. My body was in effect displaced, without a home.

These contradictory struggles with intellectual work and their uneasy fit with traditional paradigms of familial and social life are articulated in Kathleen Rockhill's powerful and moving article, "Literacy as Threat/Desire: Longing to be SOMEBODY." For the women in Rockhill's study, the knowledge and power made potentially available to them through becoming literate also repositioned them in ways that threatened familial, conjugal and economic relations. The article, published in 1991, explores women's contradictory reality as an educational dilemma:

> It is common today for education to be ideologically addressed as the pathway to a new kind of romance for women, the romance of a "career," a profession, a middle-class way of life; the image is one of the well-dressed woman doing "clean" work, important work. As such, it feeds her yearning, her desire, for a way out of the "working-class" life she has known. It is precisely because education holds out this promise for women that it also poses a threat to them in their everyday lives. This is especially true for women in heterosexual relationships when their men feel threatened by the images of power (independence and success) attached to education.[23]

As Elizabeth Grosz states, the inscription of bodies is a process that produces social texts that can be interpreted and read and that consciousness is a result of these inscriptions. We are constructed by these societal inscriptions of who we should be as men or women, yet there is nothing "natural" or apriori about such categorizations.[24] My body has been shaped by these scripts of what it means to be a mother and a wife. As Foucault states: "the body is the strategic target of systems of codification, supervision and constraint."[25] For women, the option of choosing both a job and motherhood, often labels us inadequate in both. It is even more pronounced when we choose academic careers, where "success" is often more intangible than in careers that reward us with material gains. The world of the intellect is less visible, less definable, than other work arenas.

My subsequent marital separation and similar personal narratives of many of my female colleagues are not necessarily centred in a loss of love and caring for our partners; in many cases, they seem a result of the inability to negotiate the societal constructions that circumscribe our notions of gender roles, our sexuality and our roles as women in academic life. The category "mother" is marked as a social position that both gives and denies access to social process in specific ways.[26] Thinking beyond these processes is often difficult and painful, yet necessary as we vacillate between the contradictory desires for our children and ourselves. Adrienne Rich expresses these contradictions:

> My children cause me the most exquisite suffering of which I have any experience. It is the suffering of ambivalence: the murderous alternation between bitter resentment and raw-edged nerves, and blissful gratification and tenderness. Sometimes I seem to myself, in my feelings toward those tiny guiltless beings, a monster of selfishness and intolerance ... There are times when I feel only death will free us from one another, when I envy the (childless) woman who has the luxury of her regrets but lives a life of privacy and freedom. And yet at other times I am melted with the sense of their helpless, charming and quite irresistible beauty — their ability to go on living and trusting — their staunchness and decency and unselfconsciousness. *I love them.* But it's in the enormity and inevitability of this love that the sufferings lie.[27]

I struggle with the possibilities of storytelling, of recounting my narratives in a world of work in which academic discourse traditionally excludes close scrutiny of our personal lives as work of intellectual merit. Academic discourse has traditionally ignored acknowledgement of the eros of everyday living. Our personal narratives of reading and writing the body might be perceived as indiscretion, telling too much, signs of inadequacy in the lack of separation of public and private experience. But ultimately I, like other feminist scholars, teachers and writers, seek alternative forms of textualizing my world. In Jeanette Winterson's novel *Written on the Body,* the narrator says: "There's a story trapped inside your mouth."[28] If I am "storied" by my society and my culture as well as my own particular pleasures and desires, breaking free from the "texts" of my culture challenges me to stretch beyond these scripts by rethinking the assumptions that structure societal codification.

Choosing to write and to teach, I am cognizant of the need to nurture and deepen understandings of the limitations of standard knowledge paradigms and the importance of breaking out beyond them. In the emancipatory process that is writing, the body ceases to remain purely biological; it is written and socially constructed from an early age. Some concept of the body is essential to understanding social production, oppression and resistance. In this sense, the body must not be considered simply a biological entity, but can be seen as a socially inscribed, historically marked, psychically and interpersonally significant product.[29]

MULTIPLE BODIES: RECAPTURING THE EMOTIONAL IN TEXTUAL FEMINISM

Feminist commitment to pedagogy begins to shape itself in my mind as one that evokes a critical consciousness of the places of writing and teaching in a life that includes familial bonds and the indelible, powerful traces of the multiplicity of women's bodily experiences that infuse our lives with emotional intensity. This feminist commitment requires a recovery or reinvention of a rhetoric of textual feminism: as Krista Ratcliffe states, "a rhetoric of textual feminism that exposes the emotional which has been relegated in our culture's dominant discourse to what Julia Kristeva calls the 'speech of non-being.'"[30]

Such a recapturing of the emotional offers us immense possibilities for drawing on our experiences as women, finding in these embodied texts wellsprings of creativity and aesthetic possibilities for learning and teaching. Maxine Greene perceives educational experiences as ways to "come in contact with the concreteness of things, to experience tension, to feel what remains to be done."[31] Greene refers to Sartre's notion that the world with all its deficiencies and injustices gives rise to a moral imperative at the heart of the aesthetic imperative which can be a "desire to repair."[32] This desire to repair is embedded in specific human experiences that are inclusive of our texts of women's lives and bodies. Such a curriculum and such an academic environment is not in itself devoid of problems, paradoxes or ethical complexities, as the narrative contexts of this essay have acknowledged. The "desire to repair" is necessarily subject to oppression that our own individual contexts will create.

Language brings to life what it addresses. Therefore, as I contemplate the multiplicity of roles that form an individual in teaching and learning communities, language becomes a site of multiple subjectivities. As the individual is both site and subject of discursive struggles for identity, subjectivity is constantly shifting, often contradictory and never fixed.

I imagine curriculum in an academic environment that returns us to sites of the body and of the emotional, echoed in the words of poet

Elizabeth Bishop: "it is like what we imagine knowledge to be."[33] A place in academic life that embraces passion and emotion can negotiate our lives as mothers and daughters and in all the multiple texts of women's embodied experiences in ways that are transformative. Maxine Greene writes, "an emotion, a passion can be a transformation of the world."[34] This quest for scholarship that embraces the heart in an understanding of the world and selves is eloquently expressed by Carol Christ, who envisions the root of scholarship as "eros, a passion to connect, the desire to deepen our understanding of ourselves and our world, the passion to transform or preserve the world as we understand it deeply.[35]

WRITTEN ON THE BODY

> Written on the body is a secret code only visible in certain lights; the accumulations of a lifetime gather there.
> — Jeanette Winterson, *Written on the Body*

I acknowledge the constructedness of our stories. As I construct my own narratives, the moments stopped are lifted from multiple lives, enacted in the roles of woman: mother, lover, wife, daughter, sister, friend and teacher/scholar. As Madeleine Grumet states, phenomenology takes me home, extending the "horizons of educational theory" to embrace the passion, politics and labour of human reproduction.[36] I turn to the body, to my woman's body, to my maternal body, as the site of passion, of richness, of significance and of understanding, as I struggle to make sense of educational experience and teaching life. It is primal intimacy that informs my writing, threaded through my body, inextricably intertwined, tangled through the systems of public experience. I envision writing as evoked by Anaïs Nin. She attempts to perceive writing as music that should penetrate the senses directly. "For this poetry is necessary ... I want meaning to enter the body ..."[37]

I return to the familiar. The conflicts of the inner self are reflected in the struggles between creation and maternal love; between realism and romanticism; between past, present and future; in the Socratic dialogues and tensions between teacher and students; between educators and colleagues; and through the attempt to find significance through the articulation and reconstruction of the writer's world. It is an attempt to voice Barthes's comparisons of "teaching to play, reading to eros, writing to seduction."[38]

As poet, as writer, as mother, as feminist scholar and as teacher, I choose to write and to encourage my students to experiment in discursive practices that attempt to evoke lived, embodied experiences. I seek language to express lived and felt experience, trying to come close to Anaïs Nin's idea of writing that enters consciousness through the senses. The words of this language are tasted, lingering on the tongue, touched by flesh and bone, echoed resounding and whispered and scented. It is a writing that heightens the senses, tastes life twice, in the present moment and in the retrospection.

This choice to write is political, passionate and personal. Perhaps we might envision our writing and consequently our education, as being about rewriting and reinscribing our normative structures. While feminist notions of caring and connecting are valuable, they are not enough to effect change in schooling. It is necessary to develop new forms of analysis, new frameworks for thinking that expose deeply embedded structures and discursive formations that covertly shape both our consciousness and our socioeducational institutions. As Shirley Kincheloe states, "in this context we can begin to replace the masculinist discourse that negates body and feeling with a new female expressiveness that draws upon personal experience."[39] In this context, our maternal voices can enrich and strengthen our scholarship, our teaching and our writing. These are voices that speak eloquently and powerfully. The choice to envision education and teaching in an embodied way becomes therefore a choice to challenge social constructions by reclaiming language in efforts to effect social change through transformative practices.

Through a pedagogy that embraces our maternal, our personal and our intellectual narratives as sites of knowledge, we may be able to come closer to the worlds of our teaching classrooms in meaningful ways. This pedagogy seeks to relate to students and members of our academic communities by providing multiple opportunities for a wide range of discursive practices and for engagement in dialogues that reclaim the body. These are dialogues that have the potential to inspire us, to reach into our hearts and into our senses to form connections in our minds and in our written, our spoken and our unspoken texts. *And we are undone, here and here.*

Notes

1. Maurice Merleau-Ponty, *Phenomenology of Perception* (London: Routledge and Kegan Paul, 1962).

2. Rishma Dunlop, "Aubade to a Newborn," *Room of One's Own* 18, no. 1 (March 1995), 73.

3. Madeleine Grumet, *Bitter Milk: Women and Teaching* (Amherst, MA: University of Massachusetts Press, 1988).

4. Julia Kristeva, "Stabat Mater: The Paradox: Mother or Primary Narcissism," in Leon S. Roudiez, trans., *Tales of Love* (New York: Columbia University Press, 1987), 234–235.

5. Rishma Dunlop, "Narrative, Literacy and the Quest for Self: Tango Through the Dark" (masters thesis, University of British Columbia, 1994), 44.

6. Jacques Lacan, *Écrits* (New York: W. W. Norton, 1977).

7. Julia Kristeva, in John Lechte, ed., *Julia Kristeva* (London: Routledge, 1990), 229.

8. Ibid., 80.

9. Ibid., 81.

10. Adrienne Rich, *Of Woman Born* (New York: W. W. Norton, 1986), 255.

11. Ibid., 225.

12. Susan Sulieman, "Writing and Motherhood," in Shirley Nelson Garner, Claire Kahane, and Madelon Sprengnether, eds., *The (M)Other Tongue: Essays in Feminist Psychoanalytic Interpretation* (Ithaca: Cornell University Press, 1985).

13. Grumet, *Bitter Milk*, 70.

14. Rishma Dunlop, "Route 97," *English Quarterly* 28, no. 1 (1995), 45.

15. Grumet, *Bitter Milk*, 28.

16. Rich, *Of Woman Born*, 249.

17. Ibid., 248.

18. Luce Irigaray, "This Sex Which is Not One," in Elaine Marks and Isabelle De Courtivron, eds., *New French Feminisms* (New York: Schocken Books, 1981), 99–106.

19. Hélène Cixous, "The Laugh of the Medusa," in Marks and De Courtivron, eds., *New French Feminisms*, 245–264.

20. Rebecca Martusewicz, "Mapping the Terrain of the Post-Modern Subject: Post Structuralism and the Educated Woman," in William Pinar, ed., *Understanding Curriculum as Deconstructed Text* (New York: Teachers College Press, 1992), 131–156.

21. Magda Gere Lewis, *Without a Word: Teaching Beyond Women's Silence* (New York: Routledge, 1993), 98.

22. Hélène Cixous and Mireille Calle-Gruber, *Rootprints: Memory and Lifewriting* (London: Routledge, 1997).

23. Kathleen Rockhill, "Literacy as Threat/Desire: Longing to be SOMEBODY," in

Jane Gaskell and Arlene Tigar Maclaren, eds., *Women and Education: A Canadian Perspective*, 2d. ed. (Calgary: Detselig Enterprises, 1991), 315.

24. Elizabeth Grosz, "Inscriptions and Body-Maps: Representations and the Corporeal," in Terry Threadgold and Ann Cranny Francis, eds., *Feminine, Masculine and Representation* (North Sydney, Australia: Allen and Unwin, 1990), 65.

25. Michel Foucault, in Grosz, "Inscriptions and Body-Maps," 64.

26. Julia Kristeva, in Lechte, *Julia Kristeva*, 186–213.

27. Rich, *Of Woman Born*, 21–22.

28. Jeanette Winterson, *Written on the Body* (New York: Vintage Books, 1994), 117.

29. Elizabeth Grosz, "Philosophy, Subjectivity and the Body: Kristeva and Irigaray," in Carole Pateman and Elizabeth Grosz, eds., *Feminist Challenges: Social and Political Theory* (Boston: Allen and Unwin, 1986), 12.

30. Krista Ratcliffe, "A Rhetoric of Textual Feminism: (Re)reading the Emotional in Virginia Woolf's Three Guineas," *Rhetoric Review* 11, no. 2, (1993), 400–417.

31. Maxine Greene, "Breaking Through the Ordinary: The Arts and Future Possibility," *Journal of Education* 162, no. 3 (1980), 24.

32. Ibid., 24.

33. Elizabeth Bishop, in Greene, "Breaking Through the Ordinary," 18.

34. Maxine Greene, "Reflection and Passion in Teaching," *Journal of Curriculum and Supervision* 2, no. 1 (1986), 81.

35. Carol Christ, "Toward a Paradigm Shift in the Academy and in Religious Studies," in Christie Farnham, ed., *The Impact of Feminist Research in the Academy* (Bloomington, IN: Indiana University Press, 1987), 58.

36. Grumet, *Bitter Milk*, 63.

37. Anaïs Nin, in Gunther Stuhlman, ed., *The Diary of Anaïs Nin 1944–1947* (New York: Harcourt Brace Jovanovich, 1971), 40–41.

38. Susan Sontag, ed., *A Barthes Reader* (London: Jonathan Cape, 1982), xvi–xvii.

39. Shirley Kincheloe, "Early Education as a Gendered Construction," *JCT: An Interdisciplinary Journal of Curriculum Studies* 12, no. 2 (1996), 34–35.

Part II

Maternal values and Identities in Transition from Adolescence to Mid-Life

Chapter 6

TEENAGE GIRLS MAKING SENSE OF MOTHERING: WHAT HAS (RELATIONAL) EQUALITY GOT TO DO WITH IT?

Arlene Tigar McLaren & Ann Vanderbijl

WHAT DOES MOTHERING mean to teenage girls? They do not have to be mothers in order to have rich and complex sets of meanings about what mothering entails or about how these meanings affect their current lives. In this chapter, we examine how teenage girls weave together an imagined portrait of domesticity as they attempt to reconcile the many, and often contradictory, cultural discourses about motherhood. In particular, we focus on how girls talk about equality and what that means to them as they contemplate their future lives as potential mothers and domestic partners.[1]

Our analysis builds upon recent studies on the meanings of domesticity[2] by looking at (1) how girls use diverse, and often seemingly incompatible discourses concerning education, waged work and domesticity, and (2) how they try to relate these discourses to the practice of equality. By using the term discourse we are referring to a set of stories, texts, versions of events, people and places that generate social phenomena. When these phenomena circulate in society they attach themselves to strategies of domination as well as to those of resistance. When girls reflect on their imagined careers following the completion of school, they generally use well-developed liberal notions of equality that stress individualism. When imagining combining domesticity with employment, they use less officially scripted notions of equality that imply intersubjectivity, and, furthermore, a radical dependency.

Our research on domestic-equality discourses helps to explain why girls are not easily susceptible to gender reforms that promote nontraditional courses and careers. While girls may use individualistic equality discourses in thinking about their education and future paid work, they often simultaneously use relational equality discourses in thinking about their future domestic relationships. As Jane Kenway argues, a particularly astonishing feature of school-gender-reform discourse that promotes nontraditional courses and careers is its lack of interest in bringing about gender justice in the family.[3] We suggest that girls' conceptions of equality in domestic life reflect their knowledge about how gender is culturally organized and how their future may, in fact, be radically dependent on their familial contexts — on who they love, with whom they live and with whom they have children.

Our analysis provides a glimpse into the discursive density of powerful ideologies related to domesticity and renders visible their entangled hold on girls' imaginations and practical lives. We reveal how girls are enticed by paradoxical social injunctions and, in particular, how they are often enjoined to relinquish the idealized and normative version of agency operative in the North American cultural context, while simultaneously being called upon to invest heavily in it.

In this chapter we briefly review how the girls in our study used self-deterministic notions of equality in the context of schooling and of anticipated waged work, and show how the girls used distinct "relational" forms of equality discourses in their imagined future contexts of domesticity and employment.

GIRLS' USE OF THE CONCEPT OF EQUALITY

THE CURRENT SCHOOLING AND FUTURE WAGED WORK CONTEXT

In previous research, we traced the various ways in which high school girls understood and strategically used discourses of equality to negotiate the many contradictions they encountered within their educational settings and to envision and construct their ongoing and future social positioning in employment.[4] We examined how the girls were able to manoeuvre through the rich fields of interwoven, competing discourses of equality, thereby enabling them to believe that, indeed, gender equality generally exists in school and the wider society.

To accomplish this, the girls invoked discourses that variously linked the notion of equality to their "treatment" by teachers and by boys to "opportunity" (that is, gaining access to various kinds of coursework and careers), and to "skills," "ability," "effort," "interest" or "fortitude." The following interview excerpts provide examples of this variety of discourses. To differing degrees, these conceptualizations of equality are often simultaneously infused with rigorous notions of self-determination.

Brenda,[5] for example, suggested that schools have no choice but to treat everyone equally: "Yeah. Everybody seems to be treated as an equal at school. Maybe that's just because it's school and everyone has to be, but ..." Anne emphasized that she has "always had" equal classes, that "everybody gets along, there's no discrimination between the people." Students were generally eager to offer an image of "equal treatment" as an indication of "equality."

When the girls considered evidence of discrimination and sexism by teachers or classmates, they were able to draw upon deeply elasticized notions of equality to help sustain the idea that equality was possible or that it existed. Robyn said:

> Well, a lot of girls are discouraged about it because ... you know, science is a man's world ... But I don't know ... it seems like there are some things the guys understand ... better, [but] ... the stereotyping ... can really get to you. Like if a teacher favours the guys over the girls and gives them more attention, or whatever. But I don't know, I guess it depends on the person as well.

Robyn's talk is riddled with seemingly confused and contradictory evaluations: the idea that "science is a man's world"; that boys have a greater understanding of science; recognizing teacher bias and "stereotyping"; the role of individual personality. She implies that the guys' "understanding" might be related to stereotyping, but also concludes that what happens depends largely on the individual. Having suggested that teachers' biases might have an impact on girls' classroom experiences, Robyn later insisted:

The teachers encourage everything, encourage it all. They treat us all equal ... the boys tease [us] by saying things like, "Oh, I got better on a test than you," or "You don't get it? It's so easy." Like most of the time it's more as a joke, but ... still, the repetition of it all just really gets to you. It's the same everywhere, no matter what guys are in it, they always gang up on the girls.

Here, Robyn shifts her focus from the sexism of teachers to that of boys. Her analysis is unusual in that, ultimately, she cannot dismiss discouraging or sexist behaviour or sustain an explanation of it as a mere "joke."

Most of the girls, however, invoked a beguiling variety of equality discourses in ways that did downplay whatever sexism they identified as existing. Kathleen, for example, claimed that despite instances of gender "difference" (or what might be called men and boys "doing gender"), what matters are students' interests and willingness to learn:

... but guys are better at math than girls ... I guess the teachers kind of point it out too if they're men sometimes. But I don't really think it's a big deal. I don't think it makes a difference if you're male or female, just how interested you are and how willing you are to learn.

As contradictions to apparent equality became more insistently evident, the girls were forced to adduce that equality, as a practical achievement, is dependent on a strong individualism. Girls unable to withstand putdowns by boys could thus be logically dismissed as lacking in character strength. Poignantly, this assessment was often accompanied by a perception that such girls were potentially relinquishing their foothold in the realm of opportunity. Trish, for example, pointed out that this was the case in her physics class: "Just because the guys get on this power trip. Because the girls who can't stand up to that get put down, they give up on certain things." Relinquishing "certain things," in this case the decision to take science and maths courses, incurs far-reaching consequences because, in their view, these courses can form the scaffolding for future success in the working world. Individual fortitude thus appears not only to serve as a lynchpin for the successful application of the ideology of equality, but also as the necessary factor enabling the negotiation of all the contradictions which the concept of equality simultaneously renders visible. This affiliation of "equality" with self-determination became even more apparent as students struggled with a variety of allied issues regarding relations with teachers, access to courses, academic ability and the opportunities of the work world. Repeatedly, the girls' rhetoric of equality became harnessed to the rhetoric of self-determination. Most of the girls saw "inequalities" in their material conditions as potentially surmountable through individual effort and by virtue of their ability to exercise individual choices.

The students' identification of self-determination as central to both educational and career success is not surprising given their perception of schooling as an indispensable vehicle to obtaining a career. That a career might amplify their relational needs and responsibilities is never fully elaborated for them, however, as schools appear to encourage an insular portrait of employment uncontaminated by any larger social context. Because salient notions of equality engendered in the context of school are deeply individualized, girls particularly have few or no opportunities to grapple openly with their intersubjective realities. A lack of "sensible conversations" (as Paula described it) in school about their domestic lives gives girls little ground for developing unmitigated confidence in their imagined trajectories from coursework to career.[6]

THE FUTURE CONTEXT OF DOMESTICITY AND WAGED WORK

The girls' confidence in a relatively unobstructed path from school to career was disrupted by intervening images of adult domestic life. A few girls did remain unconvinced about the effect of domesticity on waged work and others simply wanted to defer thinking about it. The vast majority of the girls, however, talked about domesticity as a major, reverberating set of strained possibilities and constraints in their future lives.[7] Most girls perceived themselves as almost inevitably destined for a life stretched between waged work and motherhood, and typically referred only to possibilities for mothering practices stemming out of culturally normative heterosexual couplings. Drawing on culturally dominant images and discourses concerning family and mothering, most girls subsequently found themselves disoriented by the persuasive sway of conflicting social imperatives.

The girls' consideration of a potential family generally threw the combining of school and career — where equality based on individualized qualities is realizable — into question. The malleable ideology of self-determination, which had supported their school-based discourses of equality, became challenged in the less flexible context of the male-breadwinner, nuclear-family model. The girls' investment in this culturally normative model of family often ended up justifying in their minds such unequal conditions as pay differentials between women and men, women's secondary job status, flexibly designed jobs and "career" deferral.

For example, according to Jodi, the economic demands placed on men to support domestic life justifies such realities as unequal pay.

> I think because the responsibility is on the man to get a good education because he is the one that he feels has to support the family, pay the bills and things like that, so he obviously has to have a better paid job, he has got to have the education to get the better paying job you know ... like if he makes forty thousand a year the woman would probably be making just twenty thousand, so that's still within the range of good money, right? At least it's something. Obviously it's not going to be the same.

The expectation of becoming a male breadwinner was shared by many of the young men. Antonio, for example, put it this way:

> I would have to support two other people, or whatever, oh, unless my wife works. Hopefully she will ... Like I'll still be working and I'll just be supporting them. That's about it.

Most of the girls envisioned taking time off to care for young children and expressed hope for a career that afforded accommodating hours. Kathleen said:

> Um, I don't really think it'll affect my working life because I think [as] a dental hygienist it's pretty flexible and I've heard that you can ... work three days a week, you can take maternity leave if you have to ...

(IN)EQUALITIES OF MOTHERING AND FATHERING

The girls' investment in combining waged work with family life was sustained by many practical concerns and desires, but their certitude about accomplishing this faltered when confronted with the realities of adult life. When asked specifically about motherhood, the girls often became uncomfortably conscious of the contingent character of domesticity. Their recognition of relational contingency strengthened as they began to iterate popular cultural understandings of domestic equality, some of which seemed to produce conflicting or incompatible images of mothering and fathering. These included the idea of: (1) a fifty-fifty sharing of responsibilities; (2) lending a hand; (3) equal "quality" of parenting; (4) negotiable choice and rejection of "traditional" roles; and (5) shared values, goals and pleasures. As Lee put it:

> No, I think it should be equal, fifty-fifty. They should both do their equal share of housework and looking after the kids.

Students' reflections regarding "shared responsibilities" were occasionally limited to the notion of "lending a hand." The idea of "lending a hand" often surfaced as a concession to the idea of equality in the face of simultaneous investment in full-time mothering. Irena said:

> But somehow, just from my own self, I think a woman's place is sort of in the house but at the same time she can go out and work and do whatever else she wants. I think the husband should share to a certain extent ... He can always lend a hand.

For others, like Robyn, equality meant spending equal time, or at least, involved relationships of equal quality with their children.

> I think it should be equal. So I think it should be shared so that the kids get ... good relationships with both parents ... so they get the same amount of quality time with both.

Some young women focused on equality as choice, as did Suk Ching, who wistfully constructed an image of negotiated equality based on the hopeful prospect of a nontraditional partner.

> Yeah. Like I have a choice. I don't have to wash dishes if I don't

want to. I don't have to take care of the children if I don't want to. He wants it, he can do it. If I want to, I can do it ... I want to see things his way. I want him to understand my way ... obviously [there is] compromise, right? ... I guess the most important [thing] is that he doesn't treat me as his wife, you know. Hopefully, by ... my future, you know, ... the future age won't be stereotypical ... the wife [won't have] to stay home ... [if] she doesn't want to stay home, and I know that she's not going to want to stay home ... she's not going to want to take care of the children ... I want him to know that.

Salina hoped her partner would have similar attitudes to child discipline, would share in the actual discipline itself and would enjoy the pleasures of prospective children.

I'd want it to be equal. Like say in the area of discipline ... I wouldn't want [it to be] like ... some families you see where ... the child is like, "Okay if I go to mom, she'll let me, if I go to dad he won't let me." I mean that's in every family but ... it's in some more so than others. And I would ...[want] everything to be equal, the discipline and the joys and the happiness and everything.

Students' understandings of equality in the context of the domestic domain, therefore, largely involved the notion of shared responsibilities, shared pleasures and negotiable choices. School-related versions involving equal ability, value, treatment or opportunity did not even surface here. As they contemplated family life, in other words, girls were forced to redefine equality to accommodate an entire complex of economic and intersubjective realities, which in the school context were either erased or obscured through the lens of self-determination. These realities not only seem to require situational compromises among parents as adults, but involve responsibilities toward and the needs of children, necessitating a conceptual framework that is more or less incompatible with the strategy of self-determination. Whether students envisioned reversed roles or shared parenting, the girls perceived themselves as deeply vulnerable and subject to the future uncertainties of interpersonal negotiations.

The version of home typically drawn on by these students conforms to a deeply "traditional" view of nuclear family life in North America. The desirability of equality as a general goal becomes a particularly poignant issue as, repeatedly, female students appear to sense that equality somehow means something different for boys than it does for girls. Success of equality, in its general sense in the family, is not just a matter of individual fortitude, determination, desire or even choice. For girls, it is felt to be radically dependent on the co-operation of a partner.

RADICAL DEPENDENCY IN REALIZING EQUALITY

School-based versions of equality as "ability" or "fortitude" are attributional qualities that students could mobilize to counter unequal treatment, and with the adjuncts of hard work and motivation, to take up opportunities. Self-determination here involves individualized decisions and choice-making in the context of perceived opportunities already felt to be available to them. Equality as shared responsibility and negotiated choices, however, requires the situated and ongoing construction of equality. Whether preparing for the exigency of divorce, recognizing the "normal" economic demands of family life or negotiating a less conventional familial configuration, the reality that equality as a lived concept is intrinsically relational is finally brought home to the girls in a completely new way through having to think family. Here, in the murky contingencies of domestic life, equality comes to be seen by girls as conditions of possibility that are actively constructed and negotiated between persons/partners, rather than as a characteristic or a quality that they could develop, possess or achieve through self-determined effort.

This became especially clear when the girls were asked how they envisaged their partners' role in childcare. Recognition of the intersubjective underpinning of domestic life often derails their sanguine apprehension of the future. Many either reluctantly or somewhat disbelievingly agreed that a husband could take the responsibility for childcare, if "he wanted to." Suk Ching maintained, "Sure, if he wants to take care of the children ... if he wants we can send the children to the daycare." Many of the girls expressed anxiety about their ability to hang on to their career, and felt themselves likely to be dependent on either the approval or understanding of their partners to negotiate the shape of their family and career lives. Leona, for example, envisioned sending her children to private school or daycare when she was away at work, recognizing that she'd have to build in time to see her children. She also acknowledged the importance of the type of career her husband would have.

> Maybe I'll marry someone who is in the same job, same kind of position, not position, but same kind of field, ... if I am doctor, [he] should be a doctor, because he will understand my problems ... Otherwise, [he] won't like me being out at night time.

Jessie made it even clearer the role her husband would have in determining whether or not she returned to work when she had children.

> ...if I have any children I might ... [give] more attention to my family, or I can always go back to work later, right? After a while. Or, I don't know, I'll compromise and talk to my husband.

Still others demonstrated an awareness of the normalized constraints and wider social expectations related to childcare. Amy depended on her evaluation of her current boyfriend as reasonable and openminded to construct a hopeful vision of shared parenting. "Actually, we'd probably wind up taking turns. He's not the type to make me stay home. I don't know how it would work."

Some girls, like Kim, relied on their image of the slowly changing nature of familial obligations and responsibilities to normalize their desire to remain in their career and have their partner assume responsibility for childcare. She expressed her concern that her partner be available to help her:

> Well, if I had kids, if I had children, ... I know I'd stay home and take care of them for a couple of years or until they grew up a bit, and then I'd have to go back to school and start all over again. Almost all over again ... I don't like that too much, cause I don't want to go through the same thing again, I don't. But then if I had a husband who'd take care of the kids for like a year or two, that'd be fine ... I'm just saying that ... most women do [take care of the kids], but nowadays [there are families] where they both do so.

That students felt dependent on the voluntarism of their partners to assume childcare was pervasive, whether this childcare took the shape of "help" or actual role reversal. Moreover, the cultural scripts that encourage both career and mothering created endless confusion and mixed loyalties among the young women. Bhinder said:

> Sometimes males tend to want to have you stay home and tend ... the children and ... I guess it would depend on your partner. But it would have a part to play cause women do love children. So having children, you'd want to stay home with them. But, then again, you know, you do want to get out and have a career as well as a partner.

The girls' perception of inevitability regarding their dependency on a partner's voluntarism tended to result in an overwhelming sense of resignation concerning mothering roles. The girls talked about probably "having" to stay home, about wishing for things they "probably" won't get, about the futility of making plans because these are most likely to change in the face of actual family practice. Clarissa, envisioning working at home, said:

> I guess I could stay home, but if I was a psychiatrist I could stay home or have a nanny. It would be ideal, to have a nanny and your office in your house. But that probably wouldn't happen.

Helena was much more cautious, "I'd just take it as it comes because I don't want to expect something and then in the end something might happen, the least expected, so I'd rather just go with the flow."

Whereas the girls struggled with a variety of competing discourses related to mothering to construct a range of possible conditions of domestic equality, the boys almost exclusively relied on economic rationales to invoke their image of equality, and generally offered only cursory and reluctant nods in the direction of role reversal. Many of the boys appeared almost grudgingly concerned with "equality" as a goal, and halfheartedly acknowledged different possibilities for shared parenting, if economic circumstances either allowed for it or demanded it.

Some boys, like Rod, recognized the need for some form of negotiation in the actual practice of equality, but were forced to admit they would prefer their partner to be at home. Rod said:

We should be smart and plan to have our children after we've worked for five years and have enough money that either my wife, my wife most likely, would stay home with the children until they're old enough to have a baby sitter or my mother could take care of them ... if my wife had a better paying job then I'd let her go to work if it was possible, and I'd leave mine.

Although some boys, like Kenneth, "don't want to think about it yet," others acknowledged that their future wives might be working, and in that case, point to the possibility of daycare arrangements. Gordon's conjecturing remains simultaneously entrenched, however, in the script of traditional roles. He acknowledged that his future wife would have primary responsibility for the children until he got home from work. However,

> ... if she had a full time job too then we'd have to get a baby sitter or whatever ... I saw an ad in the paper that [is] perfect for the housewife, eh, it's a job from about eight in the morning till about three in the afternoon, it says, you know, you're not bored all day, go out to work, make extra money and come home just in time when the kids get home, eh? I think that's great ... Yeah, yeah, once they're ... in school, right? I think that's all right.

•

That equality may mean something different for girls than it does for boys suggests that boys and girls are discursively situated in different ways within culturally dominant discourses about equality.[8] As is made particularly clear in the students' discussions about anticipated family life with a partner, equality comes to accrue different meanings for boys and girls. The girls intuitively grasped this difference through their repeated acknowledgements of their dependency on their male partners for realizing their visions of equality.

Although both males and females are being prepared through the educational system to invest in the notion of career, our research suggests that males face far fewer contradictory invitations or discourses to achieve this goal and see themselves as needing to rely less on co-operation than on self-determination to achieve their ends. As contrary constructs, individualized and relational versions of equality were never forced to collide as problematically for the boys as they did for the girls. Throughout their conjecturing about domesticity, the boys conveyed a relative assurance that their trajectories from school to career would remain firmly supported by the versions of self-determined equality made salient and workable to them in their school context.

The girls, on the other hand, appeared to be much more conscious of their positioning within multiple and contradictory discourses, perceiving themselves as radically dependent on the voluntarism of their partners to achieve their career goals. Given their discrepant positions in discourses of equality, it is important to examine how this relates to larger questions of power.

Equality discourses, perforce, are directed at social inequalities and are therefore powerfully attractive to young women. However, the elasticized scripts of equality that are culturally available to girls through school-based versions of equal treatment, equal opportunity or equal ability, for example, may, in effect, end up as depoliticizing strategies. This occurs, in part, through promotion of equality as a goal most persuasively operationalized by dint of individual effort and determination. What this effectively implies is that equality as a practice might only be as effectual as individuals are able to construct it in their own lives.

The female students' confrontation with the world of relational contingencies through anticipation of domesticity and partnerships served as a jarring realization of the deeply intersubjective character of culturally organized life. Gender inequalities that were perceived by the girls as combatable in the contexts of school and a socially bracketted career world, suddenly loomed as distinct potential constraints on their imagined futures. What the girls often were not able to anticipate, in other words, is the larger social realm in which unequal conditions of power are embedded in all social practices, not just those of school, career or even family. Largely submerged in their conjecturing is recognition of the pervasiveness of gender as a structuring tool of inequality.

As Wendy Brown notes, gender continues to serve as a cultural "marker of power, a maker of subjects, an axis of subordination" in the contemporary North American context.[9] Moreover, gender remains one of the more enduring references through which political and social power has been organized, practised and legitimated.[10] Following Henrietta Moore, gender and sexual difference have historically served to legitimate the organization of many different forms of social inequity (including race and class inequalities), so that gender is arguably implicated in the concept and construction of power itself.[11] Furthermore, the stability of a hegemonic "gender system" occurs through the performance of gendered practices that operate as "material forces" in daily quotidian life.[12]

Girls are thus confronted with the fact that whereas written or spoken discourses offer opportunities for flexibility and elasticized conceptualizations, actual practice and existing social inequities may pose restraints on the limits of the possible. Inequalities of race, class, age, or physical ability are simply erased in the socially decontextualized equality discourses invoked by students at school. The practice of equality, however, is materially complex and contingent. Effective challenges to entrenched social inequalities must necessarily, therefore, address the following concerns: (1) the complex interpenetration of discursive practices, (2) the constraints of existing social practices and relations, and (3) the problematic reliance of equality discourses on a strong individualism.

Attention to cultural processes of power reveals further limitations to equality discourses. First, concepts such as equality always come to have meaning and salience for individuals who are already situated differently by virtue of class, gender, sexuality, race, age and so on. This means that equality is never a homogeneous discursive practice. Rather, it is constructed through practical, lived conditions in such a way that persons are invited into its affective web with different intensities, and with different pre-established interests, social positions or social needs. That equality often means conforming to a white middle-class male template also means that boys and girls will be drawn into practical engagements for establishing domestic equality, with different urgencies and with already disparately organized cultural positions of possibility or privilege.

Second, one of the reasons for the disparate positioning of boys and girls within the selfsame discourse of equality occurs because of its interpenetration with other, pre-established discourses. As the students demonstrated in their conceptualization of equality in the context of schooling, the discourse of equality is malleable, capable of accommodating a variety of different meanings and possibilities. Students are able to do this, in part, because they draw on pre-existing cultural discourses and concepts to fashion a more familiar and hybridized set of ideological tools for imagining their future.

Relatedly, co-existing ideologies may also serve to confuse and thwart the liberatory potential of a concept such as equality. Both the girls and the boys attempted to construct a practical concept of domestic equality through the confining lens of the male-breadwinner, nuclear-family model. For the girls, the constraints imposed by this model inevitably led to the collapse of individualized versions of equality and threatened the plausibility of developing nontraditional family practices. In their efforts to refashion domestic practice, in other words, students persistently entangled conventional and unconventional images of family. By so doing, historical patterns and inequalities were simultaneously sustained and reinscribed.

Third, contemporary social theory has been prolific in its descriptions of a "postmodern" condition, seen to be fragmented, discontinuous and shifting.[13] The concept of equality invites girls especially to be increasingly malleable, capable of negotiating, managing and shifting their desires, resources, skills and cultural capital to meet the changing demands of their social contexts. Bearing in mind the limited nature of the data (a specific set of high school students), it appears that boys, attached as they seem to be to their economic roles, view themselves as much less expected to develop an adaptive set of skills and desires to meet their social roles.

The changing and multiple demands placed on women comes to mean that women are increasingly expected to be available for "wage, labor, sex, reproduction, mothering, spectacle, exercise or even invisibility, as the situation demands."[14] The valorization implicit in much contemporary theorizing of the fragmented and therefore ostensibly less deterministic cultural terrain is misleading and troublesome, given the possibility that this fragmentation may, in fact, augur increased paradoxes for women especially.

It is clear from this research that discourses of equality never exist in a vacuum, but are dynamically engaged with a large variety of cultural scripts and norms. As students confirm, discourses of equality are deeply co-implicated with, for example, such culturally idealized practices as that of the male-breadwinner, nuclear family. Consequently, although discourses of equality may be modestly effective in interrogating traditional scripts around motherhood, the entrenchment of adjacent cultural values related to family life (including that of normative heterosexuality, for example), may, in fact, limit the ability of the concept of equality to effectively displace these traditional scripts.

To conclude, our research has three general aims. We are attempting to understand, first, how equality can be understood as an everyday discourse embedded within complex and competing discourses and contexts; second, how girls are able to read their culture — its discourses and practices — and how they define their desires and futures in its light; and, third, how gender reforms that concentrate on the school-career nexus may suffer from their inattention to family justice issues and girls' understanding of their entwined futures of employment and domesticity.

These objectives address some of the theoretical, political and practical issues raised in Jane Kenway's poststructural analysis of girls' postschool options.[15] In particular, we hope that our research helps to counter gender educational reform that naively exaggerates the capacity of nontraditional areas of schooling credentials and paid work (for example, maths, science and technical areas) to enhance girls' futures. Our work suggests that research needs to attend more closely to the intricate interdependencies of family/schooling/employment to understand the ramifications of inequalities. In particular, we encourage ongoing attention to the complicated and often vexed narratives of girls as they reflect on their imagined domestic conditions, and to the diverse ambiguities and ironies facing girls as they try to make decisions and plan for their futures.[16]

Notes

The research for this chapter was supported by a SSHRC Small Research Grant. We would like to thank Leslie G. Roman for her very helpful comments on an earlier draft of the chapter.

1. Our evidence is drawn from a study that took place in 1990 on the participation of girls and boys in senior mathematics and physical science courses. The research team interviewed students in their final year of secondary school in twelve schools located in different regions of British Columbia. We selected the schools to reflect social class, ethnic and regional variations of the province. Half of the schools are located in the Greater Vancouver area (as is the bulk of the provincial population); the other half are situated in smaller cities and communities. At each of the schools, on average, seventeen students (whom we selected randomly) participated in semistructured interviews. We also observed classrooms and interviewed teachers, counsellors and principals. We interviewed altogether 200 students (132 girls and 68 young boys) and focused upon the experiences of the girls, using the boys' responses primarily for purposes of comparison. We have based our analysis in this chapter on student (primarily the girls') interviews from six schools. For further methodological details, see P. James Gaskell, Arlene McLaren, Antoinette Oberg, and Linda Eyre, *Gender Issues in Student Choices in Mathematics and Science* (Victoria, BC: Ministry of Education and Ministry Responsible for Multiculturalism and Human Rights, 1993).

2. Recent studies suggest that girls' responses to motherhood vary depending on social context, especially those structured by class, race, ethnicity, sexual orientation and physical ability. See, for example, Alison Jones, "Becoming a 'Girl': Post-structuralist Suggestions for Educational Research," *Gender and Education* 5 (1993), 157–166; Heidi Safia Mirza, "The Social Construction of Black Womanhood in British Educational Research: Towards a New Understanding," in Madeleine Arnot and Kathleen Weiler, eds., *Feminism and Social Justice in Education: International Perspectives* (London: Falmer Press, 1993), 32–57. Furthermore, studies point out that equality discourses may take distinct forms in such diverse settings as schools, families and workplaces. Wendy Luttrell, "'Becoming Somebody': Aspirations, Opportunities, and Womanhood," in Gay Young and Bette Dickerson, eds., *Color, Class and Country: Experiences of Gender* (London: Zed Books), 17–35. Finally, and more generally, research suggests that girls' discourses about mothering and employment are intertwined in complex ways with understandings about, for example, femininity, masculinity, the family, the sexual division of labour, gender equality and nonparental childcare. Arlene Tigar McLaren, "Coercive Invitations: How Young Women in School Make Sense of Mothering and Waged Labour," *British Journal of Sociology of Education* 17, no. 3 (1996), 279–298.

3. Jane Kenway, "Non-Traditional Pathways: Are They the Way to the Future?," in Jill Blackmore and Jane Kenway, eds., *Gender Matters in Educational Administration and Policy: A Feminist Introduction* (London: Falmer Press, 1993), 81–100.

4. Arlene Tigar McLaren and Ann Vanderbijl, "The Uses of Equality: Teenage Girls' School-Based Gendered Discourses," unpublished paper.

5. We use pseudonyms in this chapter and have attempted to match them with the ethno-cultural connotations of the students' real names.

6. Students generally construed equality to mean conforming to a white middle-class male template; using certain "male experience" as the standard and the norm for comparing "female experience."

7. When we asked students about their future domestic lives, we generally talked about "partners" and children. In our questions we attempted to avoid terms like "wife" and "husband" so as not to explicitly privilege heterosexual marriage. The students did not spontaneously offer any discussions of alternative family configurations.

8. See Henrietta L. Moore, *A Passion for Difference* (Indianapolis: Indiana University Press, 1994), who discusses how poststructuralist theories of the subject and of positionality create a space in which it is possible to talk about the different subject positions offered by various discourses.

9. Wendy Brown, *States of Injury: Power and Freedom in Late Modernity* (Princeton: Princeton University Press, 1995).

10. Joan Scott, "Gender: A Useful Category of Historical Analysis," in Elizabeth Weed, ed., *Coming to Terms: Feminism, Theory, Politics* (New York: Routledge, 1989), 81–100.

11. Moore, *A Passion for Difference*.

12. Chris Shilling, *The Body and Social Theory* (London: Sage Publications, 1993).

13. See, for example, Jane Flax, *Thinking Fragments: Psychoanalysis, Feminism Postmodernism in the Contemporary West* (Berkeley: University of California Press, 1990).

14. Linda Singer, "Bodies, Pleasures, Powers," *Differences* 1 (Winter 1989), 57.

15. Kenway, "Non-Traditional Pathways."

16. Our research examined students from a wide range of communities (for example, social class and ethnocultural backgrounds), but our analysis in this chapter did not examine how girls' and boys' conceptualizations of equality may differ according to such differentiated experiences.

Chapter 7

MOTHER TO DAUGHTER:
THE SHAPING OF A GIRL'S VALUES
IN THE CONTEXT OF A PARENT
WITH A CHRONIC ILLNESS

Karen A. Blackford

THE REPRODUCTION OF powerless female identities that reflect patriar-chal gender stereotypes[1] is a long-standing concern for feminists. Yet re-search into socialization has been difficult, because the shaping of a girl's values in the context of her family, her society and her self is a subtle process difficult to discern. The experiences of families which have had to confront other oppressive stereotypes can shed light on the identity formation of girls. This chapter suggests that families in which either the mother or the father has a disability creates an environment in which daughters can learn to see beyond stereotypical notions of physical condition, family form and gender.

My own experience as a mother and as a daughter with a disability first drew me to reconsider my values about family, bodily condition, gender and age. At the same time, I came to reflect on relationships in the family before and after the onset of my chronic illness, within which these attitudes were formed. When I later came to research the lives of twenty-three Ontario children whose parents have multiple sclerosis (MS), it became more apparent that the onset of a parent's chronic illness constitutes a challenge to the long-standing attitudes of family members. Therefore, this study gave me the opportunity to learn about mothers and daughters from a unique perspective. In the context of a parent's transition from apparent health to a diagnosis of chronic illness, daughters' values and the importance of their mothers in shaping those values became evident.

MOTHERS, DAUGHTERS AND DISABILITY

Not a lot has been written in Canada about mothers, daughters and socialization options within the context of disability. Since mothers have been stereotyped as caretakers, the idea that mothers might also have a disability is foreign to our understanding of social identity. Inversely, the word disability has until recently conjured up a dependent object. Women with disabilities, therefore, have rarely been acknowledged as gendered persons, much less recognized as mothers. Consequently, the body of literature on mothering with a disability is exceedingly scarce.

Fathers with disabilities are equally invisible in the literature. They are also assumed to be made impotent by their disability and presumed to be incapable of maintaining traditional family "bread winning" roles. This chapter provides some examples of daughters who have fathers with multiple sclerosis and others who have mothers with multiple sclerosis. The focus, however, is on the daughters' responses to their mothers' influences in the context of either their fathers' or their mothers' disability.

Most early reports on family life with maternal multiple sclerosis[2] failed to take into account the broader social, economic and historical contexts which shape family relations and people's experiences of disability.[3] Thus these studies tended to characterize disabled women as inept mothers and their children as victims. Such reports only reaffirm the idea that mothering and disability are concepts that cannot come together except with disastrous outcomes.

Some of the more recent research has taken contextual influences into account, so that the strengths of disabled mothers and of their children have begun to emerge, along with the understanding that the barriers they face are not inevitable but are rooted in society.[4] Particularly exciting is the research that teases out the ironies in the family lives of parents with disabilities and their children. For example, Ora Prilleltensky provides a thoughtful analysis of the mothering choices available to disabled women, and as one outcome, brings us a fresh examination of the mothering choices available to all women. Prilleltensky identifies resilience in mothers with disabilities in spite of social, economic, political and physical barriers.[5] Focusing on children whose fathers or mothers have kidney disease, Heather Beanlands shows that children experience uncertainty in association with their parents' chronic illness. However, they also express hopefulness.[6]

Emerging studies that have compared mother–daughter dyads in general populations with mother–daughter dyads in populations with maternal multiple sclerosis have also revealed the error of relying on stereotypes about mothering, "daughtering," "able-bodiedness" and disability. Barbara Carpio's work on daughters' body image and Patricia Crist's analysis of play and work interactions between mothers and daughters, both show similarities and not differences between mothers with MS and their daughters when compared with mothers and daughters in the general population.[7]

None of these studies, however, examine the gender identity socialization of daughters whose parents have multiple sclerosis or other disabilities. Neither do they consider gender stereotypes in relation to assumptions about disability, age or family form. These are issues that emerged as I undertook my study.

THE STUDY

I recruited eighteen Ontario families through an Ontario Multiple Sclerosis Society newsletter.[8] All families participating had at least one parent with MS, at least one child between eight and sixteen years of age and spoke English. The general research question posed was, "What can we learn about family life — that is, being a child or being a parent — from families in which a parent has MS?" I visited parents, who telephoned or wrote to express interest in participating, in their homes with all their family members present. Twenty-three children and their parents gave their informed consent for recorded interviews and were then individually interviewed.

The contents of interview transcripts were then coded and analyzed using a grounded theory approach.[9] In other words, through comparing what family members reported about times before and after MS symptoms began, and through comparing descriptions from family members in one family with those in other families, certain themes were seen to predominate. Early in the analysis, values emerged as one such predominant theme. A second examination of transcripts compared the theme of values across families, ages, genders and locations. Various characteristics, antecedents and consequences of values then became visible. Values were seen to fall into the four conceptual categories of family, physical condition, gender and age. A frequent link was seen between the nature of a daughter's values in these various areas and the values expressed by her mother.

In the section which follows, case study examples are provided to show the variety of values expressed by study participants and to demonstrate links between the values of mothers and their daughters. Readers will observe that in some cases, the link between mother–daughter values perpetuated stereotypical values, while in other cases, traditional patriarchal values were transformed. Pseudonyms are assigned to participants to ensure confidentiality.

FAMILY VALUES

A common term for the oppression of women within the nuclear family is "familialism." Meg Luxton defines familialism as:

> a widespread and deeply imbedded ideology about how people ought to live ... The ideology of "familialism" is a belief system which argues that the best way for adults to live is in nuclear families: that is, as a socially and legally recognised heterosexual couple (a man and a woman) who normally expect to have children ... Basic to the ideology of familialism are patriarchal definitions and ideals of how men, women and children should behave.[10]

Familialism is particularly relevant to our understanding of participants in this study. Joanne Taylor, a single low-income mother of three, fears that her multiple sclerosis might be exacerbated to the point where she could no longer live with and care for her children. She is aware that some parents, especially low-income parents, are isolated in a care facility when they experience a progressive loss of energy and strength. She also knows that, as their health deteriorates, some mothers with MS have lost legal custody of their children. Unfortunately, with disablist judgements in the courts and insufficient social community services,[11] her fears are grounded on probabilities. However, Joanne holds strong traditional views that the care provided by a birth mother is the only natural and proper way to raise a child. The notion of paid childcare is contrary to this strong belief. She also fears any change that would take herself or her children beyond the neighbourhood and outside the circle of her parents and siblings. Governed as she is by familialism, Joanne worries that she "must keep the family together" at all costs.

Her teenage daughter Sandra also holds traditional expectations of family life. Ironically, though, Sandra Taylor's understanding of what constitutes proper traditional family life differs from that of her mother. Her concern is not focused on staying with her mother and siblings. Instead, Sandra is distressed about the extent to which her family structure, though it has stayed together, differs from what she has learned is the ideal family form. By that she means children living with a middle-class mother and father with no hint of disability. Her preference for the future is to move in with her professional "able-bodied" father and his second wife.

This example illustrates that a daughter does not always internalize her mother's values, in this case, her mother's family values. On the one hand, Joanne Taylor sees divorce as freedom from a man she no longer trusts, a low-income neighbourhood as familiarity and disability as a sign that she can and has overcome many obstacles. On the other hand, her daughter Sandra is preoccupied with how parental disability, her mother's single-parent status and their low family income construct a picture of family that differs sharply from her ideal.

Another common assumption about family life is that only biological parents can raise "natural" children. Mothers who choose to adopt and their adopted children generally face discrimination. This stigma is based on the historical importance of a man's lineage and the proper distribution of a father's property through inheritance.[12]

Two women interviewed in the study, both of whom have MS, have sons whom they have adopted. In most ways, Alice Weycamp and Leslie Anne Clifford are similar. They are both teachers and each has a husband who is also a teacher. Each lives in a suburban neighbourhood and a single-family home. In spite of these similarities, attitudes in each family toward adoption are strikingly different.

When interviewed, Alice Weycamp described how devastated she was when her own pregnancies ended in miscarriages and she had to adopt a child. She explained that her middle-class mother has very strict expectations about what being a married woman entails. Alice feels that because of fatigue associated with her MS she fails to fulfill her mother's expectations as a housekeeper, and because of her miscarriages and subsequent adoption of a child, she fails to meet her mother's expectations of "natural" motherhood. Her son represents a worry to her, because he has apparently not accepted his adopted status. It seems that when the topic is raised in his classroom, he denies that he is adopted.

Leslie Anne Clifford was also grief stricken when she had many miscarriages, but did not undergo judgement or criticism from her mother. It seems that her mother was an immigrant to Canada, open to change and versatile in seeking ways to support her children through paid employment. She encouraged Leslie Anne to continue her teaching career after MS symptoms began and later supported Leslie Anne in her idea of adoption. When Leslie Anne heard that she and her husband could adopt a toddler, she saw the adoption of the child as a gift. Her son Nathan Clifford openly and casually informs neighbours and friends of his adopted status and commonly reminds his family doctor that he is adopted during physical examinations and history taking.

What emerges from these interviews are examples that demonstrate the ways in which entrenched familialism oppresses women and how it is reproduced in the link between mother and daughter. We also see how a mother's decision to look openly at how families can be organized facilitates a daughter's transformation of family traditions and her own self-empowerment.

BODILY CONDITION

Patriarchal society assumes that both women and people with disabilities are vulnerable and in need of protection. In spite of the similarities between the concepts of womanhood and disability, bringing them together within the identity of one person is difficult for traditional thinkers. Thus the fact that a woman with a disability is a gendered person is often invisible.

Prejudice against disability as a concept and against disabled people as individuals is a broadly accepted social value. This holding up of the "able" body as a standard for humanness[13] has been termed "disablism."[14] Since academics are products of the broader culture, it is not surprising that some intellectuals are disablist in their views. Thus some of the academic literature reflects the disablism of those authors. For example, in his studies of disability and disabled people, sociologist Irving Goffman has categorized disabled people within a branch of social science called the study of deviance.[15] Though terminology has changed from adjectives such as "crippled" to "challenged," the stigma of impairment as deviance remains.

In spite of this negative perspective of impairment in the sociology of deviance and in the broader culture, a small emerging body of literature on the sociology of acceptance suggests that alternatives to disablist thinking are possible. Sociologists who introduce the notion of acceptance report that characteristics such as moral strength, pro-social attitudes and sensitivity to others have been attributed to disabled people by some people within their social circle.[16]

My interviews with parents with MS and their children provide a glimpse of how disablist notions emerge within family relationships. Betty McKenna is a mother who now has MS. However, she had the childhood experience of seeing her own mother institutionalized for tuberculosis. Betty vividly recalls waving to her mother from across the street from the sanatorium, since visits for sanatorium "inmates" were limited to seeing family members from a window. Even after discharge, Betty's mother was always careful not to kiss her or expose her to any possibility of infection. The social stigma and fear associated with illness was resurrected for Betty when her MS symptoms appeared shortly after her son was born. While nurses encouraged her to have the child visit her in the hospital, she decided that coming to hospital was harmful for children. Instead, she chose to suffer the loneliness and longing she felt for her child. She had learned from her mother that children must be protected from maternal disability.

Now that Betty's son Mark is an adolescent, he does not acknowledge her when she is outside on her scooter if he is with his friends. Though she is tearful when reporting this lack of respect, she accepts that fitting in with friends is very important for boys. Her acceptance of rejection in this way indicates that she still practises the beliefs she learned from her mother: separation from a mother with a disability is something which children require for their healthy development.

Penny Chapman's father has MS. This eleven-year-old appears to have been strongly influenced by her mother's ideas about disability. Penny points to lack of accessible public transportation as a social injustice. She and her brother Tom have marched with placards in their neighbourhood because she feels that a neighbourhood without opportunities for access "just isn't fair." Penny is pleased that her friends like to spend time with her dad when they visit the house. Clearly, these friends feel comfortable to do so because Penny respects and likes her dad. She emphasizes the help he gives her with homework.

I gained some insight into Penny's attitude toward disability and able-bodiedness inadvertently after interviews with family members were completed. As I was putting on my coat to leave the Chapman home, Penny's mother, Shirley Chapman, explained her own family history. Apparently, Shirley had a cousin injured as a youth in a car accident. This cousin, of whom she is very proud, completed high school and university and has become a scholar. The advocacy demonstrated by Shirley and, in turn, by her daughter Penny on behalf of people with disabilities, reflects their strong belief in integration and universal access.

Thus we have two examples of families in which mothers have been major influences on how their daughters view able-bodiedness and disability.

THE DIVISION OF LABOUR ACCORDING TO GENDER AND AGE

Stereotypical notions of women ironically assume that they require male protection, control and guidance while simultaneously casting them into caregiving roles that require that they be competent and strong. Many women have sought to achieve the look of femininity while managing homemaking and paid employment, suffering silently as they "Do it all." For Sheila Neysmith, current social arrangements within nuclear families allow and even encourage the existence of oppression associated with the gendered division of labour.[17] She agrees with Anne Bullock's understanding of family relations: "Family implies a privatized, hierarchical and gendered work organization that does not equally benefit its members and also foments the differences among families who are thought to comprise 'the community.'"[18] Neysmith suggests that in most families, women are "forced to care" because there is no one else available to provide care. Familialism also dictates that as well as men and women, children and adults have a hierarchical relationship.

Linda Brothers is raising her two children alone. Her husband Frank left the marriage shortly after he was diagnosed with MS. Linda assured her husband when his illness appeared that she would care for him as well as manage the children and her job. Although her husband had not been emotionally supportive during the marriage, she felt obligated to offer care for him in the face of his potential disability. In fact, her description of the marriage breakup focuses on her shock, bewilderment and even shame at the fact that he has refused her care. The notion of the "Do it all" superwoman and the expectation of suffering both appear to be part of her idea of womanhood.

Her eleven-year-old daughter Charlotte also demonstrates an obligation to care. Now that Frank Brothers has moved in with another woman and that woman's toddler, Charlotte visits in order to provide childcare and to give her father his prescribed injections. This caring is in direct contrast to the approach taken by Charlotte's brother, Simon. According to Simon, his father chose to leave and to take on new family responsibilities. Since he sees that those choices have been a loss to himself, his mother and his sister, Simon refuses to contribute his energy to supporting his father with these additional responsibilities.

In Charlotte's case, it seems that the stress of her parents' marriage breakup, of worry about her father's health and of an increased caretaking load has caused her hair to fall out. However, in spite of this sign of stress, she continues with caring for her father and supporting her mother with encouragement, while also taking on extracurricular school activities. For example, she excels in synchronized swimming lessons. Charlotte appears to be growing into her mother's version of ideal womanhood: a super achieving martyr.

Cathy Workman (sixteen) and her sister Jillian (nine) talk openly with each other and negotiate with their mother, Julia, about family responsibilities. Julia Workman is a single mother with multiple sclerosis.

She explains that since her MS symptoms started, she has had to re-think more traditional approaches to child rearing. She has shared more housework with her daughters than previously and now includes them more often in family decision making. This has increased her respect for the girls' abilities but has not reduced her sense of being their guide in matters related to their own present and future behaviours and choices.

After her divorce, Julia Workman decided to purchase a house in partnership with her retired parents. The arrangement was satisfactory to both parties in terms of shared finances. However, she now sees that her parents do not respect her judgement as a mother, nor as an adult, since the onset of her chronic illness. Her parents both insist on setting her daughters' curfew hours and examining their visitors. Her father has even threatened to "belt" his granddaughters into compliance. Julia Workman finds that she must defend her daughters and also defend her right as a mother to parent the girls. She is anxiously considering alternative living arrangements and, meanwhile, has created separate living quarters in the lower part of the house for herself, Cathy and Jillian.

In this situation, we have a clash between two generations as they disagree about how age should or should not determine hierarchy or reciprocity in decision making and about how age should or should not structure the division of labour. This clash, however, has been increased dramatically with the onset of disability. Julia Workman's parents are responding from a disablist viewpoint since the onset of her MS symptoms. Disablism has decreased the respect her parents have for her as a competent mother and has increased their own familial feelings of responsibility for intervening as substitute parents for her children. They feel an obligation to protect Cathy and Jillian from housework when they "should" be playing or studying and from responsibilities of decision making in the family when they "should" be merely following their mother's instructions. In addition, they feel responsible to assist with or take over from Julia those mothering tasks and decisions which they assume are now beyond her capabilities. Julia Workman, however, has increasingly shared her responsibilities for both decision making and work across age groups, without surrendering her role as family guide and leader. She provides her daughters with protection and wisdom while respecting their contributions.

Penny Chapman, introduced earlier in this chapter, illustrates the shared division of labour across both gender and age. Penny appreciates her father's help with homework, but also sees this help as part of his responsibility. She remembers that her father used to cook on weekends until his MS symptoms worsened. Her grandfather still prepares breakfast when he visits. In assisting her younger brother, her father and her mother, Penny shows that children sometimes care for siblings and for people older than themselves while still having their own needs met. She receives encouragement from all family members, especially with her figure skating competitions and lessons. Shirley Chapman provides transportation, her brother cheers mightily at performances, while her father analyzes video tapes of skate competitions for her and pays for her lessons.

In discussing the future, Penny hopes to teach figure skating. She also expects to marry one day and predicts that her husband will do his share of household chores and will contribute to childcare. Any children she may have will be included in task allocation. "If I have any kids, when they grow, I'll leave it to them to pick up something that's around the house." In this way, she negates the mythology that children are helpless recipients of unidirectional caring.

CONCLUSIONS

Mothers emerge as a very important part of the context in which daughters choose and are offered values about family, bodily condition, gender and age. This finding is not surprising. The strong influence that parents have on children is well documented,[19] and mothers tend to do the greatest proportion of nurturing. Furthermore, children are shown to most often identify with a same-sex adult.[20]

What is fascinating in the stories reported here are the variety of directions in which maternal influence can lead daughters. Some daughters respond by reproducing what they perceive to be their mothers' values, others by transforming those values and still others by responding with a combination of the two.

Mothers' abilities to free their daughters to think and act in new directions appear to be associated with the transitions these mothers have experienced in their own lives through immigration, physical impairment of a family member, divorce or the experience of their own impairments. This idea of a dynamic, interactive link between mothers' values and those of their daughters and between past and present lives is notable.

What allows daughters, many of whom go on to be mothers, to respond with flexibility in spite of traditional patriarchal, ageist and disablist expectations? It seems that when transitions occur in a family which recognizes that there are potential benefits associated with adjusting to a new situation, a fresh cultural perspective on family can emerge. The interpretation of events by each mother in these examples and her determination to meet events with flexibility seems critical. Immigration to Canada means employment and increased family income, as Leslie Ann Clifford interprets her family history. A cousin's car accident means increased opportunity for educational attainment, as Shirley Chapman interprets her cousin's story. Julia Workman interprets the onset of multiple sclerosis and then divorce as an avenue to resisting the ideas of abusive parents or an abusive husband. Daughters' responses also appear to vary with contextual factors such as culture, cohort and family form, while being influenced by personal and collective life histories. Most important are any particular girl's interpretation of these events and her own agency.

These findings demonstrate why studies of girls' socialization are so difficult. Populations in transition, such as those experiencing the onset of a chronic illness, provide new opportunities to researching and conceptualizing mothers, daughters and their related socialization.

Notes

I am grateful to the children and parents who agreed to allow me to record and interpret their stories. My son Chris Blackford, my mother Freda Sawyer, and York University faculty advisors Gordon Darroch, Francoise Boudreau, Livy Visano and Penny Stewart provided support. The Ontario Ministry of Health sponsored the research described here, although content and analysis are my own responsibility.

1. E. Maccoby and C. Jacklin, *The Psychology of Sex Differences* (Stanford, CA: Stanford University Press, 1974).

2. See, for example, Susan Arnaud, "Some Psychological Characteristics of Children of Multiple Sclerotics," *Psychosomatic Medicine* 21, no. 1 (1959), 8–22; M. Olgas,

"The Relationship Between Parents' Health Status and Body Image of Their Children," *Nursing Research* 23 (1974), 319–324; June Kikuchi, *Children and Adolescents of Parents with Multiple Sclerosis: Their Reported Quality of Life* (Edmonton, AB: University of Alberta, 1985); June Kikuchi and A.E. Molzahn, *Children and Adolescents of Parents with Renal Failure on Dialysis: Their Reported Quality of Life* (Edmonton, AB: University of Alberta, 1989).

3. This chapter focuses on children whose parents have a disability. However, the lack of a critical analysis is also generally true of studies of mothers with disabled children, a rare exception being Pat McIver's work with mothers of technically dependent children presented at the 1997 Conference on Mothers with Disabilities, York University, Centre for Feminist Research.

4. Centres for Independent Living and the DisAbled Women's Network have addressed structural barriers for mothers with disabilities, as well as the strengths of disabled women, through pioneering research, supportive and educational networks, newsletters and conferences. At the University of British Columbia, nursing professor Elaine Carty's work with disabled women specifically around maternity issues reflects similar themes.

5. Ora Prilleltensky, "Motherhood in the Lives of Women with Physical Disabilities" (PhD diss., Ontario Studies in Education/University of Toronto, 1998).

6. Heather Beanlands, "The Experience of Being a Child in a Family Where a Parent is on Home Dialysis" (master's thesis, School of Nursing, University of Toronto, 1987).

7. Barbara Carpio, "Mothers' and Daughters' Perceptions of Adolescent Health Needs in Families with and without Maternal Multiple Sclerosis" (master's thesis, School of Nursing, University of Toronto, 1981); Patricia Crist, "Contingent Interaction During Work and Play Tasks for Mothers with Multiple Sclerosis and Their Daughters," *American Journal of Occupational Therapy* 47, no. 2 (1993), 129–131.

8. A more complete description of this study is available in my doctoral dissertation, Karen A. Blackford, "Children Whose Parents Have Multiple Sclerosis: An Historical Sociological Perspective" (PhD diss., York University, 1995).

9. Anselm Strauss, *Qualitative Analysis for Social Scientists* (Cambridge: Cambridge University Press, 1987).

10. Meg Luxton, "Thinking About the Future," in Karen Anderson, et al., eds., *Family Matters* (Scarborough, ON: Nelson Canada, 1988), 238.

11. Sandra Goundry and Yvonne Peters, *Litigating for Disability Equality Rights: The Promises and the Pitfalls* (Winnipeg, MB: The Canadian Disability Rights Council, 1994).

12. Diana Gittens, *The Family in Question* (London: MacMillan Education, 1985).

13. A. Wohl, *Endangered Lives* (London: M.S. Dent, 1983).

14. The term disability is used interchangeably with the term chronic illness in this chapter. Symptoms of the chronic illness multiple sclerosis do not always include evident impairment. However, the identity of disability that usually accompanies the MS diagnosis is disabling, whether or not physical impairment is present. A

critical analysis of this process and an explanation of disablism can be found in Philip Abberley, "The Concept of Oppression and the Development of a Social Theory of Disability," *Disability, Handicap and Society* 2, no. 1 (1987), 5–19.

15. Irving Goffman, *Asylums* (Harmonsworth, UK: Penguin, 1961).

16. R. Bogdan and S. Taylor, "Relationships with Severely Disabled People: The Social Construction of Humanness," *Social Problems* 36, no. 2 (1989), 135–147.

17. Sheila Neysmith, "From Community Care to a Social Model of Caring," in C. Baines, P. Evans, and S. Neysmith, eds., *Women's Caring* (Toronto: McLelland and Stewart, 1991).

18. Anne Bullock, "Community Care," in R. Ng, G. Walker, and J. Muller, eds., *Community Organisation and the Canadian State* (Toronto: Garamond Press, 1990), 75.

19 Michael Hutter, "Symbolic Interaction and the Family, Foundations of Interpretive Sociology: Original Essays in Symbolic Interaction," *Studies in Symbolic Interaction*, Supplement 1 (1985), 117–152.

20. Maccoby and Jacklin, *The Psychology of Sex Differences.*

Chapter 8

MOTHERHOOD, CHANGING RELATIONSHIPS AND THE REPRODUCTION OF GENDER INEQUALITY

Bonnie Fox

"IT IS THE MOMENT when she becomes a mother that a woman first confronts the full reality of what it means to be a woman in our society," according to feminist sociologist Ann Oakley.[1] Feminist theorists typically have assumed that motherhood is central to women's position. Since Adrienne Rich's recognition that it is the "institution" of motherhood — the way mothering is organized in our society — and not the mere "fact" of having children that handicaps women, a number of arguments have been made about the ways in which motherhood is connected to gender inequality.[2] In contrast, later but no less influential arguments have been developed about motherhood by cultural feminists that aim to positively value what is unique in women's experiences.[3] This chapter reviews the arguments that link motherhood to inequality and then suggests a line of enquiry that complements them — specifically, a focus on the social relations that both shape motherhood and which mothers create to help them adjust to the demands of motherhood. I draw on interviews from my study of forty first-time mothers, involving in-depth interviews from the last trimester of their pregnancy through the first year of motherhood, to examine some of the patterns common to the social relations of new mothers.

MOTHERHOOD AND WOMEN'S OPPRESSION

Perhaps the most influential argument about how motherhood reproduces gender inequality is Nancy Chodorow's.[4] Chodorow argues that the source of gender inequality in society is the gendered identity and different "relational capacities" of children produced in heterosexual nuclear families, in which women mother. The key argument that she makes is that masculine identity depends upon opposition to, and superiority over, the feminine; the misogyny in men is then reflected in a social order that oppresses women. What is logically problematic about Chodorow's argument is her reductionist assumption that the characteristics of the social order derive from those of the individuals who live within its constraints. The political implications of her argument show the same problem: operating at the level of individual differences, Chodorow's solution to inequality is a private one — men sharing parenting with women.

In contrast, Marxist arguments that stress the social control of mothers by capital, men or the state focus specifically on social organization. The nub of these arguments is that women are exploited because their domestic labour is appropriated by the capitalist class or men in general. Arguments about capital were made in what has become known as the "domestic labour debate." Concerned primarily about inequality based on social class, writers in this debate focused on how women's unpaid housework benefits capital. A common claim was that housework — and presumably childcare — reproduces "labour power," the workers' capacity to work, which is the primary commodity upon which capital relies.[5] It seems reasonable that exploitation is located in the fact that homemakers do the work of caring for their spouses for "love," work which otherwise would have to be paid and from which their employers benefit. Arguing that "motherwork" is similarly appropriated by capital seems more problematic, however; so much of what goes on when women are nurturing children is not of value to capital.[6]

Writers critical of these Marxist arguments for their avoidance of gender (that is, it is women who do household work), argue that it is primarily individual men — as spouses and not as capitalists — who appropriate the unpaid household work of women.[7] Yet, although it is

clear how men benefit from women's housework, it is not so obvious
how they benefit from "motherwork." Not only does women's attention
to children detract from the services they render their male partners but
it also deprives the men, who have no hand in raising their children, of
a relationship with them.

Arguments about the state's control of women's roles as biological
and social reproducers have been made by social historians.[8] The focus
of these arguments range from laws prohibiting reproductive choice to
"experts" advice to mothers. Details about social control and exploitation aside, these arguments are important for their structural approach.
The effects of motherhood are dependent upon the social context in
which it occurs, so it is important to understand that context. Moreover, it is significant that since the development of a capitalist labour
market, motherhood — at least women's position in the home — has
defined the position of all women in that marketplace.

In addition to Chodorow's and the Marxist arguments, another
type of argument connecting motherhood with women's subordination
also develops the theme of social control. Writers with a cultural focus
have criticized the *ideologies* of motherhood that have been imposed on
women. This school of thought holds motherhood ideologies responsible not only for the fact that women assume the responsibilities attached to mothering but also for the vastness of the task of mothering.[9]
The focus on ideas is problematic, as it tends to underestimate the importance of social context — the history and resulting social order that
produced the ideas. Furthermore, as with all arguments about social
control, there is a tendency in these arguments to ignore the agency of
women.

There are two more promising arguments to consider that focus on
interpersonal relations and personal experiences, in a way that clearly
locates them within a particular social context. The first of these understands the experiences of mothering as important to how mothering
produces gender differences and inequality. This argument comes from
a number of studies that describe the daily experiences of mothers of
young children. The research emphasizes the significance of the privatization of mothers' responsibilities, which often results in an experience
of social isolation, stress and lack of time for meeting personal needs,
and divides the lives of women from those of their male partners.[10] In

detailing the daily experiences of mothers, this research has been richly revealing. Nevertheless, perhaps because it comes out of the early years of feminist research when a key objective was to make the case that women are oppressed, insufficient attention is paid to women's agency in some of this work. Women are seen to derive meaning from being mothers and as being severely restricted in their daily lives. It is not surprising, then, that the more recent arguments highlight women's agency.

The second important and more recent argument, which has been the more dominant approach to the study of motherhood, is the social constructionist approach. Beginning with Sarah Fenstermaker Berk's *Gender Factory*, a number of researchers have argued that women create gender through the daily practices of doing housework — making meals, cleaning the house and otherwise caring for family members.[11] The main point in these arguments is that the household work women do expresses a sense of their identity as women — their subordination as well as the love relations in which they are enmeshed.[12] Reviewing this line of enquiry, Myra Marx Ferree states, "Being a man or woman socially is not a natural or inevitable outgrowth of biological features but an achievement of situated conduct," and especially that involving the work done in the home.[13] The emphasis in this school of thought is, then, on the symbolic nature of everyday life and interactions and on the role of that meaningful activity in creating gender — defined as personal identity. With respect to parenthood, the argument is that "through their interactions, parents construct gendered parenting."[14] Martha McMahon's *Engendering Mothering* argues that mothering transforms women so that they come to identify with conventional notions of motherhood — which, in turn, are conventional ideals of womanhood.[15]

While the studies of mothers' experiences make clear how motherhood restricts women's lives in this society, by invoking the meaning women attach to childcare and even housework the social-constructionist approach helps explain why so many women embrace domestic responsibilities, which then restrict them. The social constructionists' arguments lend support to feminist assumptions about a "community of women" or a commonality of interests among many women. In so doing, they share an affinity with older arguments that find the roots of women's common interests in motherhood.[16] From Nancy Chodorow's position that women's "relational capacity" leans toward union with people while men's leans toward independence, to Mary O'Brien's claim that the physiology of reproduction connects women existentially to the universe while it separates men, these arguments have made their case for women's different and separate nature by elevating motherhood.[17] Barbara Katz Rothman's argument about a unity of interests between mothers and their fetuses makes the point well: "And against this [technological society] we have motherhood, the physical embodiment of connectedness."[18] A major problem with these social constructionist arguments about woman's union with the world is the omission of any notion of difference — with respect to race and class especially — about which so much has been written in the last decade by feminists.[19] The abstract nature of these arguments seems to be one of the sources of the problem: an examination of the motherhood experiences of women in different circumstances surely would preclude sweeping generalizations about similarity.

The literature specifically on housework and motherhood is at issue here, however. In this literature, the turn toward cultural analysis threatens to leave some issues unaddressed. The focus on the symbolic enables understanding of why women typically do the bulk of housework and childcare, and especially why some *like* doing the work.[20] In so doing, however, it ignores the profound limitations, even oppressiveness, about privatized motherhood and homemaking. From the mass appeal in the 1960s of Betty Friedan's indictment of full-time homemaking to the large numbers of women suffering from postpartum depression, there is clear evidence of a different set of experiences than this literature indicates.[21]

Generally, this approach threatens to overlook the power dimension in the negotiations between women and men around domestic chores. More problematic, in the work of some theorists more so than others, is the tendency not to analyze the power dynamics in family relationships: the focus is on the discourses of mothering rather than on the social relations of parenthood. Power is implicit in discourse, but we do not learn about how it unfolds in interpersonal relations through a focus on the symbolic.

Part of the reason women are able to fulfill their domestic

responsibilities, and many women may even like fulfilling them, is that they receive various (although usually insufficient) kinds of help with the work.[22] The demands and obligations of motherhood require the attention of more than even two parents, regardless of how little support this society offers. There is, then, a need to examine the social supports that mothers receive, and thus mothers' changing relationships with family and friends (at least) — albeit, recognizing that in this society, childcare is ultimately the mother's responsibility. Some mainstream sociological research has been done on the changes women experience in their friendships and relations with kin and even in their relations in the wider community as they become mothers, but little attention has been given to the implications of these with respect to gender inequality.[23]

Interview material from my study of first-time mothers and their partners indicates how inequality is promoted by the changes women experience in their social relations when they become mothers. The women in this study were interviewed between 1991 and 1996. They were interviewed during their pregnancies, shortly after they gave birth and at two months, six months and a year after the births. They volunteered to take part in these in-depth interviews — along with their male partners, who were interviewed separately — in childbirth classes. The majority of the women were white middle-class Canadians whose first language was English.

BECOMING A MOTHER, BECOMING RESPONSIBLE FOR A BABY

The first, obvious change women experience after the birth of their babies is that they assume a huge responsibility for totally dependent beings. While the focus in much of the literature is on the social definition of that maternal responsibility, turning the focus to the relational consequences of women's assumption of the responsibility reveals some obvious but overlooked consequences. In fact, how mothering is defined evolves over time and is partly a product of negotiation between the woman and her partner. A woman may choose "intensive mothering" — one woman in the study described herself as "wearing her baby" all day — but ultimately such a choice requires the consent of her partner; without his consent and support she is likely to change her definition of what the baby needs and what she must provide.[24]

Let me explain. Basically, women have virtually no choice about accepting responsibility for their babies, however that is defined. Of course, many (if not most) new mothers want to do so, given the strength of the feelings they have for their babies. Fathers, however, have *choice* about how actively they will be involved in their babies' care. While women's identity may depend on fulfilling the duties of motherhood, fathers are beyond the grasp of ideologies of "intensive mothering." Fathers can, then, accept or reject women's definitions of their responsibilities. Consequently, men are in a stronger bargaining position in the negotiations over how life will be rearranged in the household once the baby comes — and whose needs will be met.

To do intensive mothering, new mothers are in fact dependent on their partners' consent — their agreement not to expect to receive any attention to their own needs and to "help out." This is especially so if the woman has no other family to help support her. Nearly all of the women in this study who did intensive mothering — that is, who always responded to their infants' needs, who always put their babies first — had partners who were very involved fathers. In response to a question about what they needed from their partners in order to take care of their babies, all of the women in the study talked about their partners' support. In the words of one woman who was fully engrossed in motherhood, "I guess the most important thing is that he be supportive of me being so absorbed with [baby]." She continued, "And that he himself is equally fascinated with [baby]."

New mothers depend upon their partners to do all that they cannot, from earning money to doing some of the housework and providing them some "help" with the baby. A mother of twins responded to a question about whether she had become more dependent on her partner with, "Yes, I'm more dependent on him ... I couldn't do it without him. I just couldn't. He has to be there. I don't know, he has to tell me a lot that I'm doing a good job, that the kids are good. Yes, I am very dependent on him." And for the man to be able to provide and to help out at home, he needs to be healthy himself; for that reason alone, the father's needs often come before the woman's.[25] One of the new mothers, who is married to a professional, explained why she got up with her infant every night while her husband slept: "I'd much rather have him stable and healthy so that he can help me when I really need it."

The man's co-operation — whether that means his consent that the woman do intensive mothering or his active support — is contingent upon his forming a relationship (a "bond") with the baby, as the quote from the woman engrossed in motherhood indicates. And this relationship often depends upon the mother's active promotion of it. Accordingly, new mothers may become responsible for relationships in their reconfigured families. New mothers may find themselves working at creating the conditions for the development of the relationship between father and baby. Thus, the woman's concern about her baby may necessitate attention to the father's needs, in order to ensure that the father "bond" with the baby. One woman explained that since her baby's birth her priorities were "totally different, totally different," and involved her baby and husband rather than herself and her career. She explained, "Maybe because of me identifying with [my baby's] needs, I'm more conscious of [my husband's] needs." Other women ended their battles over housework for the sake of peace in the family once they became mothers. One woman gave up efforts to have a career that her husband did not want her to have; he wanted her home, for the sake of their "family life." "I'm not the most important thing anymore. You learn to sacrifice so much," she explained.

If a man fails to consent to the woman's definition of the baby's needs, or if he fails to "fall in love" with the baby, the mother may be in the position of *owing* him for the time and attention she gives the baby.[26] She may then cater to his needs in order to make up for the attention the baby receives and that he does not. One woman with a family background of abuse, who was in her second marriage and without the support of family or even friends, bowed to the demand of her partner that they resume "normal" sexual activities a few months after the birth, and to do so modified her definition of the baby's needs (that is, putting him to bed and letting him cry).

In short, how a woman defines mothering is a product of negotiation with her partner. Because intensive mothering requires considerable support, it is contingent upon the consent and active co-operation of the partner, which makes for all sorts of subtle inequalities in the relationship.

BECOMING A MOTHER,
BECOMING MORE DOMESTIC

Many social scientists have reported that parenthood produces a more conventional division of labour in the home.[27] Yet the voluminous body of research on the allocation of housework neither distinguishes the two nor assesses the relationship between childcare responsibilities and housework.[28] In my study, the division of the housework became decidedly more conventional for twenty-five of the couples over the first year of parenthood. For five of the couples, a conventional household pattern that had been in place remained so, and for another five couples, housework changed to a much more conventional pattern at first — while the woman was home — but returned to its more non-conventional arrangement in place before the birth after the woman returned to her paid work. The division of the housework actually became more equitable with parenthood for the remaining five couples. In short, there is a pattern of a more conventional sexual division of housework, although that is not inevitable, and this has obvious implications for women's position in the family.

Why does the pattern become more conventional? First, staying home influences what a woman does. With one exception, each of the twelve women in the study who stayed home over the course of the year either already did nearly all of the housework or came to do nearly all of it. The reason is clear: they inhabit the house most of the time, so they have time to notice and care about the state of the place; in turn, whatever "down time" they have during the day occurs while they are at home. A woman whose partner was at home full time best explained the connection between being home and doing housework and how her partner had to realize this: Housework is "part of your job [when you are home], you know ... He's not just looking after the baby. He's got to be able to do some of the other things that *come with the territory* [emphasis added]." In this case, the father was staying home full time but not doing much around the house. He was the one exception to the rule that parents who stay at home do housework.

The reasons women take on more housework are more complicated than simply that they are at home. The social-constructionist school argues that women do housework because the work is so connected with their sense of identity as women — if not a personal sense, part of the public presentation of self (for example, the neighbours would be harsh judges of the woman with the dirty house). This may explain why some women seem far more driven by standards of cleanliness than their partners. More is at issue here, however. That women assume *responsibility* for their babies — even if partners take care of them during the day — seems to entail responsibility for a clean house as well. One new mother was concerned that her floors were too dirty for her baby who was increasingly exploring the environment.

A problem with the social-constructionist stance is its leaning toward an explanation of the status quo, rather than discovery of inherent contradiction or tension in current arrangements. Accordingly, these theorists emphasize women's general satisfaction with the unequal distribution of housework. Apparently, survey research supports this conclusion.[29] Indeed, in this study the vast majority of women asserted both that the way housework was allocated in their homes was fair and that they were satisfied with it. In fifteen of these cases, however, the details of the first year of parenthood told a very different story: pitched battles had occurred over the housework, and housework was *the* issue that provoked agitated responses during the interviews. And, of course, these fifteen households included all of those in which the division of housework had not become more conventional with parenthood: these mothers fought the development of that pattern.[30]

It is not sufficient, then, to invoke its symbolic value in order to explain why women do housework. Indeed, the women in this study who had very high standards of cleanliness (for whom the symbolism was probably more salient) were among those most persistent about struggling with their partners over the work. Furthermore, the other factors at work in shifting the housework toward the woman indicate another kind of agency than a desire to derive meaning from domestic responsibilities or to meet the expectations of neighbours. Another source of the shift of housework toward women was their active promotion of the relationship between the father and his baby. When the men came home from work, many of the women put daddy's time with the baby first; who was doing the housework came second. In turn, some of the same women found doing housework — while their partners played with the baby — to be a welcome "break" from baby care.

That motherhood promotes women's responsibility for housework indicates a clear way in which it produces gender inequality. That this is not inevitable shows how complicated are the sources of women's subordination in this society. In fact, because women may do more housework as a result of their promotion of their partners' "bond" with the baby, their increased domesticity is in part a product of their own agency.

BECOMING PARENTS, BECOMING A FAMILY

The transition to parenthood not only creates gender differences and inequalities, it also transforms couples into nuclear families. Specifically, couples who were fairly autonomous individuals, leading nearly separate lives because of demanding jobs or active social lives with same-sex friends, became more home-based. For some of the couples in this study, that change began with marriage and progressed with age, but for others (the younger parents) there was a dramatic change with the birth of the baby. Many couples talked about how the baby "brings us home more," or about how "friendship took a back seat" after the baby was born. Twenty-five of the couples became decidedly more family focused when they became parents; six couples were already that way before they became parents.

For many of the couples, this more family-focused existence meant a change from participation in situations in which gender was not particularly salient (for example, socializing with same-sex friends) to immersion in a very gendered situation. Moreover, when life is centred on the home, the woman tends to experience more pressure to create that home and family life. And in the interests of a happy home, she may give in more during quarrels about housework — or avoid them altogether.[31] A number of women in the study mentioned avoidance of long-term sources of disagreement for the sake of peace in the family.

A more obvious consequence of the "nuclear turn" for women is the loss, or weakening, of their support networks composed of women. One of the most dramatic changes in the lives of the women in this study was that they saw their friends (most of whom were women) considerably less once they were mothers than had been their practice. Friends without children were very likely to disappear (or virtually disappear) from their lives. When attempts were made to prevent this from happening, the women often decided those attempts had been a mistake, given the insensitivity their friends showed them about the needs of both their babies and themselves. One woman decided that she could see only those friends who now understood that she was "not a separate person anymore."

At the same time, however, considerable numbers of these new mothers spent a lot more time with members of their extended families, whose interest was primarily in the baby. New mothers living in Toronto were as active socially as they had been before motherhood because of other new mothers they met in their neighbourhoods. Interestingly, in these cases, these new relationships developed in "new mothers' groups" organized by Toronto's Public Health Department — a service available in Toronto but none of its suburbs.

Social isolation was a problem for twenty-two of these new mothers. It became a problem for others when they returned to their paid jobs; they simply had no time for socializing. Immersion in the demands of motherhood seemed a more common situation than isolation.

For all of the women, there was a shift, then, toward spending time at home, socializing with their male partners and spending any other time in the company of relatives or friends who had babies. In short, life was focused around the baby. Altogether, it seems that these new mothers experienced a loss of life outside their lives as mothers. While it has been claimed that socializing only in the company of mothers reinforces the privatization of mothering responsibility and standards of intensive mothering, that seems less true in that it heightens the salience of being a mother, and a woman.[32]

Becoming a Mother, Becoming a Daughter Again

One of the most dramatic changes in the lives of these women was the importance that their own mothers assumed with the arrival of the baby. In all but two of the twenty-one cases where the women's mothers lived in the same town, the mothers became the women's main support — sometimes a more important source of support and active care-giving than the father of the baby. In a few cases, mothers with whom women had scarcely been close since adulthood became their "best friends." Some of the new mothers spent several days a week at their parents' homes, eating and even sleeping there; others regularly relied on the prepared food their mothers would bring them. A number of grandmothers cared for the babies several days a week; one grandmother cared for her grandchild every weekday and some nights after her daughter returned to her paid job.

What is significant about these mother–daughter relationships is that they can push the new father away from active involvement in either parenting or housework. In some cases, this happened through the mother-in-law's active intervention. A few European grandmothers challenged the domestic contributions of the men and insisted that baby care especially was "women's work." More commonly, the active help given by new mothers' mothers seemed to allow their daughters to do both intensive mothering and much of the housework, and as a result their partners were left with little that needed to be done. Sometimes the mother–daughter team was so strong that the man felt excluded. This effect is not, of course, inevitable: in one couple, a very involved mother/grandmother supported her son-in-law in his struggle with his wife to actively care for the baby, and do it his way.

In general, however, it seemed that the nineteen women who were without the help of their own mothers had more need and greater incentive to push and encourage their male partners to actively parent and to do housework. In ten of these couples, the fathers were fairly active with respect to either housework or baby care, or both. In contrast, in the majority of the couples with whom the new mothers' mothers were actively involved in support (eighteen of the twenty-one), the new fathers did less housework than they had previously and, in one case, the father did less baby care than he intended.

Oddly enough, then, breaking down the privatization of mothering improves the lives of new mothers but does not necessarily improve the division of labour in their homes. The introduction of the woman's mother may enhance the shift toward a more conventional division of labour, in fact. There was one couple in this study that set out to combat any tendency toward an unequal allocation of domestic responsibilities. They were immersed in a large, very active support network of friends; the woman's mother was not available to help her. In this case, and amidst considerable support from friends, the household patterns remained egalitarian.

•

The early declaration of the Women's Liberation Movement that "the personal is political" oddly directed much less attention to motherhood than to housework. Yet motherhood is not only implicated in why women do housework; it is also important in the development of inequality in heterosexual relationships. And while nearly all stereotypes about women's inferiority to men have been seriously attacked if not dismantled, beliefs in the importance of full-time mothercare for babies remain virtually unshaken.

It is time to both acknowledge how meaningful motherhood is to women and to insist that privatized mothering bears tremendous costs for women — and thus for their children as well. The latter message remains very muted, even among feminists.

Notes

Support for the research reported here came from the Social Sciences and Humanities Research Council of Canada and from the University of Toronto. Thanks go to Diana Worts and Sherry Bartram for excellent research assistance, and to Rebecca Fulton, Liz Walker and Ann Bernardo for dedicated transcribing of interviews.

1. Ann Oakley, *Becoming a Mother* (New York: Schocken, 1980).

2. Adrienne Rich, *Of Woman Born: Motherhood as Experience and Institution* (New York: W. W. Norton, 1976).

3. Heather Jon Maroney, "Embracing Motherhood: New Feminist Theory," in Roberta Hamilton and Michele Barrett, eds., *The Politics of Diversity* (Montreal: The Book Centre, 1986), 398–424.

4. Nancy Chodorow, *The Reproduction of Mothering: Psychoanalysis and the Sociology of Gender* (Berkeley: The University of California Press, 1978).

5. Margaret Benston, "The Political Economy of Women's Liberation," *Monthly Review* 21 (1968), 13–27; Wally Seccombe, "The Housewife and Her Labour Under Capitalism," *New Left Review* 83 (1974), 3–24; Margaret Coulson, Branka Magas, and Hilary Wainwright, "The Housewife and Her Labour Under Capitalism — A Critique," *New Left Review* 89 (1975), 59–71; Jean Gardiner, "Women's Domestic Labour," *New Left Review* 89 (1975), 47–59; Bonnie Fox, ed., *Hidden in the*

Household (Toronto: Women's Press, 1980).

6. Sharon Hays, *The Cultural Contradictions of Motherhood* (New Haven: Yale University Press, 1996), points out that the ideology of motherhood also contains a critique of marketplace logic and values.

7. Christine Delphy, "The Main Enemy," in *Close to Home* (Amherst: University of Massachusetts Press, 1984), 57–78; Heidi Hartmann, "The Unhappy Marriage of Marxism and Feminism," in Lydia Sargent, ed., *Women and Revolution* (Boston: South End Press, 1981), 1–43.

8. Christopher Lasch, *Haven in a Heartless World* (New York: Basic Books, 1977).

9. Betsy Wearing, *The Ideology of Motherhood* (London: George Allen and Unwin, 1984); Hays, *The Cultural Contradictions of Motherhood*. See also, Kathryn Backett, *Mothers and Fathers* (London: Macmillan, 1982).

10. Jessie Bernard, *The Future of Motherhood* (New York: The Dial Press, 1974); Oakley, *Becoming a Mother;* Meg Luxton, *More Than a Labour of Love* (Toronto: Women's Press, 1980); Mary Boulton, *On Being a Mother* (London: Tavistock, 1983); Harriet Rosenberg, "Motherwork, Stress and Depression: The Costs of Privatized Social Reproduction," in Heather Jon Maroney and Meg Luxton, eds., *Feminism and Political Economy* (Toronto: Methuen, 1987).

11. Sarah Fenstermaker Berk, *The Gender Factory* (New York: Plenum, 1985).

12. Candace West and Don Zimmerman, "Doing Gender," *Gender and Society* 1, no. 2 (1987), 125–151; Myra Marx Ferree, "Beyond Separate Spheres: Feminism and Family Research," *Journal of Marriage and the Family* 52 (1990), 866–884; Susan Walzer, "Thinking About the Baby: Gender and Divisions of Infant Care," *Social Problems* 43, no. 2 (1996), 219–234.

13. Ferree, "Beyond Separate Spheres," 869.

14. Linda Thompson and Alexis Walker, "Gender in Families: Women and Men in Marriage, Work and Parenthood," *Journal of Marriage and the Family* 51 (1989), 864.

15. Martha McMahon, *Engendering Motherhood* (New York: The Guilford Press, 1995).

16. Laurie Umansky, *Motherhood Reconceived* (New York: New York University, 1996).

17. Chodorow, *Reproduction of Mothering;* Mary O'Brien, *The Politics of Reproduction* (Boston: Routledge and Kegan Paul, 1981).

18. Barbara Katz Rothman, *Recreating Motherhood* (New York: W.W. Norton, 1989), 59.

19. See Evelyn Nakano Glenn, Grace Chang, and Linda Forcey, eds., *Mothering* (New York: Routledge, 1994) for articles on motherhood that emphasize differences among women.

20. Myra Marx Ferree, "The Gender Division of Labor in Two-Earner Marriages," *Journal of Family Issues* 12, no. 2 (1991), 158–180.

21. Betty Friedan, *The Feminine Mystique* (New York: Norton, 1963); Rosenberg, "Motherwork, Stress and Depression"; Verta Taylor, *Rock-A-By-Baby* (New York: Routledge, 1996).

22. Evelyn Nakano Glenn, "From Servitude to Service Work: Historical Continuities in the Racial Division of Paid Reproductive Labor," *Signs* 18, no. 1 (1992), 1–42; Arlie Hochschild, *The Second Shift* (New York: Viking, 1989).

23. Lydia O'Donnell, *The Unheralded Majority* (Lexington: Lexington Books, 1985); Allison Munch, J. Miller McPherson, and Lynn Smith-Lovin, "Gender, Children and Social Contact: The Effects of Childrearing for Men and Women," *American Sociological Review* 62, no. 4 (1997), 509–520.

24. This is Hays's phrase, in *The Cultural Contradictions of Motherhood*.

25. Luxton, *More Than a Labour of Love*, describes this dynamic well.

26. See Hochschild's *Second Shift* for a discussion of the "economy of gratitude."

27. Carolyn Cowan and Philip Cowan, *When Partners Become Parents* (New York: Basic Books, 1992); Ralph LaRossa and Maureen LaRossa, *Transition to Parenthood* (Newbury: Sage, 1981).

28. See Linda Thompson and Alexis Walker, "Gender in Families: Women and Men in Marriage, Work and Parenthood," *Journal of Marriage and Family* 51 (1989), 845–871, for a review of this body of research on who does the housework. See Masako Ishi-Kuntz and Scott Coltrane, "Predicting the Sharing of Household Labor: Are Parenting and Housework Distinct?," *Sociological Perspectives* 35, no. 4 (1992), 629–647.

29. Ferree, "The Gender Division of Labor in Two-Earner Marriages," 158–180.

30. Meg Luxton, "Two Hands for the Clock: Changing Patterns in the Gendered Division of Labour in the Home," *Studies in Political Economy* 12 (1983).

31. See also, Holly Waldron and Donald Routh, "The Effect of the First Child on the Marital Relationship," *Journal of Marriage and the Family* 48 (1981), 785–789.

32. Hays, *The Cultural Contradictions of Motherhood*.

Chapter 9

UNRAVELLING THE MYTH OF THE PERFECT MOTHER WITH MOTHERS OF EARLY ADOLESCENT GIRLS

Elizabeth Diem

I UNDERTOOK A STUDY with mothers of early adolescent girls to explore whether using an empowering small-group strategy would foster emancipatory knowledge and liberating changes in mothers' roles and relationships. The women came to the group burdened by the myth that they could be perfect mothers who are always calm, caring and knowledgeable. Their striving to attain perfection seemed to interfere with their ability to form realistic and meaningful relationships with their daughters. In this chapter, I focus on some of the aspects of the perfect mother myth that were woven into the fabric of the women's expectations of their roles and on the relationships and the group process that contributed to the unravelling of this myth.

In April 1995, I initiated a feminist participatory research strategy with two groups of mothers of early adolescent girls. Initially, there were eleven and twelve women in each group, between the ages of thirty-two and fifty-four. Their daughters ranged in age from ten to fourteen. The mothers and their daughters lived in the two lowest socioeconomic status areas of a city in Ontario. The groups met for two hours each week for ten weeks to discuss their concerns and an additional four times over the next nine months to assist me in analyzing their discussions.

During the group discussions, I discerned three aspects of the perfect mother myth that emerged and that were unravelled: having intuitive knowledge, having a happy relationship with their daughters and being selfless without anger. By using the change in the emotion of the groups from meeting to meeting and the accomplishment of certain tasks, I also identified three phases in the group process that blended into and supported subsequent phases. The three phases were seeking connection, testing connection and exploring connection. I use these three aspects of the myth to illustrate the three phases of the group process. Pseudonyms for the women are used throughout. I am the "Liz" in the discussions.

SEEKING CONNECTION

The seeking-connection phase began during recruitment, reached a peak during the third and fourth meetings and continued until the last meetings. The women were drawn to the groups because of their frustration with their daughters and their desire for help in dealing with them. Their desire was not consistent with the impossible ideals of the perfect mother that divides mothers and denies them the opportunity to use one another for support and counsel.[1]

They found commonality in the discomfort they experienced if any indication was made that their mothering may not be perfect. For example, the ideal of having intuitive knowledge was apparent in the women's initial uneasiness with the term "support group." They felt that it indicated that something was wrong with them or their children. They also felt somewhat defensive about their mothering.

> *Josie:* I'm a very tough person.
>
> *Toni:* I came here because I was interested in what I could learn or anything that I could pass on or I don't know, I'm a pretty tough person like Josie too, where you tow the line, or as my husband would say, "It's my way or the highway." It's worked pretty good so far.
>
> *Gail:* I don't know. A lot of things that I do are totally off the wall, but they work for me.
>
> *Bev:* Recently, one of the things [I've learned] is that [I'm] not alone, there's a lot of people in the same situation as me.

Bell: Reassurance.

Pam: Reassurance, and [you're] not the only one going through it.

By coming to the meetings to seek reassurance, they were bucking the norm that expected them to have all the answers, and they were brave enough to admit that they did not.

Another force that drew them to the meetings and enforced their sense of commonality was their concern about their unhappy relationships with their daughters and their desire for better ones.

Lee: Maybe we'll be able to learn, to communicate better here and, without hollering, be able to sit and have a decent discussion.

Marg: Without the tears and the slamming of doors and the "I hate you's." That would be nice.

Kris: Wouldn't it? Wouldn't it be wonderful?

By simply asking them what they would like from the group and providing a supportive feminist process,[2] their feelings and experiences with their daughters poured out. They found connection through their commonality in problems and desires.

The women did not accept this feeling of connection passively. As they experienced comfort and energy from being in the group, they began to reflect on the reasons for their responses.

Toni: I enjoy the meetings all the time too. I really look forward to coming here. I think it's wonderful that we're able to say some of the things that we do say. Sometimes it's easier to talk in front of people who aren't around you all the time, and I hope that everyone's able to get something out of this. I really enjoy it.

Bev: One of the things that Toni said, about talking in front of people, I think that that's probably what I enjoy too, 'cause the people that you're around all the time, like your family or whoever, they seem to judge you more. It's easier to talk here without worrying about that.

In these statements, the women identified that they usually faced criticisms from others about their mothering. That did not happen in the group, and they attributed the difference to the nonjudgemental attitude of women that they did not know as well as family and friends. This was emancipatory for them because the group gave them the opportunity to learn that women could be supportive, and they came to realize that others around them often were not.

They also appreciated that this group was made up of women beyond their own immediate circle of friends and who expressed many similar concerns and shared common experiences. This served to enhance their sense of self-worth and credibility. In one meeting, they said:

> *Kris:* It's nice to have another point of view. Certain things you can't get from your friends. I think you choose your friends but you don't choose who's in here and I think because you don't choose who's in here you might have somebody who's got a different opinion on something.
>
> *Pam:* [It's a nice] cross section.

They recognized that women in a variety of situations provided them with a broader source of information and reassurance, not only for themselves but also for their children. When they heard about the experiences of the other women and found similarities, they were able to confront their fantasy that there were some women "out there" who could manage being perfect mothers.[3] They also started to look for broader reasons for problems, rather than blaming themselves or their children.

Once their commonality was recognized, the women began actively giving and receiving support. They seemed to fall naturally into a group problem-solving process by helping one another with determining logical consequences for discipline problems. They tried their new skills out at home and brought back their successes to the group. After these changes, they began reporting a change in their relationship with their children.

> *Marg:* And I'll tell you something, ladies, since I have been coming here my daughters have benefited from that ... [I'm] letting them take risks. Because I have lightened up a bit.
>
> *Pam:* My daughter has told me in the last couple of weeks that I'm just so cool!

These changes in their attitude and behaviour were liberating because they had the opportunity to break through the "persecutory anxiety,"[4] and they were able to learn, connect and be energized by their relationships with their daughters.[5] By seeking connection through commonality and giving and receiving support, they were empowered by the group and could feel reassured about their mothering and relax their control, which gave them more choices in their relationship with their children.

The expectation of intuitive knowledge and a harmonious relationship with their children began unravelling easily and quickly simply because they were able to share their experiences and help one another. The ideal of selfless love or living just to please others was woven in more tightly and only emerged after they had gained some success in dealing with their immediate problems and were willing to question one another and to be questioned.

TESTING CONNECTION

The connection in the first phase was tested by differences arising by the second meetings and reached a peak at the sixth meetings. Although interpersonal support or connection is important in bringing and keeping people together, it is not sufficient to bring about change in their lives. For change to occur, mothers must identify their beliefs, be challenged to deconstruct or unravel their beliefs and then reconstruct or reweave more humane beliefs.[6] I felt that the women's success in group problem solving was giving them the idea that they could deal with all their problems with the help of the group, rather than looking outside the group for some of the causes.

To stimulate a more critical view of their situation in society, I asked them to prepare a list of descriptions of a good mother and a bad mother. Many of their descriptions for a good mother would be impossible to achieve: "angel in disguise, saint," "says something nice every day to children, spends individual time with them everyday." A good mother would "sacrifice for kids, put up with things for them," while a bad mother was "selfish, puts herself always before her kids and her own interests come first." Their lists did not include descriptions of the mother's own self-esteem or self-respect. When we reviewed the list of opposing good mother and bad mother pairs at the next meeting, I focused the discussion on sacrifice and selfishness through asking these questions: What would they sacrifice for their kids? Would they sacrifice themselves and stay in a bad relationship for their kids? Would they think of themselves as selfish if they decided to go back to school? For each question there were opposing views. The following was part of their response to the last question:

> *Kris:* If a person is going back to school or doing something else they usually are aware that [it] is taking away family time or children time or whatever, and they will make a special effort to regain that time.
>
> *Pam:* Because we feel guilty.
>
> *Kris:* It's not guilt though. I don't think it's guilt. I don't think it boils down to guilt. I think that inside you have a need as much as the child has a need for you, you have a need for that child.
>
> *Marg:* Yeah, good point.

In the discussion, the importance of the mother being happy was mentioned, but Kris drew them back to feeling that the mother needed the child to feel happy if she was going to feel happy. They agreed. At the next meeting, I played the excerpt of the discussion given above and asked them to think about the questions "When should a mother not sacrifice?" and "What should a mother be selfish about?" In response to my queries, they acknowledged feeling guilty and self-indulgent if they talked about themselves or enjoyed themselves in these group sessions. As long as they talked about their daughters, they felt justified. Lori responded first:

> *Lori:* I am tired of being fractured, being a wife, a mother, being a dah, dah, dah. I [would] just like to be myself for a while a ... cause we all get tired, don't we? We just get tired of it. I'm sorry, [if] you're a mother it comes down to a great compromise and to everything you guys said on that tape — you cannot be your own self. So we're lost, ladies. We're really lost.
>
> *Marg:* I think mothers are conditioned to give up or sacrifice or do without — whatever it is if the kids need something first.
>
> *Kris:* That's not a really big deal. It's really not a big deal. No mother has to give up anything, and no mother is going to mind it. It's only a problem if the mother resents it.

Both Lori and Marg felt that mothers needed to sacrifice for their children. Kris felt that they did not need to sacrifice all the time, and sacrifice was only bad if it was resented. This exposure of the selfless ideal took three weeks of meetings and consistent prodding on my part to emerge.

Another aspect of being a selfless mother was all the contortions they went through to bury or excuse their anger. By the fifth meeting, I was challenging their actions.

> *Liz:* What about the idea that we can only be angry or be accused of being angry when we're having our period or PMS?
>
> *Lori:* Oh, they're full of shit. I mean get real. These guys, they blow off for whatever [reason] — they can't find their socks, they freak out. So, I warn everybody in my house. I've always been really good about that, and poor Jeff, there's only girls in the house ... but I announce it in the morning, "Leave me alone, I give you fair warning, stay out of my way."
>
> *Chris:* Yeah, so do I.

Although they admitted that men felt no compunction in expressing their anger, they felt compelled to protect others from their anger.

The discussions to this point had exposed the ideals that women were expected to sacrifice for their children and hide their anger. The initial unravelling became apparent at the sixth meeting.

> *Liz:* We should do our wrap up. I did have an excerpt from last week about when should we be selfish and when should we not sacrifice. I wanted everybody to hear that.
>
> *Sarah:* Yeah, that word bothered me a lot last week — sacrifice. That word really bothered me. People would sacrifice ... well, you know what, I would sacrifice my life for my kids, for anybody ... I found sacrifice was such a harsh word. And you know being selfish is one thing. You know you have to be selfish ... 'course not being selfish, that's just being you. You know you have to do something for yourself too.
>
> *Kris:* Yeah, but it makes it sound like it is bad to do that but really that's not the context that we want it to be. It's really a positive thing.

Sarah's and Kris's comments indicate that they were starting to realize that being selfish was not necessarily bad. Although my questioning and challenges had encouraged their emancipatory knowledge, their liberating changes depended on them adopting a questioning attitude. That quickly followed.

EXPLORING CONNECTION

By the seventh meeting, they were taking over and used questioning and challenging to explore deeper and broader issues. The question about being selfish and meeting their own needs as opposed to the needs of their daughters unravelled, in this phase, into a considerable debate about whether the agenda should be limited to issues related to their daughters or be more open to include their own.

> *Kris:* I know that sometimes we get off [track] and we don't talk about the kids, but I think whatever it is that we talk about is going to come around [to our kids]. What goes around, comes around. It's going to come to our kids eventually.
>
> *Marg:* And I think too that although we're not talking about our daughters, I think everything that we talk about has a definite effect on our daughters, because we have an effect on our daughters. I'm talking about our feelings and issues that are of interest to us and matter to us and in turn will matter to them, because we're their prime influence.

When the women realized that by looking after themselves, they would be benefiting their daughters, they had licence to reassess and change their role in the family. Before a mother and her child can establish a relationship, the mother needs to be able to affirm *her* own needs, desires, opinions, rage, love and hatred.[7] A more assertive role is also important at this stage of development because daughters can become angry with their mothers when they are too submissive[8] or are afraid to talk to them when they are too nice and kind.[9] Mothers also need release from unrealistic restrictions. Shari Thurer states that once mothers realize that "failures" result from myths created by the way society is structured rather than from personal faults, they may learn to select among rules and develop their own form of mothering that works for them and their children.[10]

Unravelling the myths of the perfect mother is an art rather than a prescriptive procedure. However, from this experience, the first need is to provide a safe place for women to identify and deal with their pressing issues while they seek connection. This, along with questioning and prodding from me, exposed and allowed further unravelling of the myth of selfless love without anger. With the unravelling of the myth of the perfect mother, these mothers gained emancipatory knowledge about their mothering and the importance of looking after their own needs. They also initiated liberating changes by relaxing their control over their daughters. Their interest in the discussions and analysis that lasted for most up to a year after the groups had started indicated that the unravelling and reweaving were likely to continue.

Notes

1. Elizabeth Debold, Marie Wilson, and Idelisse Malavé, *Mother Daughter Revolution: From Good Girls to Great Women* (Reading, MA: Addison–Wesley, 1993).

2. Charlene Wheeler and Peggy Chinn, *Peace and Power: A Handbook of Feminist Process* (Buffalo, NY: Margaretdaughters, 1984).

3. Rozsika Parker, *Mother Love/Mother Hate: The Power of Maternal Ambivalence* (New York: BasicBooks, 1995).

4. Ibid., 91.

5. See, for example, C. Enns, "Self-Esteem Groups: A Synthesis of Consciousness-Raising and Assertiveness Training," *Journal of Counseling and Development* 71 (1992), 7–13; Maria Mies, "Towards a Methodology for Feminist Research," in G. Bowles and R. Klein, eds., *Theories of Women's Studies* (Boston: Routledge and Kegan Paul, 1983), 117–139; Janet Surrey, "Relationship and Empowerment," in Judith Jordon, Alexandra Chaplain, Jean Baker Miller, Irene Stiver, and Janet Surry, eds., *Women's Growth in Connection: Writings from the Stone Center* (New York: Guilford Press, 1991), 162–180.

6. See, for example, Emily Merideth, "Critical Pedagogy and Its Application to Health Education: A Critical Appraisal of the Casa en Casa Model," *Health Education Quarterly* 21 (1994), 355–367; Janice Thompson, "Critical Scholarship: The Critique of Domination in Nursing," *Advances in Nursing Science* 10 (1987), 27–38.

7. See, for example, Jessica Benjamin, *The Bonds of Love, Psychoanalysis, Feminism, and the Problem of Domination* (London: Virago, 1990); L. Eichenbaum and S.

Orbach, "Feminine Subjectivity, Counter-Transference and the Mother–Daughter Relationship," in J. van Mens-Verhulst, K. Schreurs, and L. Woertman, eds., *Daughtering and Mothering: Female Subjectivity Reanalyzed* (New York: Routledge, 1994); Parker, *Mother Love/Mother Hate;* M. Whitford, *Luce Irigaray: Philosophy in the Feminine* (London: Routledge, 1991).

8. Judith Herman and Helen Lewis, "Anger in the Mother–Daughter Relationship," in T. Bernay and D. Cantor, eds., *The Psychology of Today's Woman* (Cambridge, MA: Harvard University Press, 1991).

9. Lyn Mikel Brown and Carol Gilligan, *Meeting at the Crossroads: Women's Psychology and Girls' Development* (Cambridge, MA: Harvard University Press, 1992).

10. Shari Thurer, *The Myths of Motherhood: How Culture Reinvents the Good Mother* (New York: Penguin Books, 1994), 300.

Part III

THE MOTHERLINE: PERSONAL AND HISTORICAL NARRATIVES

Chapter 10

BETWEEN EXILE AND HOME

Martha McMahon

STORIES OF MOTHERHOOD may conceal more than they reveal. My recent sociological story of motherhood concealed the hidden identities of such absent actors as myself, characters from my past, childless women and culturally improper mothers.[1] The subjects of my research include those who are "present" through omission, the significantly absent. The absent others in my story about motherhood became significant for me for two reasons. First, tension between themes of motherhood and nonmotherhood in the lives of the women I studied brought back disturbing memories of Kathleen and Alice, childless aunts of my Irish childhood. Second, my mother died shortly after I had finished the study, and learning to live with her death forced me to revisit my sociological story and to shift the focus from the meaning of motherhood in other women's lives to its meaning to me, a childless woman.

My feelings of loss and of being disconnected when my mother died echoed what many women told me about how they would have felt had they never had children. I recognized that in some ways the experiences of the loss of a mother and of childlessness are analogous. I now see that my research on motherhood was implicitly also about childlessness. I had set out to study motherhood in other women's lives only to confront the meaning of childlessness in my own. To tell this story I move between sociological theorizing and creatively reconstructed letters to a close friend.

TO BEGIN

My choice of research topic had been partly shaped by my sister Mary's decision to have a child. I had thought that Mary, like myself, would not have children. I had wanted to know why she changed her mind, and what having a child meant for her.[2] I was also curious about other women's decisions about motherhood, though uncurious about my own ongoing decision not to have children. After all, I had not changed my mind. But how had I acquired such a mind? Did it come about like this?

In our family of six children, Mary had been the leader among the three girls, the strong one, the rebel. Being called Martha with an older sister called Mary in an Irish Catholic family had its consequences. "Ah, Mary and Martha," adults would muse — they knew the Bible story about the sisters well, that when Jesus visited their home, Mary spent her time with Jesus listening to his stories while her sister Martha did the housework. And when Martha complained to Jesus about her sister's failure to help her with the domestic work, he apparently reproached her, telling her that her sister Mary had "chosen the better part."[3] I didn't think God had it wrong; I figured Martha had. Yet although Jesus seemed to have had little time for Martha's domestic efforts when he spent time with the two sisters, many of the adults of my childhood world indicated that homemaking was an entirely suitable future — for a girl. Why, I wondered, would they want me to choose an option of lesser worth? It seemed to me that no one noticed the contradiction but me — but then they weren't called Martha.

But not all the adults of my childhood encouraged young women toward domesticity. From the age of ten I was educated by an order of intellectual nuns that privileged the life of the mind, a sort of Jesuits for girls. Like Jesus, these nuns knew that in the Bible story Mary had chosen the better part and that Martha, although caring and kind, had unwisely chosen domesticity over learning. These nuns venerated the mother of God and expressed sympathy for her suffering, and the suffering we unthinking girls often inflicted on our own "poor mothers," as they put it so often. But they, like my older sister, were disdainful of domesticity — the domesticity which, in my child eyes, seemed inevitably associated with motherhood. In my convent school domestic work was not done by the (higher status) Mothers, but by the (lower status) Sisters. The irony that the Mothers didn't do domestic work is now apparent to me. They were highly educated and taught school. "Lucht na gcorcan" (the rabble of the pots and pans), sneered the head nun of my Gaelic-speaking convent school, as a few girls (usually less academically successful) excused themselves from her Latin class to take domestic science instead. Domesticity was construed as a foolish choice, or a choice of foolish girls.

I grew up with complex and contradictory messages. Motherhood, goodness and suffering were interconnected. Yet I also learned that, especially through its associations with domesticity, motherhood imperilled the mind, though it was good for the female soul. In my culturally Catholic world my mother embodied female virtue, the nuns represented disembodied commitment to God. Bounded by these competing moralities, I thought little about women who were attached neither to children nor to God. What of women like my childless aunts Kathleen and Alice, who didn't fit dominant images of moral Irish womanhood?

I moved, I emigrated to Canada and I went to graduate school. Unlike some of my new Canadian friends for whom childlessness expressed a political commitment, I felt no pressure to have children, and I did not define myself as resisting this pressure. I had not felt myself to be child*less* — lacking something to which I should be attached.

SHADOW SELVES AND OTHER SHADOWS

Writing about women's experiences of becoming mothers, I found myself thinking about my own childlessness, and the meanings of motherhood I had brought to the research. I saw that cultural meanings of motherhood are closely connected to cultural meanings of childlessness.[4] For example, mother is a moral identity for women: that which makes a woman good. Thus childless women, if not immoral (and historically they were often so construed), are not good in the same way as mothers. Childless women are not good women, not "real" women.[5] Images of good mothers or proper motherhood also express class and race relationships in the messages they carry,[6] and are embedded, for example, in media stories of young, unwed or welfare mothers or stories of overpopulation in the "third world": stories about the wrong women having babies. Personal and methodological questions became intertwined in my reflections. Why was I now troubled by memories of my aunts, and how were they or other childless women connected to my research on mothers?

Dear Sherryl,
Could it be that my story about motherhood began in rural Ireland where I grew up, and not in Toronto where the research itself was set decades later?

And did it in some way begin with childless women rather than mothers, or with my two unmarried aunts who, having taught for years in convents in Dublin and England, returned to live with their unmarried brother in the house where they had grown up?

I learned as a child that although these women had a right to "a place by the fire" in the family home, they were considered nuisances by my mother and those others who interpreted the world for me. And they were, I was told, selfish. But they were not called selfish because they did unkind things or failed in some expected performance of aunt-like behaviour. Nor were my aunts seen as selfish because they refused to marry and have children. Rather, my aunts were considered selfish *because they had not had the children who would have made them unselfish.* That is, in not having children, my aunts had not been transformed into that other category of woman — mother — an identity which, as you and I have talked about, even today in urban settings, carries themes of a female morality, the character of a caring person, of a good woman.

In post–famine rural Ireland where marriage was tied to land inheritance, many men and women remained unmarried. Yet this didn't normalize nonmotherhood in my family. Even though childlessness wasn't thought of as a choice (as it is today), my aunts could still be blamed for its perceived consequences.

My brothers taunted me with stories of how I looked like or spoke like one or other of the aunts and would turn out like them. Did I ever tell you I had one aunt's name, Alice, as my middle name? A horrible secret identity. My brothers called me Alice when they wanted to make me believe that I had a "bad character." As a child I only knew I didn't want to be like my aunts. They were seen as trivial and valueless by those family interpreters of my social world. Indeed, their small stature seemed to express their social insignificance. Both were tiny. No doubt Alice's partial deafness cut her off even more from the world around her. Then they died, one half-cared for, the other by an act of suicide, which in family whispers confirmed her essential selfishness and stubbornness, even in death. Their other childless sister died some time later, a peaceful death in a convent (my brother told me), cared for by her Sisters (she had been a nun). Perhaps because she had "given her life to God," her life option seemed to have been respected by family members. Certainly she was liked.

I feel I have entered into that never articulated but implicitly carried on conversation between my aunts and my mother as to who was "right," whose life worthwhile. I never did hear my aunts' points of view.[7]
Love, Martha

THE RE-FRAMING OF SELF THROUGH RESEARCH

Thinking about my childless aunts helped me to see that motherhood and nonmotherhood are connected. I was slower to see the analytic differences between nonmotherhood and childlessness.

Being a "nonmother" culturally signified a woman who had *not* been morally transformed by motherhood. My aunts, being nonmothers, were seen as selfish rather than good, nurturant women.

Childlessness, on the other hand, signified *an absence*. Participants in my research said that being a mother offered a special connection with another person and that childlessness would have felt like "something important was missing"; someone would have been absent. Someone special. Children, or rather "a child of one's own," are culturally represented as uniquely valuable to the female self, as priceless.[8]

Then, my mother died. Her death devastated me.

Dear Sherryl,
I find it harder and harder to separate what I am bringing to my

research from what I have learned from the mothers I interviewed, and to separate their lives and mine.

You already know much of the story I had written about other women's experiences of motherhood. From them I had come to understand the meaning of motherhood as a moral identity and to see the particularly strong, though not always positive, experience of connectedness with another person that becoming a mother often brings. Culturally, not to have children signifies an absence of certain kinds of social connection: a state of childlessness. In my research I had used the work of Mary O'Brien to talk about how women's reproductive capacities are often culturally constructed as symbolic resources with which to resist the discontinuities of death and change. I had wondered about how it is that death rather than birth is so often taken as the ultimate orienting life-event in western cultures. It had seemed to me that motherhood and the biological possibility of giving birth provides women with *symbolic* resources with which to challenge the dominant linear and male-centred representations of time that allow death to so dominate life. Surely birth too can locate the self in time and social space, making the experience of time continuous rather than discontinuous.

The words of Jenny, one of the women I interviewed, seemed personally prophetic. In explaining the meaning of motherhood for her, she likened *not* having children to experiencing one's own death while still living. Her words articulated my feelings, as she put it, of living one's own death that can come, in my case, with the loss rather than the absence of a particular social bond. Talking about childlessness she had said:

> It's like knowing death, to never have a child — to experience your own death as you are living. It's not so much that I'm going on with my daughter, it's just that *everyone* is going on. That life goes on, and that's important for some strange reason.

A story of motherhood's symbolic power to resist death, not just my own or my mother's, but that of meaningful life itself, seemed to start telling itself from my research. Women's stories of connectedness through having children pointed to solutions to the disconnectedness of my own life. "I am thinking about having a child," I tentatively wrote you, amazed to see these words appear on the screen. Now it was real. "It's not about wanting a child. It's about wanting to lose myself in relationships that endure. It's about wanting to *not* feel the centre of existence but just to be a small part of something," I tried to explain. It was similar to what Jenny had said, it had to do with extending life in time, not an individual's life, mine or my mother's, but of extending meanings in time through life. I felt so much had died with my mother, and that she had somehow bridged time in ways I had not.

You said you felt abandoned. As a voluntarily childless woman you asked if I wasn't privileging biological attachments over friendship. Clearly some "others" are culturally constructed to be more significant to the self than are others.

Love, Martha

BREAKING SILENCES

I had to confront the layered meanings of motherhood, nonmotherhood and childlessness in ways I had not before. How was I to understand mothers' accounts? What was it about their stories that was so troubling?

Dear Sherryl,

If motherhood symbolizes connectedness, then are we, as childless women, somehow especially disconnected? Disconnected is what I felt with my mother's death. With her death went not just my connections with her, but almost all my living links to the past and to sense of local space from which I had come. My mother sustained these as *my* past and *my* place with her constant "tracings" of connections with people, places and events.

My mother traced the world into being. She talked and re-talked the world, past and present, into existence. All our journeys, for example, were accompanied by stories. If we went to visit a relative or friend, my mother's voice called out the histories of the places, houses or farms we passed: That was the house where your grandmother was born; this pub should be so-and-so's today had the old man not died and his wife not remarried and her new husband not turned the first family out; that church is where a great-grandaunt is buried (she was so beautiful she always wore a veil over her face when she went to town so men would not stare); here a murder happened; there a Great House had been burned down in the Troubles.

From the time I emigrated, my mother talked our family into life on the phone, telling me about my siblings and about a world of distant relatives and once-close neighbours, often through accounts of their deaths and funerals. Like many elderly Irish women, my mother was a great funeral goer. Although my father had died over twenty years before, I hadn't felt him truly gone until she died, until she stopped remembering stories. People and local places were tied to each other in her tracings so that time, space and social relationships were all kept together through her stories, stories embedded in that other order, the moral order that "mothers" seem to carry as part of their social role.

I find myself turning to my research to help me understand my mother's death and to her death to help me make sense of my research. I weave threads of one story into the other. I see my loss as being not only of a mother to whom I was deeply attached, but also of bonds that held an older world together for me. She and her stories had located me in time and space, suspending temporarily the implications of emigration and childlessness as forms of exile.

I felt uncomfortable with this idea of having a child to help me live with loss, as though I felt that drawing on "the body" (in this case, my female body) as a resource to resolve existential problems was somehow inauthentic.

Despite their very different empirical meanings for women, perhaps I understand motherhood and childlessness metaphorically, as providing guiding imagery for contrasting visions of the individual and social relationships. Motherhood calls up an image of a nonmodern self, embedded and embodied in local enduring relationships, while childlessness carries an image of a modern self established as an individual through separateness and independence from others.

If this metaphorical reading of motherhood and childlessness helps my understanding, it also constrains it. I see traces of the repressive either/or reading of the Mary–Martha story secretly replaying itself in my metaphors and my stories as a tension between what I am and am not, threatening me with the consequences of making the wrong choice, of living the wrong life. But my life lies not just between what I am and am not, but between what I am not and what I am (also) not, for I am neither Mary nor Martha, at home in neither the past nor the present. So too my stories of women's lives can slip the oppositional cultural frames of work or family, of motherhood or childlessness, and of a sociological storytelling that contains them as one or the other, or reduces them to the tension in between.

Images of children in other women's lives unsettled the stories I told myself about my life. Like the dark watery pool homes of the Sidhe (faery people), the shifting surfaces of mothers' stories refract images of a world inside out, and I dare not look too closely for fear of being "taken."[9] Did I quietly slip by rather than take on being Irish Catholic and being a woman by emigrating and by not having children: take on by talking back? It was easy to emigrate or not have children while my mother embodied home: I had the comforts of home, abroad from its claims. Could this mean that I have lived like the fictitious modern (masculinist) individual of much western social and political thought? That disembodied cognitive self who is blind to ties of local place and noncontractual attachments to others. Have I so taken for granted the others who constituted me, just as women and nature are backgrounded in images of modern men's lives of achievement or adventure?[10] The meanings I read in and out of my stories and their characters shift. At times I read my research stories through feminist tensions around issues of caring, connectedness and autonomy in women's lives; at other times through my growing feelings of exile since my mother's death. Are my feelings of disconnectedness expressive of some existential plight or what sociologists call the disembeddedness of postmodern life, rather than a consequence of my mother's death and my private decisions to emigrate and to remain childless? If I think of my distress as an existential crisis, not of some abstract human condition, but of my "condition" of not wanting or being able to live like a modern, masculinist, dislocated individual, then having (or not having) a child is not the issue. To be sure, having a child, with its symbolic meaning of unconditional connectedness, offered to replace my desire for my mother and the other world she held quiet in my life — offered to make absences untroubling. How do I keep faith with the dead and "wriggle out of their shroud?"[11]

Grief unsettled the accommodations of gender and exile in my life, revealing them as strangely fused and, like ghosts once disturbed, they will not be laid to rest. How coldly blind to my presence. And in their absence lies the sweet, evocative power of the dead to tell of worlds in which I do not live, of a time that is not now and a place that is not here, of a self I never knew, of loves caught only in backward glances. My mother undoes me with her milky eyes. Who, I wonder, is the ghost ...

Love, Martha

ON OTHER TERMS?

I look back to the original story.[12] How easily I accepted the distinction between mothers and nonmothers, much, I suppose, as I had assumed a long time ago that my mother and my aunts were qualitatively different kinds of women. I didn't ask, How are such categories created and made significant in women's lives?, until I was troubled by the significance of childlessness in my own.

I also see that for all the richness of connectedness in my mother's tracings, some connections were included and some excluded, some valued, others not. My aunts' stories were not part of the order she helped tell, an order in which my life also does not fit. I can take up threads of her stories, but on different terms.

My feelings of loss made me aware that the identities of mother and childless woman don't express experience but organize it, providing a way of distributing certain kinds of cultural resources, emotional experiences and social obligations among different women. Mothers, but not nonmothers, are understood to experience special kinds of love, may claim family-like connectedness with children and can access the symbolic resources of female morality and caring.[13] The categories of mother and nonmother appear unquestionable because they are apparently grounded in nature, in a woman having or not having given birth to a child. Therefore women who adopt children construct an equivalent claim; they see their prospective children as uniquely theirs, "somewhere out there" waiting for them to become their parents.[14] Thus the meaning of motherhood in some women's lives is connected to its *absence* in other women's lives.

The identity of mother also organizes the distribution of unpaid, caring and domestic labour among women. All women, whether mothers or not, are expected to care for others. Mothers, however, are allocated the daily domestic work, as well as the ultimate responsibility for the life and well-being of those who are at once both their children and culturally sacred objects.[15] Childless women, on the other hand, are often seen as selfish, escaping dirty dishes and diapers by deciding not to have children.

Not all mothers have their claims to connectedness with children socially validated, nor can all women claim "mother" as a moral identity. Poor, unwed women may be unsuccessful in either claim when they deal with child custody or social service agencies. Even conventional mothers are expected to be attached to a man to justify their claim to motherhood. Thus men stand invisibly behind motherhood or are socially significant by their absence. A child who has "two moms" is not seen as getting double the care from her or his lesbian mothers.

The distinction between mother and nonmother is insidious yet consequential. In practice, or in the long run, motherhood may not fulfill the cultural promises of love and connectedness. Mothers often pay a high price for what may be transitory or illusory moral or emotional rewards. They may come to feel unappreciated, isolated or abandoned rather than connected.

Yet, for mothers and nonmothers, few social relationships carry the cultural power to symbolize the sort of love and connectedness socially indicated by bonds with children — with one's *own child*.[16] Is not part of the cultural meaning of having children the promise to transform individuals and couples into families and thus to offer the possibility of being at home in the world? "My home," "my child": but boundaries exclude as well as include.

Our most valued social bonds need not rest on expulsions of self or other, of us or them, of me or not me, framed by sharp distinctions rather than exploring what lies between, in the hidden connections of selves–others. Rather than policing the boundaries between self and other in our sociological work, why not work the hyphens?[17]

If I think of motherhood and childlessness metaphorically, as raising questions about how to live in a postmodern world without either abandoning or obsessively clinging to the conventional equivalence of mother and home[18] and as being a problem of gendered identity and exile, then perhaps my challenge is to learn to live closely and creatively *with* significant absences. And to learn to work without traditional authority, in some unfixed place between exile and home: to live with ghosts.

To End

My tale brings no truth from the field but a narrative with which I may weave more livable identities.[19] We need to ask who and what is excluded in our research and with what consequences. What policed borders order our work, and how are they guarded? Boundaries can contain disturbing knowledge. On what silences do our stories rest, and who, if they spoke, would tell different stories that might unravel us and our tales of self and other, us and them, as they fill the empty, sometimes dread-filled, spaces that seem to set us apart?

Recognizing that time, space and identities are fluid doesn't mean that I am unable to learn about others' lives. It suggests that, in the process of learning about others, I shift my understanding of my own life in ways that change the stories I can tell about others. I borrow shadows from the living and the dead. My research stories are haunted with absent selves and others who invisibly hold up both my accounts and the social world.

Notes

An earlier version of this paper was published in *Qualitative Inquiry*. See Martha McMahon, "Significant Absences," *Qualitative Inquiry* 2, no.3 (1996): 320–336.

1. Martha McMahon, *Engendering Motherhood: Identity and Self-Transformation in Women's Lives* (New York: Guilford Press, 1995).

2. My sister talked about the importance of her partner in her decision to have children. For sociological discussions of how women decide about having children, see Elaine Campbell, *The Childless Marriage: An Exploratory Study of Couples Who Do Not Want Children* (London: Tavistock, 1985); Kathleen Gerson, *Hard Choices: How Women Decide about Work, Career, and Motherhood* (Berkeley: University of California Press, 1985); Jean Veevers, *Childless by Choice* (Toronto, ON: Butterworth and Company, 1980).

3. I have just recently learned that the Mary–Martha story could be, some say should be, read the opposite way to my childhood reading, if it was read in its historical context. Jesus could be understood as supporting Mary rather than putting Martha and domesticity down. Mary's behaviour could be interpreted as a challenge to a gender order that normally excluded women from engaging rabbis in intellectual and theological conversation. Thus I can understand my childhood reading to have been based on the suppression of a more liberatory meaning. I enjoy the irony. However, either version of the story leaves me with a Martha identity I don't want.

4. I say "childless" rather than "childfree" because the former captures the cultural expectation that most, if not all, women will have children. The term childfree, of course, may be used to express freedom from such expectations. But the term childfree can also suggest that having children is mostly or exclusively a burden.

5. I think it is no accident that the major counter-feminist, antiabortion women's movement in Canada calls itself REAL Women.

6. For example, white middle-class women who stay home to care for children are deemed unselfish, but "welfare mothers" are seldom represented as good mothers on the basis of the time they spend at home with their children.

7. Nor did I learn the point of view of the wider community in which they lived. Looking back from here I suspect it was partly my aunts' challenge to conventional gender expectations that occasioned such unkind family responses. They broke family gender rules in their lives and passions. Alice had been an outstanding violinist and a member of the national philharmonic orchestra earlier in her life. Yet even her accomplishments at the violin seemed to matter little to those closest to her in later years. I never heard her play. Her sister, my other aunt, was a greyhound racing enthusiast and recognized locally as something of an expert on dogs. I saw a lot of them as a child but I hardly knew them.

8. See V. Zelizer, *Pricing the Priceless Child* (New York: Basic Books, 1985).

9. An expression used in Irish folk stories to tell of someone "taken" by the Sidhe (faeries) to their world.

10. Val Plumwood, *Feminism and the Mastery of Nature* (New York: Routledge, 1993).

11. This expresssion is borrowed from the Irish-language poet Biddy Jenkinson in reply to Maire Mhac an tSaoi, who describes her own commitment to writing poetry in that marginalized language as a refusal to consign her ancestors to silence or leave their graves untended. See Mary Harris, "Beleagured but Determined: Irish Women Writers in Irish," *Feminist Review* 55 (1995), 26–40.

12. McMahon, *Engendering Motherhood.*

13. Among white middle-class North Americans, it is not usual for non-kin to get close to other people's children. The poor Black communities described by Carol Stack and the social construct of the "play child" described by bell hooks stand in contrast to these exclusionary practices around children. See bell hooks, *Outlaw Culture: Resisting Representations* (New York: Routledge, 1994); Carol Stack, *All Our Kin: Strategies for Survival in a Black Community* (New York: Harper and Row, 1974).

14. M. Sandelowski, B. Harris, and D. Holditch-Davis, "Somewhere Out There: Parental Claiming in the Preadoption Period," *Journal of Contemporary Ethnography* 21, no.4 (1993), 464–486.

15. Zelizer, *Pricing the Priceless Child.*

16. Some friends responded to this point by telling me about their close bonds with aunts, uncles, siblings, children or fictive kin. And I feel a special bond with one of my nieces. My point isn't that such special relationships among extended kin don't exist or aren't valuable, but that the privileging of parental–child relations and modern-living arrangements means there is often little cultural or institutional recognition of these and other kin-like relationships.

17. Michele Fine, "Working the Hyphens: Reinventing Self and Other in Qualitative Research," in N. Denzin and Y. Lincoln, eds., *Handbook of Qualitative Research* (Newbury Park, CA: Sage, 1994), 70–82.

18. See Anna Antonopoulos, "The Politics of 'Home,'" in E. Godway and G. Finn, eds., *Who is This 'We'?: Absence of Community* (Montreal: Black Rose Books, 1994), 57–82.

19. Laurel Richardson, "Writing: A Method of Inquiry," in N. Denzin and Y. Lincoln, eds., *Handbook of Qualitative Research*, 516–529.

Chapter 11

BLACK WOMEN AND THE MEANING OF MOTHERHOOD

Nina Lyon Jenkins

PATRICIA BELL-SCOTT, a noted scholar on women's issues and mother–daughter relationships, participated in a keynote panel discussion at the Mothers and Daughters Conference at York University in September 1997.[1] In her discussion, she stated that it takes more than data and facts to tell the stories of Black women's lives. In keeping with that idea, I'd like to share with you my personal experience of how I came to choose the topic of Black motherhood. Even though I am a mother of three, the idea of exploring Black motherhood as a research study was not something I had given much thought to. The idea came to me when I took my first graduate feminist studies course. I entered the class with great enthusiasm and a sense of expectancy that this class would do for me what no other class was able to do — that it would provide for me an environment where my voice would be heard, my experiences validated, and where I would see representations of myself in the readings, in the experiences of my classmates, in the dialogue. I expected to no longer feel marginalized as a result of race, sex or gender.

Unfortunately, I cannot say that this was what unfolded. I did feel marginalized, but not because of sex or gender. I felt marginalized based on my race, social class, marital status and motherhood. The following excerpt from Adrienne Rich best describes my sense of inadequacy:

> When those who have the power to name and socially construct reality choose not to see you or hear you, whether you are dark-skinned, old, disabled, female, [a mother], or speak with a different

accent or dialect than theirs, when someone with the authority of a teacher, say, describes the world and you are not in it, there is a moment of psychic disequilibrium, as if you looked into the mirror and saw nothing.[2]

As I looked into the mirror image of my classmates to see a reflection of myself, there was nothing there. There was virtually nothing to validate my reality as a Black middle-class, professional, married mother. Out of this experience, however, which seemed to silence my voice, a seed was planted. I became pregnant with ideas; with new knowledge; a paradigm shift had occurred in my thinking. I began to understand that feminism is not necessarily synonymous with inclusiveness. My struggle to make sense of it all and to give birth to the expression of my ideas and experiences was slow, deliberate and often painful. I was being stretched and pulled in ways that were unfamiliar to me and quite uncomfortable. The birthing process very often is. But I pushed and pushed some more and birthed the topic of my research: Black motherhood.

MOTHERHOOD

Motherhood is a central part of many women's lives. "As an institution with significant and powerful symbolic content in our culture, motherhood has an impact on all women independent of the individual choice about whether to become a mother."[3] This impact comes from the durability and tenacity of the assumptions made about any individual woman that are forged in the context of the cultural and social forces that define the "essential" or idealized woman.[4] Mother is so interwoven with the notion of what it means to be a woman in our culture that it will continue to affect our individual lives.

There is no single meaning or given experience of motherhood. The very term "motherhood" connotes a falsely static state of being rather than a socially and historically variable relationship. The experience of motherhood is highly complex and full of contradictions.[5] It is not simply a biological phenomenon or the expression of nurturance and care. Motherhood is often a socially constructed identity. Ultimately, however, what being a mother means will depend upon a number of factors:

socialization; the condition under which women become pregnant and give birth to children; the social and cultural context of child rearing; the beliefs and expectations that women hold about motherhood; and the intersection of race, socioeconomic status, age, sexual orientation and culture on these beliefs and expectations.

Motherhood shapes women's relationships with other people, their opportunities for paid employment, their leisure, their self-perceptions and their individual identities.[6] Yet despite this reality, relatively little has been written about Black mothers' subjective experiences. Very little research takes into account the perspective of Black mothers, their individual diversity and the coping strategies they use.[7] In a few instances, Black mothers have been the major focus of investigation, yet even in these studies the use of quantitative methodologies has limited the subjective knowledge about Black motherhood.[8]

Some of the literature that does exist emphasizes a narrow range of issues or uses a pathological perspective or deficit model to examine Black motherhood. For example, early researchers, mostly Black and white men, have excluded Black women from studies of "normal" motherhood, focusing instead on Black motherhood as "deviant." This is evident in the number of studies on Black women who are single teenage mothers or who are poor single teenage mothers. These mothers have come under harsh attack in the social science literature and in the popular media. They have been accused of raising children with limited language, cognitive, affective and intellectual development, low academic achievement and low self-esteem. The research not only criticizes teenage mothers, it criticizes all Black mothers for failing to discipline their children, emasculating their sons and defeminizing their daughters.[9] The male researchers conclude that Black mothers who head their own households cannot possibly value themselves.[10] The assumption of this view is that the only stable family structure is the patriarchal family with both parents present. These studies have painted a very distorted picture of Black mothers. They lead us to believe that Black mothers are deviant and harm their children, and, furthermore, that the experience of motherhood negatively affects the self-esteem of Black women.

BLACK MOTHERS AND SELF-ESTEEM

The interrelationship of race, sex and self-esteem in Black women has not been fully explored and is a source of continual controversy. We live in a society where Black women experience a double jeopardy, that of being Black and female. The dual stigmas of racism and sexism enhanced by exposure to the outside world tends to reflect the notion that to be Black and female is to be second class. For many Black women, the attempt to develop and maintain a positive sense of self-worth is often bombarded by the "cold winds of multiple counter-opinions."[11] Examples of these counter-opinions can be found in two conflicting views of Black women's role in the family: 1) Black women are domineering, castrating females under whose hand the Black family and the Black community are falling apart, and 2) Black women are romanticized, strong, self-sufficient females who are responsible for the survival of the Black family and the Black community.[12] Neither of these viewpoints provides an accurate picture of Black motherhood, as they are both one-sided.

A number of recent scholars, including Margaret Anderson, Patricia Bell-Scott, Patricia Hill Collins, Bette J. Dickerson, Andrew Billingsley, Robert Staples, Norma Burgess and Paula Giddings, have called into question the negative perceptions and characterizations of Black mothers. The works of these writers are examples of works that encompass African-American women's feminist thought, Afrocentricism and "relevant ingredients contributing to theory-building in the examination of Black motherhood."[13] Such ingredients include, but are not limited to, the use of an Afrocentric paradigm that takes into account the cultural, historical and current experiences of African-Americans. Additionally, the use of Black feminist thought, which moves the experiences of Black women from the margins to the centre of analysis, must be a part of the theory-building process. Challenges to the basic tenets of positivist science, which supports the notions of one truth and expert knowledge, must be made. Similarly, Burgess argues that combining interdisciplinary scholarship on African-Americans provides greater opportunities for explanation. We must provide a "new" knowledge of old works. We must challenge the old ways of thinking, such as that used by deficit model theorists, who supported the Moynihan report.

The Moynihan report, produced by an American federal government agency, officially labelled the African-American female-headed family inferior, nonproductive, pathological and dysfunctional. The thesis of the Moynihan report was that family disintegration continued from slavery into the twentieth century as African-American families remained locked in a "tangle of pathology."[14] Scholars such as Harriet McAdoo, Andrew Billingsley, Paula Giddings, Velma McBride Murry, among many others, challenged these characterizations. They have changed their approach to studying Black families by using a wholistic, more culturally relevant approach. These researchers recognize and have documented the resourcefulness and resilience that Black families possess.[15] They understand the sociocultural, historical, economic and political contexts of African-American family life. Rather than interpreting the strength of Black women as dysfunctional, they see the strength of Black women as indispensable to their families' health and survival. Bette Dickerson, in her work on African-American single mothers, provides culturally relevant "lenses" through which to examine, interpret and understand the enduring resiliency of Black women and their families. Her synthesis of a culturally relevant approach with feminism is to make clear the ways in which race/ethnicity and gender intersect to simultaneously shape the experiences of all Black women.[16]

BLACK MOTHERHOOD

One of the more outstanding Black feminist scholars to analyze Black motherhood is Patricia Hill Collins. She points out that Black motherhood consists of a series of constantly renegotiated relationships that African-American women experience with one another, with their children, with the larger African-American community and with self.[17] For most Black women, irrespective of these differences and renegotiated relationships, family is extremely important. As a matter of fact, "the strongest and most fundamental allegiance of African-American women is to home and family."[18] How Black women define, value and shape Black motherhood as an important familial role reveals the diverse characteristics of Black women. It reflects both the dynamic and dialectical relationship that Black motherhood as an institution represents.

According to Collins, motherhood can serve as a site where Black women express and learn the power of self-definition, the importance of valuing and respecting themselves and the necessity of self-reliance and independence. It is a site where they can develop a belief in their own empowerment. Black women can see motherhood as providing a base for self-actualization, for acquiring status in the Black community and as a catalyst for social activism. This multidimensional role is central to many Black women's lives. Yet, according to Collins, for some women motherhood serves as a constant reminder of the oppressive state of women. For these women, motherhood is a truly burdensome condition that stifles their creativity, exploits their labour and makes them partners in their own oppression.[19] Whether it be a source of fulfillment and accomplishment or one of oppression, the multidimensional role of motherhood is central to many Black women's lives and connects them to their community.

The role of Black mothers is very complex. Many Black women have grown up with multigenerational models of mothers. Mothering is usually not an isolated activity but is shared with others — multiple mothers. Multiple mothering is such a common occurrence in the Black community that many Black women who raise their children far away from the extended family create substitute "mothers," "grandmothers," "othermothers" and "fictive kin."[20] Motherhood, whether bloodmother, othermother or community othermother, can be invoked by Black women as a symbol of power, community activism and a commitment to the future of their communities.[21]

COMMUNITY OTHERMOTHERS

African and African-American communities have recognized that vesting one person with full responsibility for mothering a child may not be wise or possible. As a result, "othermothers," women who assist bloodmothers by sharing mothering responsibilities, traditionally have been central to the institution of Black motherhood.[22] The centrality of women in African-American extended families is well known. Organized, resilient, women-centred networks of bloodmothers and othermothers are key to this centrality. Collins notes, "Grandmothers, sisters, aunts, or cousins acted as othermothers by taking on childcare responsibilities for each other's children."[23]

Black women's experiences as community othermothers have provided a foundation for Black women's social activism. Their feelings or responsibility for nurturing their children in their own extended family networks have stimulated a more generalized ethic of care, where Black women feel accountable to all the Black community's children.[24] The significance of community othermothers is particularly useful in understanding their role. As othermothers, Black women are allowed to treat biologically unrelated children as if they were members of their own families. An example of this is recounted by Elsa Barkley Brown in her article, "Mothers of Mind." Recalling her wedding day, she writes:

> One of my mothers/aunts sat me down to talk about my things ... she said to me, "Your mother is my sister, my daughter, my mother, my cousin, and to you I have been and always will be your aunt, your mother, your grandmother, your sister; your children will have an aunt, a grandmother, a great grandmother, a mother, a sister, a cousin."[25]

The role provided by this othermother is specific to the nurturing not only of other women, but of their children as well. Collins notes that "community othermothers work on behalf of the Black community by trying, in the words of late-nineteenth-century black feminists, to 'uplift the race,' so that valuable members of the community would be able to attain the self-reliance and independence so desperately needed for Black community development under oppressive conditions."[26] Othermothers often play central roles in defusing the emotional intensity of relationships between bloodmothers and their daughters (and sons) and helping daughters understand the Afrocentric ideology of motherhood. This, Collins, asserts, is the type of power many Blacks have in mind when they describe the "strong, Black women" they see around them in traditional African-American communities.[27]

FEMINISM AND THE STUDY
OF BLACK MOTHERHOOD

In order to adequately study Black motherhood, a theoretical framework that incorporates the experiences of Black women is needed.

Black feminist thought is such a framework. Traditional feminist theory is inadequate for this task. Feminism has at its core three major assumptions. The first is the need to investigate and document the unique voices and experiences of all women.[28] By listening to the voice of Black mothers, we can fill voids in our existing knowledge about the diversity of Black women's experiences. The second assumption of feminist theory involves the social construction of gender roles as the bases for the unequal distribution of power between women and men in the family as well as in the larger society. Not only is gender a socially constructed phenomenon, but also the self and self-conceptions are likely to reflect the gendered structures and processes of the worlds in which they arise.[29] Socially constructed gender roles affect women's identity in a variety of ways. For example, Black women receive subtle but very potent messages from parents, significant others, the media and mainstream society about what it means to be a woman. Sometimes these messages are contrary to the meanings Black women define for themselves. "The counter-opinions threaten to attack the new self-perceptions" and many Black mothers, in light of limited social support, may not "possess the ability to combat these external voices."[30] One of the biggest challenges Black women face is resisting the negative controlling images and learning how to hold on to the "me" in their own individuality.[31] The third assumption of feminist theory is the focus on women's empowerment — the type of empowerment that results from an understanding of one's own expression, that is, the ability to organize against the oppressions of marginalization, victimization, trivialization, powerlessness and exploitation.[32]

Feminism and some aspects of feminist theory are particularly problematic for women of colour. Feminism's limitations stem from its failure to consider the diversity of the women it seeks to empower, to understand that not all women's experiences are the same and that not all oppression is based on a patriarchal system. For the most part, traditional feminist theory has failed to consider the intersections of race, class and gender in society. Much of traditional feminist theory has been constructed from the particular experience of white middle-class women, and some feminist analyses have conveniently excluded the experiences of women of colour — with the same result of androcentric analysis.[33]

Given such inadequacies and gaps in feminist theory and praxis, it has taken the independent development of feminist theory by women of colour, particularly Black women, to produce new analyses that are grounded in their own experience. These analyses provide not necessarily new but different starting points for feminist thought and action. Black feminist thought helps to capture and illuminate the experiences of women of colour in ways that traditional feminist thought had not done previously.

According to Patricia Hill Collins, Black feminist thought is a way of reconceptualizing feminist theory, using the experiences of women of colour and analyzing race, class and gender as intersecting and interlocking systems of oppression. It is a theoretical framework that places women and their experiences at the centre of the analysis, making women become subjects rather than objects. Black feminist thought is a theoretical framework that "taps the multiple relationships among Black women needed to produce a self-defined Black women's reality by those who live it."[34]

The use of a centred approach speaks to "the need for theory, frameworks, and language through which the complexity and diversity of Black women's lives can be considered and named from Black women's viewpoints."[35] When women's voices are included in a study and a centred approach is used, the quality of women's lives is revealed in ways that have otherwise been silenced by the nature, scope and methodologies of the research. The power of women's voices expands our conceptions of their experiences. New conclusions can be drawn and new directions forged that have implications for policy, programs and research.

CONCLUSION

Little inductive research exists and scant attention has been given to examining the subjective meaning of motherhood for Black women. Given the dearth of literature on Black motherhood, there is a tremendous need to devote attention to this topic and to offer a new way of examining the experiences of Black mothers on their own terms. Black motherhood is particularly important to feminist scholars and researchers as we attempt to reconstruct knowledge about Black women and the roles they perform. Historically, Black mothers have been viewed in negative terms; however, scholars who are committed to changing and reconstructing knowledge have an opportunity and obligation to engage in scholarly research and writing that captures and illuminates the experiences of women of colour.

The Black women in historical and contemporary North American society has been viewed from a weak, disorganized and pathological perspective rather than from one of strength and resiliency.[36] Distortion, myth and outright lies have been part and parcel of the currently dominant characterization and knowledge base on Black mothers.[37] Placing racial/ethnic women's motherwork in the centre of analysis, as Black feminist thought does, recontextualizes motherhood. We cannot continue to allow themes of survival, power and identity to remain muted when the mothering experiences of women of colour are marginalized in feminist theorizing.

Finally, it is imperative that we shift the centre of analysis to accommodate the divergent experiences of motherhood. Research on Black mothers must be culturally sensitive and must carefully consider the sociohistorical context of their experiences. To do so promises to recontextualize motherhood and point us toward feminist theorizing that embraces difference as an essential part of commonality.[38] As Dickerson asserts, Black women's experiences must be relocated from the margins of other's experiences to the centrality of their own experiences.

Notes

1. Patricia Bell-Scott, "Mothers and Daughters: Race, Class, and Sexuality," panel presentation at "Mothers and Daughters: Moving into the Next Millennium," a conference held at York University, Toronto, Ontario, September 26–28, 1997. Dr. Bell-Scott presented excerpts from her co-edited book, *Double Stitch: Black Women Write about Mothers and Daughters* (New York: HarperPerennial, 1993).

2. I first saw this quote from Adrienne Rich, *Of Woman Born: Motherhood as Experience and Institution,* in an essay by Frances A. Maher and Mary Kay Thompson Tetreault, "Learning in the Dark: How the Assumptions of Whiteness Shape Classroom Knowledge," *Harvard Education Review* 67, no. 2 (Summer 1997), 321–349. In their essay, the authors state that they first saw the quote in a paper

by Renato Rosaldo, entitled "Symbolic Violence: A Battle Raging in Academe," presented at the American Anthropological Association Annual Meeting, Phoenix, Arizona, 1988.

3. Martha L. Fineman, "Images of Mothers in Poverty Discourses," *Duke Law Journal* (1991), 276.

4. Ibid., 276.

5. Alice Adams, "Maternal Bonds: Recent Literature on Mothering," *Signs: Journal of Women in Culture and Society* 20, no. 21 (1995), 414–427; Yael Oberman and Ruthellen Josselson, "Matrix of Tensions: A Model of Mothering," *Psychology of Women Quarterly* 20 (1996), 341–359; Ellen Ross, "New Thoughts on 'The Oldest Vocation': Mothers and Motherood in Recent Feminist Scholarship," *Signs: Journal of Women in Culture and Society* 20, no. 21 (1995), 397–413.

6. D. Richardson, *Women, Motherhood, and Childbearing* (New York: St. Martin's Press, 1993).

7. See, for example, Joyce Ladner, *Tomorrow's Tomorrow* (Garden City, NY: Doubleday, 1972); Robin Jarrett, "Living Poor: Family Life Among Single Parent, African-American Women," *Social Problems* 41, no. 1 (1994), 30–48; Carol B. Stack, *All Our Kin* (New York: Harper and Row Publishers, 1974); and Constance Willard Williams, *Black Teenage Mothers* (MA: Lexington Books, 1991).

8. A few researchers have made Black mothers the centre of analysis or have attempted to gather information from the mother's perspective. See, for example, Robert Strom, "Perceptions of Parenting Success by Black Mothers and Their Preadolescent Children," *Journal of Negro Education* 59, no. 4 (1990), 611–622; Williams, *Black Teenage Mothers;* and Lena Wright Myers, *Black Women: Do They Cope Better?* (New Jersey: Prentice-Hall, Inc., 1980).

9. For additional discussion, see Robert Staples and Leanor Boulin Johnson, *Black Families at the Crossroads: Challenges and Prospects* (San Francisco, CA: Jossey-Bass Publishers, 1993), and Andrew Billingsley, *Climbing Jacob's Ladder: The Enduring Legacy of African American Families* (New York: Simon and Schuster, 1992). Suzanne M. Randolph, "African American Children in Single-Mother Families," in Bette J. Dickerson, ed., *African American Single Mothers: Understanding Their Lives and Families* (Thousand Oaks, CA: Sage Publications, 1995), provides an excellent discussion of the state of Black children being raised by Black single-parent mothers.

10. Myers, *Black Women: Do They Cope Better?*

11. Terry D. Cooper, "The Plausibility of a New Self: Self-Esteem from a Sociology of Knowledge Perspective," *Counselling and Values* 35 (1990), 32.

12. C. A. McCray, "The Black Woman and Family Roles," in LaFrances Rodgers-Rose, ed., *The Black Woman* (Thousand Oaks, CA: Sage, 1980).

13. Norma J. Burgess, "Female-Headed Households in Sociohistorical Perspective," in Dickerson, ed., *African American Single Mothers*, 21–36.

14. Daniel P. Moynihan, *The Negro Family: A Case for National Action* (Washington, DC: U.S. Government Printing Office, 1965). See Dhyana Ziegler, "Single Parenting: A Visual Analysis," in Dickerson, ed., *African American Single Mothers*,

80–93. Ziegler provides a discussion of the Moynihan report and its impact on the study of African-American female-headed families.

15. Paula Giddings, "Foreword," in Billingsley, *Climbing Jacob's Ladder*, 11–16.

16. Bette J. Dickerson, "Introduction," in Dickerson, ed., *African American Single Mothers*, xix.

17. Patricia Hill Collins, *Black Feminist Thought: Knowledge, Consciousness and the Politics of Empowerment* (New York: Routledge, Chapman and Hall, 1991), 118–119.

18. Dickerson, ed., *African American Single Mothers*, 4. See also, Collins, *Black Feminist Thought*, 115–137.

19. A more detailed discussion of Black motherhood is provided by Collins in *Black Feminist Thought*.

20. Collins explains these terms in detail in her essay, "The Meaning of Motherhood in Black Culture and Black Mother-Daughter Relationships," in Patricia Bell-Scott et. al, *Double Stitch: Black Women Write about Mothers and Daughters* (New York: HarperCollins, 1991). See also Chapter 6, "Black Women and Motherhood," in Collins, *Black Feminist Thought*. The key to understanding Black motherhood is to realize that mothering in the Black community is not just a biological function, but that the role of mother is a multifaceted one that takes on different meanings for individuals within the Black community.

21. Collins, *Black Feminist Thought*, 132.

22. Ibid., 119. Refer also to Rosalie Riegle Troester, "Turbulence and Tenderness: Mothers, Daughters, and 'Othermothers' in Paule Marhall's *Brown Girl, Brownstones*," *Sage: A Scholarly Journal on Black Women* 1, no. 2 (1984), 13–16.

23. Collins, "The Meaning of Motherhood in Black Culture," 47.

24. Ibid., 49.

25. Elsa Barkley Brown, "Mothers of Mind," in Bell-Scott et al., eds., *Double Stitch*, 74–93.

26. Collins, "The Meaning of Motherhood in Black Culture," 51.

27. Ibid., 51.

28. Marie Withers Osmond and Barrie Thorne, "Feminist Theories: The Social Construction of Gender in Families in Society," in Pauline Boss, William Doherty, Ralph LaRossa, Walter Schumm, and Suzanne Steinmentz, eds., *Sourcebook of Family Theories and Methods* (New York: Plenum Press, 1993), 591–672.

29. See Martha McMahon, *Engendering Motherhood: Identity and Self-Transformation in Women's Lives* (New York: Guilford Press, 1995).

30. Cooper, "The Plausibility of a New Self," 31.

31. Julia A. Boyd, *In the Company of My Sisters: Black Women and Self-Esteem* (New York: Dutton Books, 1993).

32. Patricia Hill Collins provides a very thorough discussion of feminist theory and Black feminist thought.

33. Collins, *Black Feminist Thought*, 348.

34. Ibid., 22.

35. Patricia Bell-Scott, Beverly Guy-Sheftall, and Jacqueline Jones Royster, "The Promise and Challenge of Black Women's Studies: A Report from the Spelman Conference, May 25–26, 1990," *NWSA Journal* 3, no. 2 (1991), 284.

36. Andrew Billingsley, in *Climbing Jacob's Ladder*, provides an excellent discussion of the adaptive-resiliency model that is needed to adequately study Black families. He urges the use of a wholistic perspective that attempts to broaden and deepen our understanding of the Black family in general and Black motherhood in particular.

37. See Dickerson, ed., *African American Single Mothers*. Several authors in the book refer to the stereotypical distortions that emerge from the deviant approach to analyses of African-American motherhood. For example, see Dickerson, "Introduction" and "Centering Studies of African American Single Mothers and Their Families"; Norma Burgess, "Female Headed Households in Sociohistorical Perspective"; and Sharon Elise, "Teenaged Mothers: a Sense of Self."

38. See Collins, *Black Feminist Thought*.

Chapter 12

THE EXPERIENCE OF MOTHER LOSS:
VOICES OF ADULT DAUGHTERS AND
IMPLICATIONS FOR FEMINIST PRACTICE

Mary Valentich & Catherine Foote

CATHERINE FOOTE, Mary Valentich and Leslie Gavel have been friends for many years and have known each other in various roles as student, professor and professional colleague. As social workers we have all had some experience with illness and dying, but nothing had formally prepared us for our own mothers' illnesses and deaths and for the period after. Our mothers, Laura Foote, Catherine Valentich and Midge Gavel, died in 1988, 1989 and 1991, respectively. In 1995 we wrote the following accounts of their illnesses and deaths.[1]

> My mother, Laura Foote, was diagnosed with breast cancer in the summer of 1980, when she was fifty-one and I was twenty-five. After she had a mastectomy and radiation therapy, the cancer went into remission for three years. Then it spread to her liver, and for the next four years, Mum alternated between periods of chemotherapy and remission. With each cycle, the length of remission shortened. Early in 1988, the cancer returned to much of her liver and to her bones, and I knew she was going to die. One problem after another surfaced, and she was not able to receive further treatment. During the last six months of her life, I was her primary caregiver, physically and emotionally. My father and two brothers chose to remain uninvolved, and we all — including my mother and her doctors and nurses — pretended that she was not dying.

The last night of her final hospital admission, I stayed in Mum's room all night. I don't know if she knew I was there. I went home the next afternoon to make some phone calls and to get cleaned up and changed. She died Sunday, August 7, 1988, while I was in the shower. She was fifty-nine. For eight years I had gone through all her cancer with her, but I was not with her when she died. And we had never talked about what was happening to her, what our lives together had been, what we had learned from each other, how I could go on without her, or what she hoped for me.

During the eight years since her death, I have yearned for Mum every day, doubly so in the past three years since the birth of my daughter. I need her as my mother and as the grandmother of my Kate Libbey; I envy women who are rediscovering their mothers as they watch them grandmothering. I will live the rest of my life with more questions than answers about my mother. I never really knew her.   — Cathie

In 1988–89, my mother lived with my family for eight months while she received treatment for cancer of the uterus. She had tried to keep the symptoms from us, but on a brief visit in October 1988, we recognized that she had a serious medical problem and made arrangements for her to be treated almost immediately in Calgary. In some respects, it was a happy time: she moved through various phases of treatment well; I could mother her; and she and our son, Stuart, could be together as they were in his first years when she cared for him.

On July 13 we took my mother to my brother's home in Toronto, where she held her new grandchild, Laura, for the first time. It was a special moment. Mother had her last radiation treatment, radium implants, a month before and had been pronounced in excellent medical condition. She was eager for life and fitter than she had been for years. We believed we had snatched her from death's door, but we did not know how weakened her immune system was.

We left on vacation, revelling in a job well done, only to receive a phone call from my brother the next week that my mother had acute diarrhea. Although the substitute family physician had her medical records, he treated her symptoms as a stomach upset. My brother finally took our mother to the emergency room of a hospital in her hometown on a Friday night, only to have her admitted to a palliative care unit, with no access to medication for a day or to a specialist. Thanks to the misdiagnosis, the delay in getting treatment, the absence of medical personnel on the weekend, and the general disregard for an "elderly" person of seventy-three, my mother was in enormous distress. On Tuesday, a specialist finally noticed that her kidneys were failing and that she had a Stage III e coli bacterial infection, complete with a rare blood disease, that would lead, ultimately, to seizures and death.

My brother and I stayed with our mother during the last awful week, doing what we could, but nothing altered her steady deterioration. When the medical system of the large city hospital to which she had been moved finally rallied, it was too late. My brother and I sat with her through hours of dialysis and plasmapheresis and protested her removal from the intensive care unit the next Friday. We left her swollen body on Saturday night; every movement was agony for her. Yes, the resident physician looked in on my mother Sunday morning, but nothing alerted her to the heart failure that followed shortly thereafter. Mother struggled on; she had more seizures, and the doctors took more heroic measures.

When we arrived at 1:00 p.m. on Sunday, our mother was again in intensive care. By 3:00 p.m., my brother and I decided not to let her linger. Were we premature? We cradled her and sang to her. Once she looked at me. She died at 7:15 p.m., and I despair and rage at the senselessness of it all. *I'm sorry, mother; you wanted to stay with us, but we couldn't save you. Now we are lost without you.* — Mary

Mom hardly left her bedroom in late December 1990 because the stairs in the condominium had become too difficult to manage. We were lying on her bed watching *The Young and the Restless* on her portable television, and I was drinking hot chocolate that, although she was dying, she had willingly prepared for me. My younger sister, who had been caring for my mother for the past

month, was annoyed with me for what she perceived to be my in-
considerate treatment of my mother, although Mom *had* offered
to make the hot chocolate. Watching my mother make hot chocolate allowed me to pretend, albeit briefly, that she was not ill with
breast cancer and would be there to mother me indefinitely.

Mom and I both knew she was dying. I said, "I love you.
What will I do without you? How will I look after my children?"
"I love you," she replied, and pragmatic as always, she added,
"You will muddle through."

Muddling through is very much how I have led my life for
the past five years. Anxious muddling; devastated muddling; ecstatic muddling; but mainly contented, vaguely satisfied muddling. I know life, in general, is about muddling through, but I
am certain it would have been more straightforward and pre-
dictable if Mom was alive. Maybe not. Regardless, I am without
her, and I count this as the biggest hurdle that I have faced so far.

— Leslie

When we asked ourselves whether we would change anything in
our accounts, the answer was no. Our words etched our despair, anger
and feelings of loss in a timeless fashion. We can go forward from the
time of their deaths, but we can never go back. The words stand. We
can, however, elaborate and do so, to ourselves and others who will listen. Mary can take moments on that last ambulance ride and string
them together like rosary beads on a well-worn chain. Mostly she can
see her mother's face and her looks — her eyes are filled with a mixture
of hope, even excitement. They are on a journey together and they are
close. She always wanted Mary to come back home to live in the area.
Mary visited but never returned to live near her. Mary now knows why
her mother wanted her to be near. Because one day she would leave
Mary. She had a knowing glance — was this the day? She had always
told Mary that the day would come.

For Cathie, the three words that come to mind are regrets, anger
and empty spaces. With respect to "empty," she observes all the places
and ways in her life her mother ought to be, but she is missing. She
notes that the losses she has experienced because of her mother's death

have increased in number and clarity over time. As more and more things happen to her in her life (becoming a mother, having a breast biopsy, facing re-entering the workforce in her forties), she feels as though she can understand her mother and her mother's life better. Thus Cathie misses her even more, because she sees all the things they could have shared and helped one another with, and all the ways in which they could have grown closer — "all the places in our lives that would have overlapped and brought us together, to appreciate, understand, enjoy, forgive, support each other — to become friends."

As time goes along, Cathie notices the many things she wishes to know from and about her mother that she will never be able to know — all the questions she should have asked her and information she should have gathered — all the answers now missing forever. For example, what were her mother's pregnancies and experiences of giving birth like; what was she, Cathie, like as an infant/baby/child; how did her mother experience menopause; was she menopausal or post when first diagnosed with breast cancer?

Leslie has recently written a more extensive account of the loss of her mother.[2] She tells the world of her grief, that her mother has gone, and that so many questions remain unanswered. She knows that her mother is present in the opinions that have become a part of Leslie's world view; she is present in the lessons she has taught Leslie (life is arbitrary) and she is part of the quirky, bouncy, expressive self that Leslie brings to her encounters.

The experience of mother loss remains prominent in our lives, but it changes and develops. It does not leave one. And while it remains painful, we prefer to live with the reality. As Cathie once noted, her mother's illness and death have become incorporated into her sense of identity. Thus Cathie will always be the woman whose mother died when Cathie was thirty-three and childless.

Now that Cathie has a daughter herself, she misses her mother as her mother and as a grandmother to her daughter. She believes this shared mothering would bring much comfort, confidence and competence to each of them; that loving and caring for Kate together would help them close old gaps in their relationship. Cathie also believes she would develop more of a sense of her own mothering and identity as a mother if Laura were here, providing the primary context for that understanding of motherhood. And Cathie is saddened by the fact that Laura died before becoming a grandmother — she never felt the happiness of seeing her own good mothering reflected in the joys of her daughter and granddaughter.

Since the time of our mothers' illnesses and deaths, we have spoken to many women about their fears about or their experiences of their mothers' deaths. It is not so unusual now, but still very poignant, to read of another woman's story of her mother's battle with cancer:

> Later, watching Mom fade in and out of consciousness, I wondered how I could possibly live without her. Who would I tell first about my writing successes or go to when I needed the unconditional love she's always provided? ... She was the centre of our family. It would fall apart if she were gone.[3]

The centrality of the experience of mother loss for adult daughters has been brought home to us in three ways. First, by Mary's mother, Catherine, who told Mary that not seeing her own mother before she died was a wound that never healed. Catherine Valentich left Croatia in 1939 at age twenty-one. Many years later, she learned of her mother's death from cancer. Catherine's mother had refused the recommended treatment of amputation of her arm. Catherine never recovered from the shock. She likely never forgave herself for leaving her mother and yet what choice was there for her in Croatia with no marriage prospects, the promise of a hard life in the village and Europe itself on the edge of war? A marriage was arranged. As a dutiful daughter, she had to leave to meet and marry the stranger in Canada. In going, she lost everything that was familiar.

Second, a student of Mary's recently noted that her eighty-seven year old grandmother was upset because her illness and age prevented her from travelling from Alberta to British Columbia to attend the funeral of her hundred-and-two-year-old mother.[4] She wanted to say goodbye and be physically present. There was no help for her turmoil.

Third, we were moved by the voices in *Our Mothers*, a book that speaks eloquently to the issue of mother loss by adult daughters.[5] Seventy-two women photographers were asked to take portraits of their mothers and to write a commentary. Although the photographers were free to follow their inclinations, their words often focused on their mothers' deaths. The following selections all affirm the fact that facing one's mother's death is beyond anything most of us have ever experienced.

> Today my father is dead, my mother is eighty-one. I am haunted by the thought of her death, which may not be very far away: His death still haunts me. Before it is too late, I want to say: "Mum, I love you. Thanks for being there."[6]

> I know that when she dies it will be impossible to try anymore. "Mama! Let's not wait until it's too late!"[7]

> On the very day I was about to write this piece, I dreamt that my mother died.[8]

> Another image, on her death bed: the translucent, smooth skin and an expression of softness that I had never seen before. She was ninety-seven years old.[9]

> She would kiss me and say, "Sweet dreams. Don't forget to say your prayers." I would close my eyes and the next thing I knew I would be soaring, flying into the dark starry skies.
> When my mother died, the dream ended. I came down from the stars to the earth I was born.[10]

> When my mother died, everyone said she was like a saint ...
> Who was she really, and what were her dreams? These are questions I can never answer. This is the void that can never be filled.[11]

THE DYNAMICS OF LOSS

In order to appreciate the nature of the loss of a mother, one must recognize the centrality of the relationship between mothers and daughters. Many authors have focused on the mother–daughter bond and made the point that mothers and daughters are especially close.[12] As Adrienne Rich so eloquently puts it, "The first knowledge any woman has of warmth, nourishment, tenderness, security, sensuality, mutuality, comes from her mother."[13] Margaret Notar and Susan McDaniel write, "The mother ... serves as a central female role model, defines the meaning of femininity and womanhood, and often provides the most solid and longest lasting woman-to-woman ... relationships that the daughter experiences."[14] Andrea Schluter, writing in *The Globe and Mail*, acknowledges that mother love is like no other love; it is biological, unconditional and eternal.[15]

It is not surprising that one searches for such love. The dynamics of mother loss focus us on our wanting to recapture, re-experience or find for the first time that all-encompassing love. When Cathie writes that she never really knew her mother, she may be saying that she and her mother never had a chance to immerse themselves in their love. Mary could see that Cathie's mother, Laura, was so clearly proud and happy for her daughter, but Cathie didn't know this love directly from her mother. Mary, on the other hand, had felt her mother's love directly, and she had also learned from her mother's friends that her mother often spoke proudly of Mary and of Mary's brother, Tom. How we know our mother's love influences how we experience the loss. If a daughter doesn't know her mother's love, there is a void, a sense of eternal emptiness when the mother dies. If a daughter does know her love, then she recognizes such nurturance more readily in other relationships.

From a developmental perspective it would seem that the base of a daughter's identity would be stronger if the death occurred when the daughter was an older woman. If the daughter is in her twenties, it is more difficult to understand her mother's life and context. The daughter would likely feel more vulnerable to life's hurts, she might feel lost and confused as if in a vacuum. If the daughter is in her sixties, it is possible that she and her mother would have grown closer together or at least come to terms with some of the common relationship problems. Perhaps the daughter would feel somewhat more at peace with her mother's death, especially if her mother had resolved some of her dilemmas and had experienced honesty, openness and pleasure in being valued. With each phase of life, the daughter would have had a chance to know her mother again — as a grandmother, as a friend, as a traveller on a similar journey.

Recognition of the mother's nurturance has finally taken hold in the feminist community. The psychodynamic traditions that facilitated mother-blaming have been difficult to eradicate. In professional practice situations, one can still find remnants of mother-blaming. As Kathy Weingarten notes, "The ideas about mothers and mothering that are familiar to me are replete with idealization and blame, both of which depend on an acceptance of absolute maternal responsibility."[16]

These psychodynamic traditions have served to constrain one's experiences of positive mothering. If we didn't separate from our mothers, become individuals, become independent, we would be enmeshed, immature and unready to take our place in the world. As we have previously noted, psychodynamic explanations tend to ignore that mothers have traditionally been assigned to low-status, undervalued work (bearing and rearing children, keeping up the home); that their power has been restricted to the home front; and that daughters have been seen as extensions of their mothers and subject to control.[17] As Marcia Westkott states, "In short, the story of mothers and daughters takes place in the world of the father. To try to understand the mother–daughter relationship apart from that world is to abstract it from the patriarchal society in which it is embedded."[18] Perhaps this is the heart of the issue: however we value the loss we experience when our mother dies, her loss is not valued by society because she as a mother is not valued — she has secondary status in patriarchal society. So how can we be so forlorn? We haven't lost much if in society's view she is a person without status. We therefore become trapped by the dominant society's standard of motherhood.

Feminism has had a difficult time in acknowledging or accepting a more positive vision of mothering. Christina Looper Baker and Christina Baker Kline observe:

> Yet, in this fundamental visioning of woman's role in society, many second-wave feminists saw little room for motherhood. Reacting to a not-so-distant past when women were valued primarily for their reproductive role, feminist leaders frequently devalued motherhood and sometimes actually opposed it ... Feminist motherhood has been a topic deferred because it complicates the role of the emancipated woman ... Even today, the women's movement has a hard time reconciling motherhood with sisterhood.[19]

The delegates who participated in and presented papers at the 1997 "Mothers and Daughters: Moving into the Next Millennium" conference, at York University, suggest otherwise, as do artists who seem more free in their photography, film, poetry and artwork in their search for their mothers. One does not search for her mother if one does not value her. The seeming silence about wanting our mother's love can come to an end. We no longer need to feel ashamed for wanting that love to continue after the death of one's mother. This changing feminist perspective on mothers and daughters dovetails with the changing expression of grief in our society.

THE EXPRESSION OF GRIEF

Many people in North America have been shielded from illness and death by well-meaning family, friends and professionals. Apart from the sensationalized deaths in the media, some of us have little experience with illness and dying. There is social anxiety about death and a denial of the grief one may feel. There are at least two messages that society sends to the bereaved: (1) it is good to express feelings of grief, but do not express them too much for too long, and (2) get over your grief as quickly as possible, put it behind you, get back to normal, and move on with your life.[20] These messages are particularly unhelpful because they leave the bereaved persons feeling unsupported, isolated and abnormal, and they disparage the depth and breadth of the loss the bereaved are experiencing. The bereaved person must struggle to make sense of the loss throughout her lifetime and these societal messages tend to hinder and impede.

Fortunately there is recent change evident in the grieving process, particularly with respect to privacy. As W. F. Deedes notes:

> There were times, not so long ago, when incurring the loss of a family member was essentially a private matter. I can think back to the times when blinds were drawn in the house of mourning. Silence prevailed ...
>
> Any tribute to the departed, unless he or she was well known, came from the pulpit. Death did not raise voices, it lowered them. The bereaved were not expected to utter a word, even to close friends. Their silence in grief was understood, respected.[21]

The outpouring of grief in public and tangible ways for Princess Diana in August 1997 may indicate that we have passed a turning point with respect to Anglo-Saxon societal constraints on grieving. We have been witness to a prolonged, open, visible, shared and socially approved experience of grieving such as has never been experienced before. The grief of a nation and of thousands of people around the world allowed us to confront our grief and to learn more about ourselves. This was especially so for the British:

> The most fascinating thing about the Diana phenomenon is how, almost overnight, the British national character seems to have changed. In their grief over Diana's death, the British have been everything they are not supposed to be: emotional, demonstrative, rebellious, classless, informal.
>
> Out the window has gone emotional reserve, verbal circumspection, deference to royalty and blind respect for protocol and hierarchy. In has come frank talk, open tears and a new democratic, almost revolutionary, spirit. If the symbol of Eastern Europe's revolution was the crumbling of the Berlin Wall, the symbol of Britain's was the quivering of the stiff upper lip.[22]

Although many of the traditional attitudes about grieving will not change quickly, and grief for Diana was an unusual situation, we have witnessed people's use of publicly approved mourning and ritual as a chance to express personal grief that otherwise would have been repressed.

Within this changing social context, it will be easier for feminist ideas about grief to take hold. Ideas that allow us to acknowledge a continuing relationship with the person who died and to know that time won't necessarily heal the loss. We can also allow ourselves to know that life won't get better every day and that there is no set period for grieving, correct times to carry out certain post–death tasks or proper ways to grieve.

LIVING WITH LOSS

As social workers, we have applied our feminist understanding of mother loss to the range of personal and professional actions women may take to ease their pain. Personal actions may include memorials, rituals,[23] religious expression or the development of friendships with women for support or reconstruction of aspects of the mother–daughter relationship. Other reconstructions of the relationship may involve storytelling, artwork, creating a garden or preparing the mother's special foods.

Professional bereavement practice facilitated by a feminist practitioner includes individual, couple, family and group approaches, each of which can be adapted to the adult daughter's developmental stage.[24] Grieving is seen as open-ended and nonpathological. If medication is desired, it may be used, not to eliminate emotions but to enable the woman to function while incorporating the loss into her being. Counselling will be more complex if the mother–daughter relationship was characterized by negative interaction. With time and careful review, the daughter may gain insight into herself and her mother and become free to grieve what was and might have been. At any point, prior to or after the mother's death, a workshop experience with small group discussion, rituals and artistic expressions may be helpful.

Feminists cannot, of course, leave to others the education and advocacy needed to help change attitudes about mothers and mothering. Long overdue, feminists can begin to reclaim motherhood and speak about the meaning of their mothers' deaths and the ways in which individuals seek solace. Feminist social workers may be particularly helpful in recognizing the diverse cultural expressions of grief. Adult women usually welcome a chance to let down the barriers, and recognize that they too can cry for their mothers, thereby moving closer to the legacy of their mothers. A mother's heritage may not make its way into a will, but it can thrive for generations if it is revealed and nurtured through education and social commentary that encourages valuing mothers, recognizing their worth and grieving their loss. Feminist practice can enable us all to gain the riches mothers so quietly leave behind.

Notes

1. These women's stories first appeared in print in Catherine Foote, Mary Valentich, and Leslie Gavel, "When Mothers of Adult Daughters Die: A New Area of Feminist Practice," *Affilia* 11, no. 2 (1996), 145–148. (© 1996 Sage Publications, Inc.)

2. Leslie Gavel, "Missing Mom," *Modern Woman Magazine* (October 1997), 67–68.

3. S. Hunt, "Blessing," *Homemaker's Magazine* (September 1997), 13.

4. Laurel Hvingelby, interview by Mary Valentich, August 31, 1997.

5. V. Esders, ed., *Our Mothers* (New York: Stewart, Tabori and Chang, 1996).

6. P. Agosti, "Our Roles Have Changed," in V. Esders, ed., *Our Mothers*, 10.

7. J. E. Atwood, "Before It's Too Late," in V. Esders, ed., *Our Mothers*, 22.

8. M. Broekmans, "Rites of Passage," in V. Esders, ed., *Our Mothers*, 34.

9. D. Colomb, "An Image Ingrained Forever," in V. Esders, ed., *Our Mothers*, 40.

10. S. Metzner, "Recollections," in V. Esders, ed., *Our Mothers*, 98.

11. J. Tenneson, "What Were Her Dreams?," in V. Esders, ed., *Our Mothers*, 134.

12. L. R. Fischer, "Between Mothers and Daughters," *Marriage and Family Review* 16, nos. 3–4 (1991), 237–248.

13. Adrienne Rich, *Of Woman Born: Motherhood as Experience and Institution* (New York: W. W. Norton, 1976), 218.

14. Margaret Notar and Susan A. McDaniel, "Feminist Attitudes and Mother–Daughter Relationships in Adolescence," *Adolescence* 21, no. 81 (Spring 1986), 1.

15. Andrea Schluter, "It Is a Strange Thing, the Love of a Mother," *The Globe and Mail*, 6 May 1994, A20.

16. Kathy Weingarten, *The Mother's Voice* (New York: Harcourt Brace, 1994), 43.

17. Foote, Valentich, and Gavel, "When Mothers of Adult Daughters Die: A New Area of Feminist Practice," 154.

18. Marcia Westkott, "Mothers and Daughters in the World of the Father," *Frontiers* 3, no. 2 (1978), 16.

19. C. L Baker and C. B. Kline, *The Conversation Begins: Mothers and Daughters Talk about Living Feminism* (New York: Bantam, 1996), xiv–xv.

20. Foote, Valentich, and Gavel, "When Mothers of Adult Daughters Die: A New Area of Feminist Practice," 150.

21. W. F. Deedes, "Two Worlds," *Calgary Herald*, 6 September 1997, J6.

22. M. Gee, "A Change in British Character," *The Globe and Mail*, 10 September 1997, A23.

23. J. W. Boyce, "The Day We Buried Our Father," *The Globe and Mail*, 3 August 1994, A22.

24. E. Myers, *When Parents Die* (New York: Penguin, 1986); F. Walsh and M. McGoldrick, eds., *Living Beyond Loss* (New York: Norton, 1991).

Chapter 13

IF YOU DIE IT WILL KILL ME: ABORTING MATERNAL HISTORY

Erin Soros

Funerary speech and writing do not follow upon death; they work upon life in what we call autobiography.
— Jacques Derrida, *Memoires for Paul de Man*

"*If you die it will kill me.*" I begin with my mother's words, with a sentence she whispers to me on the day of my grandmother's funeral. The words are familiar, she has used them before, but given the recent death of her mother they resonate with a certain fear. She leans herself into my body as if she were surprised that she is not already dead, as if the death of her mother should have also been her own, as if I were all that keeps her alive. If you die it will kill me. But how, I wonder, could the death of a daughter mean the death of a mother? How could my death be hers? Is it not true that no one but me can die my death, that I can give my death to no one?

In *The Gift of Death*, Jacques Derrida defines death as that which can never be taken or given by another: "Death is very much that which nobody else can undergo or confront in my place. My irreplaceability is therefore conferred, delivered, 'given,' one can say, by death."[1] I am myself because no one else can die my death. The irreplaceability of one's death makes one unique — oneself — and hence makes one uniquely responsible for one's acts. Only through the irreplaceability of my death can I claim responsibility for giving or taking from another: "Death would be this possibility of *giving and taking* that actually exempts itself from the same realm of possibility that it institutes, namely, from *giving and taking*. But to say that is far from contradicting the fact that it is only on the basis of death, and in its name, that *giving* and *taking* become possible."[2] The impossible give and take of death gives the possible responsibility of give and take. Only the irreplaceability of one's own death gives one responsibility for the irreplaceable death of another, a death which one can never give.

Death begets irreplaceability, irreplaceability begets identity, identity begets responsibility. This structure of filiation is what I intend to critique, beginning with Derrida's definition of death. But is this death indeed Derrida's? *The Gift of Death* intricately layers Derrida's argument with those of Patočka, Heidegger, Levinas, Kierkegaard and Hegel, defying a reader to determine responsibility for any given theory or to decide in whose place death occurs. While Derrida explicitly asserts that the theories of death he articulates belong to these philosophers, he also states that "the ideas that lead us to these last propositions ... have a literal place neither in Patočka nor in Levinas nor in Heidegger ..."[3] When I refer to *The Gift*, I write of a death that does and does not occur in Derrida's place.

To begin with death. But which one? Who has died? Who has killed? Who can tell?

I can only tell a story. Here I will write death: write to it; write of it; perform it. It is always there, haunting these words, giving them as they give it. I have arrived at this writing — this autothanatography — through a death that is and is not properly my own. I had an abortion. This statement mimics "I had a child," calling to memory a future I chose not to live. An abortion is a decision, a division, a split. It is the possibility of doing life and death at the same time. It means that a part of me does not exist but remains, a cinder, a burnt trace beside my current life, lining my writing with what will never be there.

Birth: death. Abortion.

Women rarely refer to an abortion with the possessive, choosing instead a definite or indefinite article to introduce the noun, as if we were unsure whose death it was. Yet although ownership here is uncertain — or perhaps *because* it is uncertain — an abortion is an act that performs one as a distinctly female subject. To be a woman is not necessarily to have an abortion, but to have an abortion is to be a woman. Like giving birth, giving death creates a gendered relation between self and other and a gendered narrative of the gift. An abortion signifies a gender that gives death and a death that gives gender.

"Everyone must assume his own death, that is to say the one thing in the world that no one else can *either give or take:* therein resides freedom and responsibility."[4] Derrida's premise is that everyone always assumes the same kind of death, an irreplaceable, singular — yet general — death. That sexual difference does not structure one's assumption of death nor, therefore, one's assumption of freedom and responsibility. Indeed, "in passing," Derrida notes that "in none of these discourses we are analyzing here does the moment of death give room for one to take into account sexual difference; as if, as it would be tempting to imagine, sexual difference does not count in the face of death. Sexual difference would be a being-*up-until*-death."[5] This speech act is slippery: Derrida states what he is tempted to say, says it while saying that he is not. His desire is declared without responsibility. Yet he gives himself away, for the assumption that sexual difference is a being-up-until death is woven throughout the text, through each analysis that fails to consider the possibility of a sexually different death and fails to elaborate how such a death would construct irreplaceability, identity and responsibility. *The Gift of Death* fails to conceive abortion.

If an abortion is a woman's choice, as I believe it should be, what does this choice entail? What are the ethics involved and how do they construct gender, identity, death? How can a woman's responsibility to the fetus be defined? If choosing abortion was my own decision, what specific knowledge enabled it, gave it to be thought, performed? Whatever calls one to responsibility calls one to memory: I can only tell a story, my story, which is never properly mine.

The late 1930s. Prince Edward Island. Tootsie's place: a local bootlegger's. My grandmother works as a cleaning lady, washing the floor, picking up the bottles the men leave behind. My grandfather is a bootlegger and rum runner. He is quiet, large, with a face plum-red when angry. No one crosses him. Phil, he's called, and the men joke about women and food, ask him if he's had his fill. She is chatty, thin, too poor for her name. The men never call her "Florence"; they call her "Doll." The improper becoming proper; the proper, improper. "My Doll," Phil calls her, erasing Florence, deflowering her.

"She was never taken with him," my Aunt Marg says. "She never wanted to go with him." But she *is* taken with him, or taken *by* him: he stalks her, harasses her, forces his way inside. She becomes pregnant. She marries him, gives birth to my mother seven months later. After nine years of battering and abuse, she escapes with her son and daughter and travels across the country to Vancouver by plane, bus and train, switching mediums, breaking the line, hoping she can't be traced.

In this story, pregnancy functions as a form of encryption — as an act of keeping a secret and a refusal to mourn. The trauma is pocketed within her womb. The other is kept hidden inside yet simultaneously kept out. The violater's body remains within her, yet is not assimilated. It is saved as an inside outside the inside, the growing fetus a visible reminder of the rape and a physical replacement for the part of herself that was lost through the trauma. Each day, the fetus swells, testimony of another's illegitimate desire. It fills her belly like a word, holding all she cannot say. She cannot say no to rape nor can she say no to forced pregnancy. With the possibility of abortion foreclosed, the only way she can remove the trace of Phil's body is by giving birth to it. The pregnancy thus acts as a negotiation of the rape: the memory of the trauma is brought in only to be expelled, screaming its first sound through her second mouth.

Phil inside outside Florence.

For almost fifty years — from her marriage to her death — she obsessively scrubs floors. She is medicated, institutionalized, given shock treatment: she always returns to the floor, cleaning that fragment of her name.

She hears voices, thinks people are poisoning her food; she refuses to eat. One by one various organs are operated on, divided or removed. Through a combination of self-starvation and surgery, she loses half of herself. Her bones click against the chair as she rocks back and forth, holding her ileostomy bag tight to her body, an inside outside the inside. When my mother tries to make her eat, coaxing the spoon between her lips, my grandmother accuses her of feeding the bag. She does not want to feed the bag. She does not want to fill it.

And she keeps cleaning, carrying the bag from room to room in our house. I wake to the sound of the vacuum, the desperate suck and whine as she smashes it against my bedroom walls.

Phil and vacuum. Vacuum and Phil.

The doctor inserts the speculum between my legs and clicks it open, inverting the interior of my body, catching the fetus within a specular gaze. She slips the speculum out, then pushes another rod in, a hollow shaft that scrapes the walls of my vagina. I dig my nails into my palm. Sweat seeps into my eyes. I breathe. I count. Rustle of paper. Thrust and twist of cold metal. Contraction. Sudden rumble and suck of a vacuum. Sound at once shocking and familiar.

"What is recalled to memory calls one to responsibility."[6] The abortion can be viewed as a response to my genealogy: haunted by my past, I assumed responsibility for my grandmother's pregnancy, aborting what she could not. Just as the speculum inverted the inside of my body, my abortion inverted her rape. What had originally been forced in was finally forced out.

Expecting. From the Latin "*ex,*" meaning "out" and "*spectāre,*" meaning "look" and source of "speculate," "speculum," "specter." Expecting: to look out ... or to out the ghost.

If you die it will kill me. When my mother said this, she revealed her belief that she could compensate for her own mother's reluctance to give birth to her — a rapist's child. My mother's statement can make sense only if my mother were inside me, if I were pregnant with her. Only then would my death be hers. Only then could my life be her own. If I were pregnant with her she could feed herself on my body, using me to fill the vacuum left by the original violation — the rape and forced pregnancy her mother had tried so desperately to erase. But the structure of this fantasy is complex, for my mother also expressed her wish to remain pregnant with me. Expecting me, she said, was the happiest time of her life. My gestation filled her. She ate little, losing weight during the pregnancy as if she expected her body to feed itself on mine, digesting my flesh into hers. "You were almost too small to be born," she said, describing how the nurses wrapped me in tinfoil to keep me warm. "You looked like a baked potato. I could have eaten you." If I could remain her fetus or her baby, she would never be hungry, would never be lacking. "I want you back, Erin," she said. "Can't you make yourself small?"

She desired that I be pregnant with her pregnant with me. Within this narrative of absolute filiation, to continue my pregnancy would involve both giving birth to my mother and giving birth to myself.

I dream that my mother is inside me, waiting to get out. I dream that we are both inside my grandmother's birth chamber, sliding to the entrance, competing for air. Florence, Gwen, Erin. One inside the other inside the other. F, G, E. G, F, E. E, F, G. The family alphabet swirls in my head as I try to determine who is pregnant with whom, who initiates the decision, which letter comes first.

I was pregnant with history, with ghosts, yet I never told the women who haunted me. I kept it secret from them, or at least I did not tell the one remaining alive. To make my choice, I needed to separate myself from outside influence. I did not want to have an abortion for my grandmother. I did not want to have a child for my mother. I wanted to act for myself, in my name alone. As Derrida asserts in his *Gift*, true responsibility must not be "motivated, conditioned, made possible by a history."[7] In order for the decision to be my own, it could not have been given to me by the other. In order to take responsibility for the event, to articulate the ethics of having an abortion, I needed to distinguish my history from my mother's and grandmother's, separate what I desired from what I felt compelled by them — or by their ghosts — to do:

> Although some might think that there is no exercise of responsibility except in a manner that is essentially historical, the classic concept of decision and responsibility seems to exclude from the essence, heart, or proper moment of responsible decision all historical connections (whether they be genealogical or not, whether their causality be mechanical or dialectical, or even if they derive from other types of motivation or programming such as those that relate to a psychoanalytic history).[8]

Responsibility arises neither from a compulsion to follow orders nor from a sense of duty. To take this analysis to its logical end, one can say that true responsibility remains absolutely separate from societal and familial expectations. It must be totally restricted to self, must never engage the other, even the other of language: "Just as no one can die in my place, no one can make a decision, what we call 'a decision,' in my place. But as soon as one speaks, as soon as one enters the medium of language, one loses that very singularity. One therefore loses the possibility of deciding or the right to decide."[9] A proper decision "declines the autobiography": it must be solitary and secret and silent, aborting all its ghosts.[10]

But can such a responsibility, a responsibility that never engages the other, truly exist? Can one ever step outside of history, genealogy, language? Can I ever make a decision by myself? The very act of reflection always involves the other. E, F, G: each letter signifies through the next, becoming itself through the other's absence. Responsibility exists only in and through language: in order for an act to be ethical, one must not only initiate it, but be ready to answer for it, in one's own name. An ethical act demands reflection, analysis, rationalization and "once I speak I am never and no longer myself, alone and unique."[11] As Derrida suggests, this given definition of responsibility contradicts itself: a responsible decision can be made only by a complete and total self, yet this self can make the decision only through language, through the other:

> Such is the aporia of responsibility: one always risks not managing to accede to the concept of responsibility in the process of *forming* it. For responsibility (we would no longer dare speak of "the universal concept of responsibility") demands on the one hand an accounting, a general answering-for-oneself with respect to the general and before the generality, hence the idea of substitution, and on the other hand, uniqueness, absolute singularity, hence nonsubstitution, nonrepetition, silence, and secrecy.[12]

In order to be responsible, my decision must be silent, secret, solitary *and* spoken, visible, shared.

"'... the instant of decision is madness ...'"[13]

I am only too familiar with this ordeal of the undecidable, this madness. At age sixteen I began eating alone, carrying small portions of food to my room, trying to escape outside influence, to consume only what I chose. But given that my mother did the shopping and cooking, I could never wholly determine when my decision was my own. She was always there, inside me. I began to buy and prepare food myself, yet still I could never guarantee that others had not somehow affected what I chose to put in my mouth. My calculations became more exact. I destroyed all food my mother gave me. I refused to eat anything she ate. I was consumed by a desperate attempt to determine what I alone desired and to find a food that did not come from an other. My diet transformed into a mad and dangerous game: in the attempt to become entirely self, I lost half my body weight. I divided in two.

E, F, G. The alphabet in its proper order.

I wanted to be the first, the origin, the absolute initiator of my acts. My body began to feed on itself as if it were an auto-sustaining system. I was almost perfect — outside need, outside time. I had carved away my body's history — the accumulated flesh of previous meals. Fat was extraneous; it was not me. I would escape it and its history of food. But this self-sufficiency demanded absolute vigilance. Each bite was a failure: I had accepted a gift, had let in the other. I waited for the day when there would be no more give and take, no more in and out, when I would be permanently closed, completely myself.

Fill and vacuum. Vacuum and fill.

If I had been pregnant with my mother, I would have killed her. But although my self-starvation can be interpreted as a starving out of my mother, it also meant that I was trapped by her, within her home, within her history. The harder I tried to become absolutely self-sustaining, the more dependent I became. My mother decided to feed me herself: sitting at the table between two starving women, she tried to nudge the spoon first through my lips, then through my grandmother's. She swivelled back and forth, facing her daughter then her mother, begging us both to eat, miming the swallowing she so desperately wanted us to enact. Framing my mother, my grandmother and I mirrored each other, together weighing enough for one person.

My stomach had swelled from the starvation, ballooning over my pants to resemble the tight belly of an expectant woman. As my mother tried to feed me, I rejected her, flailing like an infant, pulling my head wordlessly away from the spoon.

Here lies madness: the harder I tried to carve history from my body, the more pregnant with it I became. By attempting to starve out the ghost, I became one. The trajectory of anorexia nervosa, my specific form of madness, my attempt to be free of the other, illustrates the trap inherent in all efforts to deduce absolute responsibility. This is the madness of trying to make a decision that is completely independent of any historical determination. The madness of making a choice that is my own.

When I was pregnant, I was revisited by my past. Just as the anorexia performed pregnancy, the pregnancy performed anorexia: for weeks I was so nauseated I could hardly eat, hardly bring in the outside. I was separated from one of the primary forms of give and take, in and out, that constitutes human subjectivity. And just as I once had interpreted my hunger as foreign and had conceived of food as an other that threatened to overwhelm me, I experienced pregnancy as a visitation of a strange presence, or a strange absence, a haunting. I did not know how to speak of the fetus, how to name a being that would never live outside my body, how to determine who or what it was, whether it was or was not myself.

I decided to have an abortion, knowing that the decision could never be absolutely — properly — my own. I could not carve my decision free of my specific history — the stories of my grandmother, the desires of my mother, the battles with myself. I could not separate the abortion from my attempt at self-starvation. I could not keep my decision solitary or secret or silent. The instant of decision is madness: I made an *improper* choice.

What have I done? How do I conceive abortion? If the fetus can be none other than self, then I have given death to myself. How is this possible and how do I define my responsibility for the act? If responsibility is always a responsibility to an other, what is my responsibility to an other that is not one?

The crisis of identity and responsibility that abortion performs is inherent to Judeo-Christian conceptions of subjectivity as described by Derrida, conceptions based on a male model of life and death. Within this model, individuality is given through the irreplaceability of one's own death: "The sameness of the self, what remains irreplaceable in dying, only becomes what it is, in the sense of an identity as a relation of the self to itself, by means of this idea of mortality as irreplaceability."[14] No one else can take my death. I can give my death to no one. Only through the irreplaceability of my death can I claim individuality and hence responsibility:

> ... responsibility demands irreplaceable singularity. Yet only death
> or rather the apprehension of death can give this irreplaceability,
> and it is only on the basis of it that one can speak of a responsible

subject, of the soul as conscience of self, of myself, etc. We have thus deduced the possibility of a mortal's accession to responsibility through the experience of his irreplaceability, that which an approaching death or the approach of death gives him.[15]

I am responsible to the other insofar as I am myself. Yet the irreplaceable death that gives my identity can never be properly my own. I can be responsible only through the fact of the future arrival of my death, which I can never properly experience. Although I am the sole individual to whom I can give my death, I can never receive the gift. If I give myself death by suicide, I am no longer alive, no longer properly myself. At the instant when my death is mine, I am not. Death is a gift that can never be given. Identity and hence responsibility are delivered through this ineluctable fort/da of a proper death that leaves on arrival.

But to arrive at this definition of death, a death which is irreplaceable, which no one can experience in my place, Derrida has tossed out one specific form of death. In order for death to be properly itself, abortion has been aborted. Abortion forms the constitutive outside of Derrida's conception of death. As a constitutive outside, it enables death to be defined as irreplaceable and singular. This definition is possible only through the negation of its other, the replaceable and non-singular death of abortion. Abortion gives the death of Derrida by erasing itself from the scene. His death is the gift of abortion.

Who gives? Who remains? If the fetus is part of my body, then I give death to myself yet live to claim the death as my own. An abortion can then be defined as a proper death, even the only proper death, the only death I can live. But what if the fetus is other, becomes other through its death? An abortion would then be a form of death that an other experiences in my place, literally in the place of my body. The other becomes other only at the moment I give it my death. The other never is, yet it receives a gift. The other remains self until an instant of madness when it experiences my death. My death becomes mine in this instant when I give it away. The proper becoming improper, the improper proper. Abortion is the possibility of impossibility, creating a catachresis of the terms self and other, life and death: the terms are still used, but fail to deliver. Abortion gives a death which is neither singular nor shared. It gives death to *no one*.

Small wonder that I find it so demanding to conceive of my abortion. That determining individual responsibility for the act is an impossible task. That I am unsure how to define my role in giving death to an other like no other. Given an abortion brings death to crisis, unhinging the concepts of identity and responsibility dependent on it, I can hardly sign my name to the act, can hardly defend my decision as one that is ethical or proper.

This analysis of abortion reveals that there is more than one form of death, that death is gendered. Sexual difference is the aporia of death. The decision to have an abortion remains inconceivable within Derrida's *Gift of Death*. Abortion makes Derrida's gift of death inconceivable. Far from existing as a "being-*up-until*-death," sexual difference is given through death and death is given through sexual difference. A woman can live a death that is not one.

But here lies a fundamental paradox: although being a woman includes the possibility of giving death, this possibility delivers the threat of not being a woman. When a woman has an abortion, she gives a death that undermines her very definition as female. For if, according to Sigmund Freud, a woman completes herself by giving birth, then by having an abortion a woman renders herself incomplete. Only a woman can have an abortion, but an abortion negates the function which for Freud determines her as a woman. The death thus creates a chiasmus, simultaneously performing one as a woman and as a not-a-real-woman or a not-woman. Abortion is an aporia of sexual difference. Abortion gives death to women.

To explore this aporia, I must tell another story that is and is not my own. The sense of being traced by death, of losing or lacking something — this sense that ostensibly constitutes femininity — has been said by Freud to arise when a little girl sees a little boy's penis — always "strikingly visible and of large proportions" — and becomes aware that she does not have one.[16] She has nothing to see, she lacks the significant material, the material that signifies. While at first she suffers this knowledge as a confirmation of punishment for some misdeed — that originally she had a phallus and it had been cut off, presumably by the mother — she soon realizes that this lack is inherent to her sex. According to Freud, she then "makes her judgement and her decision in a flash. She has seen it and knows that she is without it and wants to have it."[17] So, as the story goes, the little girl sets her sights on her father. Because her father undoubtedly has a penis, she resolves to repudiate her own lack by having a child through him, in essence having his penis by having his baby: "the girl's libido slips into a new position along the line — there is no other way of putting it — of the equation 'penis-child.' She gives up her wish for a penis and puts in place of it a wish for a child: and *with that purpose in view* she takes her father as a love-object."[18] This fantasy penis-child (but whose fantasy?) enables the girl to fill the original lack suggested by her inferior genitals, her nothing to see. Only with this goal *in view* does the little girl become a "little woman," a proper woman.

Although the specific fantasy of bearing a child through the father gradually dissipates, a woman ostensibly remains haunted by a longing for a penis. This penis envy can be resolved only when she gives birth, when her childhood fantasy can finally be materially realized. Giving birth allows a woman to compensate for her lack, to complete herself. But such an outcome suggests that when Freud's little girl had only a fantasy to view, she was not yet a "little woman" or was perhaps *too little woman*. A woman is not a woman, or not a complete woman, until she becomes pregnant and gives birth. Only then, when she has a fetus or a baby — the "penis-child" — does she become a big woman. Paradoxically, only by supplying herself with a child does a woman become properly herself. Only with a penis is she a woman.

What is she, then, if she does not become pregnant? Can she be a proper woman without a penis-child? And what is she after an abortion? Does abortion give death to a woman who is not one?

Even when a woman finally has a baby, something remains missing. The child replaces a lack. A substitute, by definition, is never what it replaces. It signifies by not making the signified present. It signifies what is not there. The child, then, is not a penis, or not a proper penis. The child is a fetish. Here I am departing from Freud's definition of a fetish: only a boy, Freud claims, negotiates the apparent castration of his mother by telling himself that she has what is not there. A girl has no such confusion: she knows what she and her mother are missing. Only a boy can see a maternal phallus where there is not one. The fetish, like the penis, can only be his. But how can the story of a mother giving birth to a penis-child be anything but a tale of fetishism?

The child signifies a penis precisely by not being one. And just as the boy's fetish disavows castration anxiety — by both erasing and exaggerating it — the girl's fetish assures her possession of what she is missing: it both replaces and highlights the lack. Thus when a mother uses her child to complete herself, the child only symptomizes the precarious nature of her completion. The child's increasing independence threatens to take part of the mother away, a part that the mother fears was never properly her own. The instant the mother gives birth she both has the penis and loses it.

And if the mother gives birth to a girl, this child's missing organ must inevitably disappoint the mother, reminding her of what she herself can never properly own. But a daughter also offers the mother the possibility of repeating the story, of giving birth once more. Through the future pregnancy of her daughter, the mother will once again be given the chance to fill herself, to acquire a penis. Each pregnancy promises finally to replace a lack that can never be replaced. The mother's desire to have a child through the daughter is cathected with the daughter's own desire. One inside the other, the mother giving the daughter giving the mother, a chain of compulsory reproduction that always fails to fill the vacuum.

But to interrupt this familiar story. To abort or castrate it. If a baby promises to be a maternal phallus, what can an abortion be but castration? In this story, to have an abortion is to castrate oneself. In giving death, I cut off my penis, cut off myself as penis.

Abortion: castration.

I have perhaps arrived at one of the reasons people respond to abortion with such horror, why institutions and individuals, women and men alike condemn this giving death; and why men express such rage at their powerlessness when abortion becomes a woman's choice, a woman's responsibility. If women never properly have the phallus, if the phallus that a woman has is not hers, whose is it? Whose phallus is castrated? Perhaps a man who refuses a woman the right to abortion is haunted by the fear that a woman can cut off what he always believed was his own.

Imagine. A woman can cut it off; she can live without it. And with this act, we return to the beginning, to the girl who is not yet a "little woman," to the one who is always already castrated. One could argue that far from negating one's natural femininity, abortion represents a return to one's original state as female: an acceptance of one's castration, one's lack, one's sex. An abortion is a way — perhaps the only way — to make oneself a woman. Real women have abortions.

But the seduction of this logic demands that we negate the precise undecidability performed by abortion, ignoring the crisis engendered by an act that can never decide what to give. On the one hand, if women are the sex that can become pregnant, then terminating one's pregnancy performs one as a woman. But on the other hand, if a fetus is what allows a woman to compose or complete herself as properly female, then aborting a fetus performs one as a not-woman. But on yet another hand, if a woman is by definition castrated, then having an abortion — cutting off the fetus as penis — performs one as a woman. Woman; not-woman; woman. Impossible to decide which term comes first, which one is delivered, which one is given death. Abortion ties sexual difference in nots.

And still I have limited the crisis of this impossible decision by assuming that the fetus-penis is, in fact, her own. But if a woman's swelling belly attests to a man's swelling penis; if it assures a man that he has it, has it through her, has it by having her; if she can receive a penis only through a man; if the fetus as penis is never properly hers but *his*, who, then, is she castrating? And what is he after she cuts it off? Who remains the woman?

Abortion is not simply a castration of oneself or a castration of one's sexual partner, but a castration of the phallogocentric order that structures the categories of sexual difference. Deciding to have an abortion demands that one tell the old stories, but backward and upside down: the castration ostensibly inherent to a girl at birth is mirrored in the act of abortion but with the significance reversed. Castration is no longer the originary fact which differentiates one sex from another, but an act that destabilizes sexual difference. Castration does not remain in its proper place, but is repeated, cited, cut off from its origin. Sexual difference is not given, but given. It is not original, proper and stable, but delivered — precariously and improperly — through the gift of death.

Abortion. Combination of "*ab*," Latin prefix meaning "away" or "off," and "*orīgō*," Latin root meaning origin or source — point or place of beginning.

Phallogocentrism structures a coterminous relationship between phallus and origin, phallus and language, phallus and identity. Within this structure, women are expected to deliver: the phallus needs the womb, needs the womb to need it. Phallus as origin; womb as origin: an abortion cuts through both these interdependent structures, castrating the phallus and restructuring the womb outside of a reproductive imperative. And with the phallus and womb cut off as origin, the entire filiation of conceptual structures dependent on these figures begins to tremble. With the act of abortion, a woman refuses to claim a phallic identity, refuses to erect a phallic language. An abortion is a negation of full presence. It is a nothing to say.

And if a woman speaks this nothing, tells the story of a death that is not one, does she not take something away from his gift? Her gift of death must be sacrificed if she is to deliver the fetus/phallus/fetish, supplying a man with what he fears he lacks. It must be sacrificed if death is to signify as itself, as a proper and irreplaceable death, as a death with an absolute filiation with identity and responsibility. It must be sacrificed if the binaries self/other, man/woman, life/death are to remain in their proper place. Death gives irreplaceability gives identity gives responsibility gives decision: if the identity of this death is deconstructed by abortion — a woman's death — then its entire filiation is brought to crisis. As Derrida says in his *Gift*, "Dying can never be ... delivered ..."[19]

Here I come to guilt, for really it is guilt, not responsibility, that is expected of a woman who has an abortion. Etymologically, guilt is a payment or debt: guilt represents the emotional cost demanded of a woman in exchange for what she refuses to give, a debt she inherits for what she has cut off. Given her crime, she can never be guilty enough, can never make up for what she has failed to erect. But if she has an abortion *without* guilt? If she betrays the order of payment? How would this affect phallogocentrism and the compulsory reproduction which serves it?

"The Pea," I called the fetus, a common word, an improper name: "p" for payment or promise, "p," for Phil or phallus. A pea's name, a piece of a name, a fetish, failing always to bring the signified to presence. "P," an inverted "b," a pregnant belly turned upside down. Letters I refused to deliver.

I broke a promise and didn't pay for it. I denounced the reproductive imperative, refusing to supply my mother with a phallus. I failed to give birth to the past. Failed to fulfill my philiation. Although my decision to have an abortion was traced by history, it also represents a profound betrayal. But such is always the logic of a decision, of an instant simultaneously given by the past and broken from it.

Decision. From "*dē*," Latin for "off," and "*caedere*," Latin for "cut." Decision: to cut off.

To cut myself off from my mother. My experience of anorexia was intertwined with the structure of phallic motherhood, where a woman is always in danger of losing what she never properly has. In order, then, to undo the thinking patterns of anorexia, I needed to imagine a differently configured relationship between mother and daughter, a relationship that is not structured by compulsory reproduction, that does not compel a woman to replace what she is missing through the birth of a child. A relationship where a child is not forced to be a phallus for her mother, is not required to fill the vacuum.

If you die, it will kill me.

I recite her words as if they were my own, repeating them with a difference. If you die, it will kill me: if the structure of phallic motherhood dies, so does the anorexic paradigm of absolute selfhood. The two concepts need each other in order to survive. The fantasy of phallic motherhood defines a self as lacking the phallus, as dependent on another to supply it and thereby enable the mother to be properly herself. The fantasy of anorexia defines the self *as* a phallus, as completely self-contained, absolutely independent of an other. Abortion fractures both sides of the binary. As castration, abortion gives death to both the phallic mother and the anorexic girl: she dies and it kills her.

Who is left, then? What remains?

"Life," from Prehistoric Germanic "*līb*," denoting "to be left, to remain."

I remain haunted by an other that is not. I live with my death. The living death of anorexia forms a chiasmus with the living death of abortion. They cross each other, one moving toward a life that is death and the other toward a death that is life. Self-starvation was an attempt to refuse death, to be immortal, but this refusal was an abdication of life and hence a movement toward death. An abortion is an acceptance of death, an acceptance which demands opening myself to life — to the death that gives it and the death that it gives. An abortion is the gift of life.

Notes

Thank-you to Chris Bracken, Mark Cochrane, Karlyn Koh, Lorraine Weir and Michael Zeitlin for the gift of their suggestions and support. A grant from the Explorations program of the Canada Council funded the initial work on the narrative. A different and longer version of this essay is published as "Giving Death" in *Differences: A Journal of Feminist Cultural Studies* 10, no. 1 (Spring 1998).

1. Jacques Derrida, *The Gift of Death*, trans. David Wills (Chicago: University of Chicago Press, 1992), 41.

2. Ibid., 44. Emphasis in original.

3. Ibid., 44.

4. Ibid., 44. Emphasis in original.

5. Ibid., 45.

6. Jacques Derrida, *Memoires for Paul de Man*, edited by Avital Ronell and Eduardo Cadava, and translated by Cecile Lindsay, Jonathan Culler, Eduardo Cadava, and Peggy Kamuf (New York: Columbia University Press, 1989), xi.

7. Derrida, *The Gift of Death*, 5.

8. Ibid., 5. Emphasis in original.

9. Ibid., 60.

10. Ibid., 62.

11. Ibid., 60.

12. Ibid., 61. Emphasis in original.

13. Ibid., 65.

14. Ibid., 45.

15. Ibid., 51.

16. Sigmund Freud, "Some Psychical Consequences of the Anatomical Distinction Between the Sexes," *The Standard Edition of the Complete Psychological Works of Sigmund Freud,* vol. 19, trans. James Strachey (1925; reprint, London: Hogarth, 1961), 252.

17. Ibid.

18. Ibid., 256. Emphasis in the original.

19. Derrida, *The Gift of Death*, 44.

Chapter 14

AFRICAN NOVA SCOTIAN WOMEN: MOTHERING ACROSS THE GENERATIONS

Sylvia Hamilton

IN MY FILM AND RESEARCH work, my goal has been to explore the role of women of African descent in the development of Black communities in Nova Scotia and in their continuing struggle for equality. My work proceeds from a desire to answer some personal questions and to reflect on how the lives and work of these women affect our contemporary generation. The most personal and perhaps most profound of human relationships is that of mother and child. In examining the lives of African Nova Scotian women I have observed that the work they have taken on — the "mothering" of their families (blood and other) — may be extended to the "mothering" work, which I believe is also activist work, they have performed for the Black communities. This chapter is a reflection on these women's familial and community roles as mothers and community activists across several generations.

A DIALOGUE BEGINS

My interest in the social and cultural history of people of African descent in Canada is long standing. I completed high school and university without receiving any significant information about this history. Consequently, when I began my own historical research, I asked myself, What is considered "history"? What is worthy of investigation and study? Clearly, because of the dearth of material in school and university texts, as well as in other print and visual media, it was logical to conclude that African peoples' lives, and specifically Black women's lives, were not considered "history."

This realization meant that I had to begin redefining for myself what value I would place on my own research and experiences. Faced with this absence, this lack of history, I had to redefine value and worthiness. "We" were women too and, as such, we should have been included in the texts on women. However, we were not. The message transmitted and received, whether intentionally or not, was that "we" were not valued and were not worthy.

Yet I grew up within a context where I knew women who, I believed, had done some amazing things but whose lives were invisible within the dominant society, and even within the local community itself. I had also grown up with the clear understanding that each individual has a role and responsibility in the process of creating social change. In other words, if you see something wrong, you have an obligation to do something about it. "Speak the truth" and "stand up and be counted" were common phrases I heard spoken by elders throughout my early years.

In 1981, the Canadian Research Institute for the Advancement of Women (CRIAW) held its fifth annual conference in Halifax. The theme of the conference was "Women and Culture," and my mother, Marie, and I (along with filmmaker Dorothy Taud Henaut and her daughter, Suzanne) were invited to participate in a workshop entitled "Socialization: Mothers and Daughters." In our dialogue, we spoke from our respective positions. Mom spoke about her life, about how she worked and raised her family and about what she tried to instill in us, her children — her daughters and sons. I spoke about my memories of growing up, about what I was learning and about what I was doing. For me, our presentation was the beginning point for a "public" dialogue, not only about the mother–daughter relationship within the African Nova Scotian culture but also about the role and experiences of Black women within their own local communities. The following excerpt from the workshop dialogue illustrates how my mother served as a loving guide and mentor for her children:

Marie: All my daughters had their own minds and ideas. My goal was to help them become responsible and to stand up for their rights and for themselves. I wanted them to be able to come to me at all times. Now, when they visit, you will find us all in the kitchen having fun and talking, while other families would spend their time watching television. I tried to set an example for my daughters, and then left the rest to them. I did not judge them and I could not live their lives. They had to make their own choices.

Sylvia: It was during my years at university that I consciously realized I had had a somewhat privileged upbringing. I had learned life skills which other students were just becoming aware of: independence, responsibility, decision making, a sense of identity and humour, and also how to make do with very, very scarce resources.

Above all, I had learned not to be ashamed of my race, and, in fact, to be proud of it. I learned this at a time when so many things around me were working overtime to deny and invalidate our existence as a race. In the face of this, I had also learned not to hate.

If you asked me when and how I learned these life lessons from my mother, I couldn't fully tell you. Some I've learned from her direct teaching, but a lot more from her presence and her strong example. I remember once Mom had to go to the school to talk to the principal about my oldest sister Ada ...

Marie: ... I had come home from school and my oldest daughter was very, very upset. I asked her what had happened and she said the teacher had smacked her across the face. I asked her why and she told me her side of the story. Then I said, "Is this the truth?" She said, "Yes." I told her not to worry and that we would go to school together the next morning.

When I arrived at the school with my daughter, I told her to go into her classroom. When I knocked on the principal's door, she addressed me in this manner: "What are you doing here? You're supposed to be teaching." I said I had a reason. I asked her what was she supposed to be doing when she smacked Ada. So we discussed the matter and we found out who was wrong and who was right. On that particular day the principal was watching two classrooms. She walked into the Grade 7 classroom and my daughter, with a smile on her countenance as always, was blamed for making a lot of noise and laughing. It was not my daughter's fault. She told the truth. It was the fault of the principal.[1]

THE MAKING OF
BLACK MOTHER BLACK DAUGHTER

In early 1984, I was involved with an ad hoc women's film group in Halifax. We were a loose gathering of women who were interested in making films about women and by women. A number of us had very specific ideas of what we wanted to film while others were more interested in the technical-production areas. We met with the National Film Board in Halifax to discuss what we wanted to do. There were funds for only one project at a time, and the group decided that my idea should be the project to go forward . As a group, we made a commitment that women would perform all the roles in the production of the film, from camera to sound to editing.

For me, the impetus to create a film about the lives and experiences of Black women in Nova Scotia came from a strong sense of their absence in historical accounts, as well as my desire to create a visual record and memory for my daughter and other daughters of her generation.

Since I had not made a film before, I wanted to work with an experienced Black co-director who would have a shared knowledge of the experiences to be represented. I invited Toronto-based filmmaker Claire Prieto, who had just finished her film, *Home to Buxton*, to co-direct. Along with NFB producer Shelagh Mackenzie, we began the process that eventually led to the half-hour documentary, *Black Mother Black Daughter*.

The production team was racially mixed and the majority of the white team members had had little previous experience with, or exposure to, Black people. As a result, taking this team into the Black community and into Black women's homes involved more than just the usual preproduction sessions. We had to discuss history, culture and protocols to ensure that the team would understand, be sensitive to and respectful of the participants.

When I first approached a number of the women to participate in the film, they could not quite figure out why I wanted to make a film about them. No one had ever come to them with such a proposal before. They wondered what they could say that would be of interest to others. They lived ordinary lives and did what they had to do. After many discussions and several cups of tea, they realized that I was indeed serious and that I was really going to make this film. During the interviews for the film, the women spoke of family, not only in the nuclear sense but how it extended into the entire community. They spoke of their reliance on the land for the resources they needed to survive, a reliance which began with the earliest Black settlers in Nova Scotia and which is still demonstrated today in traditional crafts, market gardening and fabric weaving.

Black Mother Black Daughter was released in April 1989.[2] At the Halifax premiere, we had expected about three hundred people to attend the 8:00 p.m. screening. By 7:30 p.m., the Convention Centre was already filled and more seats had been added to accommodate five hundred people. In spite of this, there was still a line-up running along the full length of the hallway and continuing outside onto the street. Needless to say, we had not planned on a second screening. We quickly changed this decision and informed the people waiting that the film would be shown a second time. I remember walking among the crowd and people telling me they were not going anywhere, they were waiting for a second showing. In Toronto, a similar phenomenon took place when the film was screened at the St. Lawrence Centre. At both premieres, at least nine hundred to a thousand people came out. Since then, the film has been featured in festivals around the world. One of its most recent screenings was in January 1998, in Guadeloupe, where it was screened in two locations on this French-speaking Caribbean island. It is also shown in many schools, universities and community settings across Canada to audiences as young as seven and eight years of age.

Without fail, following each of the screenings, individuals of African descent would comment on how grateful they were to have been given images of themselves. Non-African people would tell me how amazed they were to learn this history — a history they knew nothing about, that they had not been taught in school or university. Certainly, no one was more surprised and elated at the response to this film than the women who appeared in it. Although several of these women, including my mother Marie, have died since its release, a small chapter of their lives remains open.

Film is at once powerful and engaging. It is also the costliest of artistic media. Consequently, the form itself brings a wealth of challenges and pressures requiring deft negotiation. In the film, I wanted to represent elements of the cultural fabric that came from the women themselves and from their use of language. For example, the common use of oratory, as in church prayers and testimony, expresses emotion and evokes a sense of being connected to others and to a higher spiritual power. During the initial stages of the project's development, I was not planning to be a participant in the film. As we continued the research and production, it made sense to include myself since it seemed the best way to tell this particular story. It was a record of how I was seeing these women, not necessarily how others might see them but how I did. Moreover, I had a personal connection with most of them and it would have been dishonest to pretend that I did not.

Film is an artistic medium and aesthetics are as important as content. Both interweave to give the work its feel. *Black Mother Black Daughter* emanated from a unique cultural context and a point of view, and, as such, presented images on screen that had never before been seen. Music, archival text, moving and still images, as well as sound, were combined to evoke a sense of place for the women and the communities represented in the film.

In telling their stories, we also used the work of local artists, musicians and poets. For example, an a capella quartet called Four the Moment performed *Lydia Jackson,* a poem written by poet George E. Clarke and set to music by Delvina Bernard. The song tells the true story of a Black Loyalist woman who, in 1783, was tricked by a prominent Nova Scotian doctor into signing a falsified indenture agreement.[3] The theme song for the film, *I Love You Woman,* with its refrain "Black mother black daughter," was written by Delvina Bernard after she had read the initial proposal I had written for the film, but long before the production began. It became a standing joke between us that Four the Moment was all over the country singing a theme song for a film that did not yet exist.

I believe every filmmaker/researcher/academic must acknowledge her own power, privilege and authority, because with power and privilege comes the moral and ethical responsibility to the individuals being studied or filmed. I think that one of the fundamental and essential principles of filmmaking must be respect for the lives being examined. This is the other "r" word, Aretha Franklin's "r" word, which is absent so much of the time from a great deal that we all do day in and day out. I have witnessed research that lacks this essential element. In carrying out my own work, I have tried to ensure that this principle is one that guides, informs and grounds me in the subject matter at hand.

ACTIVIST MOTHERS, MOTHERS AS ACTIVISTS

A key theme that emerges in *Black Mother Black Daughter* is the steady cross- and intergenerational involvement of Black women in their homes, churches and communities. Their lives are not compartmentalized — there was and is an interconnection, a cross-over among and within these spheres.

The film represents the women I had personally known and observed growing up in a small Black community: women who were Sunday school teachers in African Baptist churches, in the women's groups in the church and at the core of a variety of community-based educational and social justice organizations. They were mothers, grandmothers, foster mothers, stepmothers, godmothers, daughters, sisters, aunts and, importantly, midwives. These women were active in all of these spheres and in all of these roles, and they were as equally active in their churches.

The centrality of Black women's involvement in the Black Baptist Church is explored at length in Evelyn Brooks Higginbotham's *Righteous Discontent: The Women's Movement in the Black Baptist Church 1880–1920*. Brooks Higginbotham states that this time period was considered the women's era and the "nadir" in American race relations, and that:

> women were crucial to broadening the public arm of the church and making it the most powerful institution of racial self-help in the African American Community ... The church served as the most effective vehicle by which men and women alike, pushed down by racism and poverty, grouped and rallied against emotional and physical defeat.[4]

She argues that Black women were advocates of women's voting rights and of women's equality rights in employment and education. Further, she points out that "Black women drew upon the Bible, the most respected source within their community, to fight for women's rights in the church and society at large ... [and] during the nineteenth century they developed a distinct discourse of resistance, a feminist theology."[5]

The activism within the church, as examined by Brooks Higginbotham, was not limited to the Baptist denomination. Cheryl Townsend-Gilkes, in her exploration of women's traditions in the "Sanctified Church," found that women in this church:

> created for themselves a variety of roles, careers and organization with great influence but with variable access to structural authority ... In a variety of ways, their efforts are related to those women in other Black religious and secular organizations.[6]

Lillian Williams, in writing about Black women activists and reformers in Buffalo, New York, between 1900 and 1940, asserts that Black women were engaged in a persistent struggle for change, and that "these reformers embodied a protest tradition that had manifested itself in the secular and religious organizations of Buffalo's Black community during the nineteenth century."[7] Williams cites Mary Burnette Talbert, an activist in Buffalo, to demonstrate the wide scope of this work. Speaking to delegates at the 1916 National Association of Coloured Women Convention, Talbert urged her colleagues to "take an active personal interest in everything that concerns the welfare of the home, church, community, state and country, for, once they have struck out in this great work, they are doing the work of God."[8] This explicit message parallels the mission statement announced by the Ladies Auxiliary of the African United Baptist Association (AUBA) of Nova Scotia one year later, in 1917.[9]

In Nova Scotia, it is striking to see the familial patterns of participation of grandmothers, mothers, daughters, aunts and cousins in the Ladies Auxiliary of the AUBA, other women's groups in the African Baptist Church and in the overall community. For example, Gertrude Smith was born in East Preston, a small village near Dartmouth, in 1898. Affectionately known to many as "Nan Smith," Gertrude was a dedicated member and organizer of women's activity in the African

Baptist Church and also in the Halifax community where she lived after she was married. She was involved in the Gleaner's Women's Group and the Gleaner's Club. A number of young women who moved into Halifax from rural areas to go to school or to work often lived with Nan Smith. Doreen Paris, the current president of the African United Baptist Women's Institute, and my sister Janet lived at her home. Gertrude Smith's daughter, Bernice Powell, used to speak about how determined her mother was to serve the community and how she stayed involved even in the later years of her life — even after a serious illness that resulted in the amputation of both her legs. Like her mother, Bernice Powell was a member of the women's groups of Cornwallis Street Baptist Church and was active in community affairs. Gertrude Smith died in 1982 at eighty-four years of age.

Muriel States was Gertrude Smith's contemporary as well as her colleague. Born in 1888 in Avonport, Nova Scotia, she was the only girl in a family of six brothers. She became an official organizer for women's groups in the AUBA, work she undertook for some forty years. One of the paid positions she held was as a supervisor of girls at the Nova Scotia Home for Coloured Children. Her activism strongly influenced the next two generations of women in her family. One of her daughters, Patricia Riley, was a school teacher and active member of the Victoria Road Baptist Church women's group. Her granddaughter Sherolynn Riley, also a school teacher, is the current president of the George Washington Carver Credit Union, one of the only Black banking institutions in Canada. As an elder, Muriel States was a model of commitment. She died in 1984 at the age of ninety-five.

After raising her family, Wilena Jones went back to school at the age of sixty and graduated in 1975 with a teaching certificate. She was active in church and community work for many years and influenced at least three generations of activists in her family. Her own daughters, Janis Jones-Darrell, and Lynn and Debbie Jones, became involved in educational, social, cultural and political movements during the 1960s. Today, they are active in the African Baptist Church and in organizations which focus on social justice and equality issues.

Wilena's granddaughter Tracey Jones, the daughter of long-time Nova Scotian community activists Joan and Burnley (Rocky) Jones, is the head librarian at Halifax's North Branch Library. This library has developed a very community-centred approach to its programming and services and is a regular meeting place for a variety of organizations in the Halifax area. Tracey's advocacy work has involved race relations with the Halifax Police Department, literacy and educational initiatives, and issues of concern to women and children.[10]

The community-based activism that began in Nova Scotia during the 1940s and 1950s was taking place within the broad North American context that saw African-Americans' increased advocacy for civil rights as full and equal citizens. These same issues were in evidence in the work of Nova Scotia's voluntary organizations such as the Nova Scotia Association for the Advancement of Coloured People, the Coloured Citizen's Improvement League, the Nova Scotia Home for Coloured Children and the African United Baptist Association. Women were key players in these groups.

The fact that women organized and acted within the public sphere is not surprising. They, as were their male counterparts, were denied basic rights on the basis of race. In a similar manner to the women in Williams's study, African Nova Scotian women were involved in gender-specific groups as well as in mixed-gender groups. Their lives were simultaneously private and public, since they worked inside the home, in work sites outside the home and in a variety of community settings. For them, race was not a factor that they could ignore or remove from the way their lives were constructed. For example, if they were looking for domestic work outside the home, they were forced to respond to job ads that specified "coloured girl" wanted.

The African United Baptist Women's Institute is the umbrella organization for the women's groups within the AUBA and includes the Ladies Auxiliary, the Helping Hand Society and the Women's Missionary Society. The Institute meets annually and has been doing so since the early 1950s when it was established. This annual meeting is a further demonstration of intergenerational activism. Women greet and hug each other. A grandmother who is in her eighties attends with her daughter and perhaps her sister. They gather as if it were a family reunion and are adorned in what we would call some "serious hats." These amazing hats, decorated with feathers and nets and in pastels or deep colours, are, in many ways, symbolic of the many "hats" the women wear in the community. The issues they address represent their concern for and activism in their community. At the 1996 annual meeting, for example, a major report on a project dealing with violence against women in Black communities was presented to the membership. It laid out a detailed action plan for the Women's Institute's continuing work on the issue.[11]

CONCLUSION

As I reflect on my work, it is clear to me that the roles African Baptist women play as mothers, activists and advocates are characterized by the ideals of collective action, self-improvement, community betterment and equality. For the older generation of women, the fact that they might not see the desired changes they fought for in their lifetime did not diminish their energy, drive and commitment. Knowing that the struggle would be a long one, they passed their ideals and goals for change on to their daughters. If not in our lifetime, they reasoned, then in our children's. As my film and research work proceeds, and as I continue hearing more stories from Baptist women, I reconfirm what I already knew — that there is still so much more to explore and learn from their life stories.

By the time *Black Mother Black Daughter* opened, eight years after my mother and I first presented our dialogue at the CRIAW conference, I moved from being a daughter to also becoming a mother. My daughter Shani is thirteen years old. She was two years old when *Black Mother Black Daughter* was released. On one occasion, after a rather lengthy interview about the film before one of its premieres, a female newspaper reporter told me she really felt sorry for my daughter because she would have to live with racism and her life would not be easy. My response to her was that she need not worry about my daughter and how she would fare because her family and community would do everything possible to give her a strong sense of self-identity. Instead, I suggested to the reporter that she would do better to concern herself with what she was teaching her daughter and son at home. If our children were to meet one another, I wondered if her son and daughter would be disrespectful to my daughter because of her race.

In my work I have tried to portray the lives of African Nova Scotian women as more than mere subjects for sociological inquiry, which has so often pathologized and problematized people, especially women, of African descent. It is of utmost importance to me that we women of African descent count our lives as worthy and valuable. Equally crucial is the ongoing necessity of inculcating this sense of worth, identity and value in our daughters.

Notes

1. Marie Hamilton and Sylvia Hamilton, Dialogue Transcript, CRIAW Conference, Halifax, 1981. In the author's possession.
2. *Black Mother Black Daughter*, National Film Board of Canada Distribution Library, Montreal, 1989.
3. The story of Lydia Jackson is recounted in C. B. Fergusson, ed., *Clarkson's Mission to America 1791–1792* (Halifax: Public Archives of Nova Scotia, 1971), 89–90.
4. Evelyn Brooks Higginbotham, *Righteous Discontent: The Women's Movement in the Black Baptist Church 1880–1920* (Cambridge: Harvard University Press, 1993), 1.
5. Ibid., 2.
6. Cheryl Townsend-Gilkes, "Together in the Harness: Women's Traditions in the Sanctified Church," in Darlene Clark Hine, ed., *Black Women in American History: The Twentieth Century*, Vol. 2 (Brooklyn: Carlson Publishing, 1990), 379.
7. Lillian Williams, "And Still I Rise: Black Women and Reform, Buffalo, New York, 1890–1940," in Darlene Clark Hine, Wilma King, and Linda Reed, eds., *We Specialize in the Wholly Impossible: A Reader in Black Women's History* (Brooklyn: Carlson Publishing, 1995), 521.
8. Ibid.
9. The mission statement of the Ladies Auxiliary outlined their responsibility for "the stimulation of the spiritual, moral, social, educational, charitable and financial work of all the local churches of the African United Baptist Association." As reported in the Minutes of the African United Baptist Association of Nova Scotia, 1917. Maritime Baptist Historical Collection, Acadia University, Wolfville, Nova Scotia.
10. Wilena, Janis, Lynn and Tracey appear in the documentary film *Against the Tides: The Jones Family*, which I directed. It was part of a four-hour television mini-series about the history and contributions of Black people to the development of Canada. It was conceived and produced by Almeta Speaks of Toronto. Almeta Speaks Productions, *Hymn To Freedom*, Toronto 1994, Distributed International Telefilm, Toronto.
11. African United Baptist Association of Nova Scotia Women's Institute, Family Violence Workshops, Provincial Plan of Action, 1996. In the author's possession. This

report articulates the following specific mission statement regarding violence against women: "The Women's Institute of the African United Baptist Association of Nova Scotia, Canada, [has] awakened to the scope and nature of family violence threatening the Black Family. We will continue to seek ways to enable the Women's Institute through its member groups to advocate against violence both outside the church and within. We as God's people will learn and undertake strategies to confront this global crisis, from which we are not exempt."

Part IV

MULTIPLE IDENTITIES
OF MOTHERHOOD:
RIGHTS, CHOICES
AND DIVERGENCE

Chapter 15

THE OTHER WITHIN THE SELF:

BLACK DAUGHTER, WHITE MOTHER AND
THE NARRATIVE CONSTRUCTION
OF IDENTITY

Elizabeth Yeoman

IN THE FILM *Secrets and Lies,* Hortense, the Black heroine, seeks out her birth mother and is stunned to discover that she is white.[1] For my own daughter, Ilse, realizing that she was a different colour than her white mother was a much more gradual process. She learned this not so much through observation of physical characteristics as through discourses that taught her that people could be categorized according to these characteristics, and that the categories mattered. In this chapter, I examine stories from our family's oral history as social construction, and the conflicts between discourses about race and gender in certain narratives. In doing this, I hope to accomplish three things: to illustrate the importance of narrative forms of history in how we learn to think about ourselves, to show how complex this learning process can be and to try to find ways (that may also benefit others) in which to retell the narratives of our family history for my daughter.

There is a story about my great-great-grandmother, who was an early European settler in New Zealand, and how she "rode a hundred miles alone, while eight months pregnant, so her baby could be delivered by a white woman." When I first heard this story, as a teenager, I interpreted it unproblematically as a narrative (one of many in my family) about intrepid womanhood. A photograph of another ancestor, on my father's side, shows a woman with a full mouth, dark curly hair and eyes so dark they look black. I suggested to my mother that she may have been of partly African ancestry. "Not in that family!" my mother exclaimed. Why not? Because we know they were racists? Because a further back ancestor trafficked in slaves? All the more reason to believe they (and I) would have some of the blood of those slaves in our own veins, I would think. But that is not the story my mother likes to tell, or — I am sure — that they would have told themselves. After my own children were born, I gradually realized that my choice of stories and the ways I told them would have to be re-examined. Although many of our family narratives were about strong women, they were also told from positions of privilege at the expense of other women (and indeed men as well) — servants, slaves, factory workers, colonized peoples.

Penelope Lively writes of a past that is "more myth than history and all the better for it."[2] In this chapter, I talk about the past in this sense, as what we *believe* we know about our own history and how we use it to make sense of the present. While I do not agree that we are necessarily "all the better for it," I do believe that this is one of the ways in which history *matters*. Certain historical narratives and metanarratives become part of popular imagination. In this sense, neither literature nor oral history nor myth are completely dissociable from more traditional forms of history and all play a role in how we understand and act upon present-day events. An examination of family oral history/mythology can be a way into a clearer understanding of broader historical and cultural frameworks. As Jane Lazarre argues, "the unnatural split between individual and historical consciousness, where the one seems to emerge and prevail wholly independent of the other is ... part of an ideology of individualism fraught with false stories which are dangerous to personal as well as political life."[3]

NARRATIVES OF MY CHILDHOOD

According to family tradition, my female ancestors were endlessly brave. As well as my great-great-grandmother who rode alone through rough country while eight months pregnant, another navigated a ship to the new world when the captain and first mate both died en route, still another went alone to England to plead (successfully) in person with the king for a pension for her sickly husband, and my own grandmother supposedly swam with crocodiles and rode an elephant across India. She told me about the crocodiles when I, as a child, wept with fear at the sight of a leach. Her stories were Kiplingesque, although I believe and hope there was also something of Mrs. Moore in *A Passage to India* in her — something of a person who tried, at least, to understand and to respect, who was frustrated by the colonial system, even though she benefited from it. As a child, I was fascinated by her stories. I longed to travel and have adventures in distant lands as she had. If I grew up to be an adventurous and independent person, I believe it was in large part because of my grandmother's stories, which made anything seem possible and gender no obstacle. And yet ... when I was in my early twenties, my grandfather said casually to me that my grandmother had never liked India, that this was a main reason they had left long before the British had to leave. This is what makes me reflect now that, while she gloried in the adventurous stories she told, she was probably too independent and democratic to have really enjoyed the highly structured and circumscribed life of a British colonial in India. Her oral history probably bore only a tenuous connection to the original experience, but it was what made it possible for her to talk about it at all and for me, many years later, to believe I too could be brave.

It's difficult to talk about this personal history, and the racism and imperialism behind it. Painful now to realize, as I did not when I was a child, that the bravery of my female ancestors was empowered, directly or indirectly, by the oppression of others and that their stories must mean something very different for my daughter. Can they be retold for her, told differently? They have probably been altered and are far from being precise, factual truths by the time they are told to us anyway. For example, was our foremother really able to navigate a ship through her knowledge of mathematics? Indeed it might be possible to document this through research. It might also be important to try to do this as part of the project of recovering women's history. But what I am interested in here are very different questions about history, the questions of which stories we choose to tell, how we tell them, and what happens when discourses of race, gender and class conflict within a narrative. We cannot deny the complexities of our own histories or erase the painful parts, but we also need stories that situate us in time and place and give us courage to carry on. Carolyn Steedman, discussing differences between autobiography and historiography, emphasizes that in autobiography an event can be *psychologically* true, despite questions as to its historical veracity.[4] But an obvious (to present-day feminists anyway) psychological truth about the abilities and competences of women, threading its way through the narratives of my family, finds itself in constant conflict with the more bitter and painful truths of racism and classism.

My sister tells me the same stories overwhelmed her anyway, made her feel she could never live up to such standards of intrepidity, forced her to dwell introspectively on what she is and is not. Out of this introspection, however, came the insight that, in the dominant narratives of our family, it was the women who were strong and daring, who survived. The men, she pointed out, drawing on other narratives familiar to both of us, were a sorry lot, dying of pneumonia after refusing to take off wet socks, committing suicide by tying shoelaces together and jumping off a bridge, being eaten by cannibals and haunted by the ghost of a slighted wife. In these stories, they are the "other" — their narrative purpose is to highlight the competence of their wives, daughters, mothers and sisters. However, there are two layers of "others" here, for behind the visible other, the man, is the almost *in*visible other, the non-European. Theorists like Chinua Achebe, Toni Morrison and Edward Said have shown how the primitive or exotic dark skinned other was and is essential to European and white colonial narratives.[5] This other serves as a foil, contrasting and therefore highlighting the "civilization" of the white. So it was in our own family. The slaves sold by one ancestor, the cannibals who ate another, form nameless, voiceless backdrops to our chronicles, illuminating our own civilized state. Rarely are they mentioned in so many words and when they are, it is only to add local colour. The cannibals were, in a strange way, a mere detail in a chilling story about a great-great-uncle. The selling of slaves I found out for myself in a book about the history of Black Maritimers.

NARRATIVES OF MOTHERHOOD

I discovered the story of the selling of slaves when my own children were small. It took the form of a letter quoted in full in which my ancestor gives detailed instructions for the sale of a shipload of slaves upon arrival in St. John, New Brunswick. I showed this evidence to the children's father, who is himself descended from slaves. A year or two later, after we had divorced, they returned home from a visit to him and said to me accusingly, "Papy says you have an ancestor who sold slaves!" "Well, he's your ancestor too," I answered, "and Papy probably has ancestors who sold slaves too." I did not know what else to say, but the exchange troubled me. I suppose we all want admirable ancestors to offer our children and sometimes we don't know how to incorporate other kinds of stories into our family histories.

In reading Alice Walker's description of her great-great-great-great-grandmother, a former slave who outlived "almost everyone who'd ever owned her,"[6] a woman of courage and spirit, a survivor, I felt a certain envy, not so much for my own sake as for my daughter's. Our own ancestors, at least the ones who got talked about, may also have had courage and spirit but were imbrued with imperialism and privilege at the expense of others. About Ilse's father's ancestors I know nothing, and nor does he: he professes disinterest in roots, believes they are unimportant, perhaps in response to the pain of his own ruptured background, abandoned as a child by his father, his mother the intelligent and beautiful but rejected daughter of a Black Haitian servant and her white German employer. He cannot help me and I do not know how to be a white mother of Black children. Oral history and other narrative forms are only a part of this problem of mothering, but an important part, I believe.

Patricia Williams tells how her white friends draw on the Cinderella narrative to give meaning to their own lives, and how they attempt to impose it on her as well. (She should try harder with her appearance and make more effort to be "nice," and then she would meet someone appropriate to marry and live happily ever after.) She argues that this narrative is meaningless to her. Within her grandmother's memory were stories of runaway slaves and these were the narratives that shaped her childhood and beyond. She eloquently describes what she learned about life from oral history:

> [W]hite knights just don't play the same part in my mythical landscape of desire ... [T]he stories my mother raised me on

[were] about [women] who harbored impossible dreams of love for lost mates who had been sold down rivers of tears to oblivion ... Cinderellas who had burned their masters' beds and then fled for their lives ... women who invented their own endings, even when they didn't get to live happily or very long thereafter.[7]

When Ilse was younger, I used to assume that she *did* need the fairy tales that I grew up with, but with Black heroines. She seemed to love those old stories. But, in response to them she asked questions like, "What colour was Sleeping Beauty?" and, "Aren't there any *black* mermaids?"— questions I would never have thought of as a child, because, for a white child, colour is not an issue. It is assumed that the characters are white unless stated otherwise. We had to seek out or invent stories with heroines who looked like Ilse. She was always more comfortable with visual art than with words and I remember her drawing page after page of black and brown mermaids after seeing the Disney film *The Little Mermaid.*

Toni Morrison[8] writes about the visibility of the white and the invisible presence of the Black other, the pervasiveness of the assumption that it is white experience that matters. So is my daughter the invisible other, the exotic backdrop to her own ancestors, her own mother? Yet also of our blood and sharing our history? Her question about the colour of Sleeping Beauty, was in fact one that, as a young child, she asked frequently when I began to read a new story. It seemed as though she needed to know the colour of the protagonists before she could begin to identify with them. And, despite many years of work by multiculturalists and antiracists, there are very few children's books with Black characters (between 1 percent and 2 percent of all American children's books recently published)[9] and many of those that do exist portray these characters as victims, if not villains, or as minor characters rather than protagonists.[10] These figures are probably comparable in Canada. There is a reason white children simply assume the narratives they hear are peopled by other whites, whereas Black children need to ask about race.

I am aware, in writing this, that I am referring to my daughter as Black, when, in fact, she is more than half white. It also occurs to me that a paper entitled "Black Mother, White Daughter" would be much less likely because the daughter of a Black mother would, in most cases, still learn to see herself as a person of colour. The only time I ever remember Ilse referring to herself as white (and she often talked about race and difference) was when, at age six, she attended ballet classes in Toronto's Chinatown. The teacher and the other students were all of Chinese descent. When a neighbour's child, who was white, asked Ilse if she was the only Black girl in her ballet class, she replied "No, I'm the only white girl." The only way she could ever see herself as white, despite her white ancestry, was when it was in opposition to yet another (in this case Chinese) other. And yet her family history is peopled by the colonizers and the colonized, the slaves and the slave owners, by women who navigated ships and became suffragettes from a background of privilege, and by women who were stolen and sold and perhaps who burned their masters' beds and fled for their lives.

THEORY OF HYBRIDITY

Ngugi wa Thiong'o[11] and other postcolonial writers have suggested that one way of counteracting racist discourses produced by narratives in which it is white experience that matters is for Black Africans to work in their own traditional languages and to return to their cultural roots. This is an important possibility for many formerly colonized people but there are millions more who in their *own* history, their *own* narratives, know the tales and the languages of colonizer and colonized. Black feminist writer Patricia Hill Collins argues, from a very different background, that the fundamental problem is one of dichotomous thinking. In defining ourselves in oppositional terms we create a world where "[o]ne part is not simply different from its counterpart; it is inherently opposed to its other." A Black feminist project then, according to Collins, should begin from a more inclusive position of "both/and" rather than "either/or."[12] Notions of hybridity within the postcolonial literature are also helpful here. Homi Bhabha writes of an "occult instability which presages powerful cultural changes," and suggests that "the theoretical recognition of the split-space of enunciation may open the way to conceptualizing an international culture, based not on the exoticism or multi-culturalism of the *diversity* of cultures, but on the inscription and articulation of culture's *hybridity*."[13] Edward Kamau

Brathwaite describes the friction caused by the confrontation of slave and slave owner as "cruel but also creative." Like Bhabha, he emphasizes the rich possibility inherent in the hybridization of cultures: "Nothing is really fixed and monolithic. Although there is white/brown/black, there are infinite possibilities within these distinctions and many ways of asserting identity."[14]

Despite the now clichéd but still important feminist principle that the personal is political, it is often painful and difficult to use one's own life (let alone the life of one's child) as research material. However, it offers a lens, with which I am more than familiar, for examining discrepancies and conflicting sites of engagement. Through the complexities of negotiating what it means to be a woman in our family, I can explore aspects of what it means to be a woman in the world. Because of the fact that my children are seen as Black my world has become more difficult but infinitely richer. I did not foresee this before they were born. However, I was always interested in identity, origins and narrative. Inventing new stories for my children forced me to recognize biases and omissions (enormous omissions) I might never have seen otherwise. Being forced to confront both racism and the complexities of hybrid identity on their behalf made my life more complex and painful but also prevented me from being satisfied with a unified identity and history. It is because of my children's constantly asking, "What colour are they?" as I read to them, that I came to realize the importance of colour to them. Until then I was "blind" to colour, because to me it had never mattered.

More recently I have also learned the powerful potential of disrupting commonly accepted racial categories. On the one hand, my children have been forced to be Black whether they wanted to or not because of the way others see them. On the other hand, asserting a mixed identity can contribute to making such categorization more difficult. Maureen Reddy argues that this "destabilizes racial categories and points up their arbitrary nature. If one is neither black nor white, but *both* black *and* white, then the boundaries between racial categories are shown to be fluid rather than rigid."[15]

Practice: Mothering, Narrative and Hybridity

Six years ago my work brought us to Newfoundland, a place with a very different history from either the Maritimes or Ontario, the two places my children and I had lived previously. Newfoundlanders tend to see themselves as kind and hospitable people. Many people do not seem to believe that racism exists here, or that it can touch their close-knit homogeneous communities. Their strong sense of regional identity and the economic and environmental problems of their own region contribute to this view. And yet both my son and my daughter have experienced various forms of racism, including being called nigger by strangers in the street and being beaten up, being told by a teacher that the racism was in their heads and by another that my son's dreadlocks were "sloppy" and had nothing to do with culture. Other writers have documented how many white people deny the existence of racism in their communities and talk about it as if it were in the past or elsewhere.[16] Such attitudes are not peculiar to Newfoundland. I also want to add that yet another teacher handled a racist incident in the playground more sensitively and effectively than I could have myself and that my son has some caring teachers and scores of friends. But my daughter, Ilse, has left Newfoundland and gone to live with friends in Toronto, so isolated and "different" did she feel here.

When I presented some of the material from this paper at a conference, a young woman, the daughter of an Anglo-Canadian mother and a Nigerian father living in Quebec, as I learned later, listened intently to my discussion of hybridity. When I had finished my presentation, she responded by telling some of her own story, experiences of racism in an all-white community and within her own extended family, the richness and the pain of learning to negotiate a hybrid identity. She was passionate and articulate and I believe everyone present was greatly moved by her story. My narrative seemed to provide space for hers in some way. She told me afterwards that she had never talked about this aspect of her life before in public.

I still have not found adequate ways of providing space for my own daughter's narrative. She continues to draw people (no longer mermaids) of all shades, and she surrounds herself with friends of diverse and often hybrid backgrounds. She still lives in Toronto, in large part, I believe, so as to be able to do this, to have a context in which her own narrative becomes meaningful. For now this is her response to a complex problem of identity.

Other responses can be found in sometimes painful retellings of old stories, acknowledging, for example, that racism and the legacy of slavery are not only an American problem, not only someone else's history. As well, we can invent new stories. Within Homi Bhabha's Third Space is the possibility of such narratives, stories of hybridity that recognize the complexities of history rather than its mythic simplicities, yet speak to us also in profound psychological truths. What I have learned from my daughter is the importance of finding this possibility and expanding its creative potential.

For Ilse and for Shari Okeke

Notes

1. In laying out the framework of this chapter, I need to explain the terms I use in my discussion of race. Racial categories are never clear or measurable. Rather, they are constructed in various ways through discourse and discursive practices. Thus, to talk about race is meaningless in a biological sense, and polysemic and ideological in a historical one. However, we are forced to acknowledge the impact of its construction every day because of events and human interactions. For the most part, I use the terms "Black" and "white" here, because to be more specific is complicated, and I need terms to describe perceived difference, marked and unmarked categories imposed on us by society. Thus I write that I am white, although I may have Black ancestors, and that my daughter is Black despite the fact that she has a white mother. Whether we like it or not, we are what the world sees.

2. Penelope Lively, *Moon Tiger* (London: Penguin, 1987), 189.

3. Jane Lazarre, *Beyond the Whiteness of Whiteness* (Durham, NC: Duke University Press, 1996), xviii.

4. Carolyn Steedman, *Past Tenses: Essays on Writing, Autobiography and History* (London: Rivers Oram Press, 1992), 42.

5. Chinua Achebe, "An Image of Africa," *Christian Science Monitor* (1975); Toni Morrrison, *Playing in the Dark* (Cambridge, MA: Harvard University Press, 1992); Edward Said, *Orientalism* (New York: Ranom House, 1978).

6. Alice Walker, *Anything We Love Can Be Saved* (New York: Random House, 1997), xiii.

7. Patricia Williams, "My Best White Friend: Cinderella Revisited," *New Yorker* (February 26 and March 4, 1996), 94.

8. Morrison, *Playing in the Dark.*

9. Kathryn Reimer, "Multiethnic Literature: Holding Fast to Dreams," *Language Arts* 69 (January 1992).

10. Joel Taxel, "The Black in Children's Fiction: Controversies Surrounding Award Winning Books," *Curriculum Inquiry* 16, no. 3 (1986).

11. Ngugi wa Thiong'o, *Decolonising the Mind: The Politics of Language in African Literature* (London: James Currey, 1981).

12. Patricia Hill Collins, *Black Feminist Thought: Knowledge, Consciousness, and the Politics of Empowerment* (New York: Routledge, 1991), 50.

13. Homi Bhabha, "Cultural Diversity and Cultural Differences," in Bill Ashcroft, Gareth Griffiths, and Helen Tiffin, eds., *The Post-Colonial Studies Reader* (London: Routledge, 1995), 209. Emphasis in original.

14. Edward Kamau Brathwaite, "Creolization in Jamaica," in Ashcroft, Griffiths and Tiffin, eds., *The Post-Colonial Studies Reader*, 205.

15. Maureen Reddy, *Crossing the Color Line: Race, Parenting and Culture* (New Brunswick, NJ: Rutgers University Press, 1994), 76. Emphasis in original.

16. Both Jane Lazarre and Maureen Reddy give numerous examples of this phenomenon in their books, cited in notes 3 and 15 respectively.

Chapter 16

EMANCIPATED SUBJECTIVITIES AND THE SUBJUGATION OF MOTHERING PRACTICES

Mielle Chandler

PROLOGUE

A DOG JUMPED and the three of them had to be scraped off the tarmac. This is what I think when the child tells me: "I want a motorcycle and a fast car." The child who cannot yet ride a two wheeler without training wheels wants a motorcycle and a fast car. The negotiation is starting early — I wasn't expecting this for another ten years or so.

A dog jumped and the three of them had to be scraped off the tarmac and I didn't go to the mourning. I got the news in bits and pieces on my answering machine. At first because I wasn't home when the phone rang and then, after that, because I wouldn't answer it.

A dog jumped and the three of them had to be scraped off the tarmac and I didn't go the the mourning because I didn't want my GPA to drop. It was in grave danger of doing so, you see, because I'd yelled at the elementary school principal and counsellor and the lady at the ministry and the after-school care person all on the same day about three weeks earlier. I'd burned those bridges right to the ground — no childcare, no childcare subsidy, no kindergarten class to send the child off to for a couple of hours a day — and then I had to call my professors and try to explain why it was I didn't think I could make it to class and could I please have an extension on that paper because I won't even be able to turn on my computer until about ten every night and by then I'm tired. Tired.

A dog jumped and the three of them had to be scraped off the tar-mac and I didn't go to the mourning because I didn't want my GPA to drop. I needed every spare second to myself. I needed every spare second to myself to work on my papers. My papers. My papers which are about how we fundamentally are in-relation with. And here I was refusing to be in-relation with community because I was too in-relation with child to be able to be separate enough to struggle with Descartes, with Nietzsche, with Marx, with Mouffe, with Rawls in order to satisfy a GPA requirement which I needed in order to eventually become an individual with enough credibility to argue that we are not individuals but in-relation with.

I refused to be in-relation with others in grief in order to be in-relation with text in order to affirm that we are necessarily, rightly, importantly, crucially in-relation with.

A dog jumped and the three of them had to be scraped off the tar-mac and I didn't go to the mourning because I didn't want my GPA to drop. What have I become?

•

To write a paper is to leave mothering, or, rather, it is to leave the type of subjectivity I engage in while mothering. A clean break is neither possible nor desirable, mothering being my topic, and so integral to my identity. Indeed, to leave it would be to become someone completely different. As I write, a child asleep in the next room, part of me is still on duty, ready to battle dream monsters or change wet sheets, making a mental note to tell the babysitter (that is, the stand-in mother whose labour affords me, temporarily, a paper-writing subjectivity) that the child can't go swimming tomorrow (I'm worried the cold might turn into an ear infection), adding granola bars to the shopping list. The process is one of travelling between an individuated and separated subjectivity which allows me to write, and an actively in-relation subjectivity (if it can be called a subjectivity) which is born of mothering. It is an existence fraught with tension, for while each site demands my attention, the former requiring quiet sustained concentration, the latter the alertness of a catcher behind home plate, neither allows me to inhabit the other adequately.

A prejudice on which I build this text is that the conception of persons as separate autonomous beings has too long been predominant and privileged, that persons are also beings in-relation to and with. This idea exists in many discourses including ecological theories, economic theories, theories of socialization and consciousness, and linguistic theories. It is my position that although persons are not only autonomous, unitary, separated individuals but rather fundamentally, and at every level, encumbered; nonetheless, much modern western philosophy not only posits the self as separated, but esteems this separation as the basis of "freedom." Freedom, understood in this sense, is a fallacy — the esteeming of which constitutes one of the factors that enables and perpetuates the devalued status of the blatantly encumbered: mothers. In this chapter I deal specifically with an aspect of much feminist and lesbian feminist theory: a privileging of the emancipated subject, the free and autonomous, separated self.

In recent history, cultural feminism has tended to revalue mothering through celebrating it as a "feminine" trait, while radical feminism has tended toward a rejection of mothering, formulating it as a patriarchally defined and oppressive role of women.[1] Liberal feminism has simply argued for "fairness," claiming that men should do more housework. All three positions I find inadequate and problematic, the first for its sex and gender essentialism, the second for its antinatalism and the third because sharing devalued labour does nothing to revalue it, it simply spreads what is devalued more evenly between more persons within heterosexual nuclear families. Recent developments in feminist queer theory, however, provide a nonessentialist framework for a deconstructive analysis of both the esteeming of the unencumbered separated subject and the devalued status of mothering.

"MOTHER" AS PRACTICE

"...*mothers* refers to the maternal function of women."[2] (Rosi Braidotti, feminist academic)

"... *motherhood* is men's appropriation of women's bodies as a resource to reproduce patriarchy."[3] (Jeffner Allen, radical lesbian feminist)

"... a mother is the person who constitutes the fall-back position. A mother is the person who is there when nobody else is and when all other systems have failed."[4] (Guy Allen, gay male mother)

"Mothers must militantly make it clear that they are not expendable ... Mothers everywhere must caucus, organise unions, and put an end to their isolation through collective action."[5] (Lucia Valeska, lesbian working-class mother)

"... 'maternal' is a social category."[6] (Sara Ruddick, white academic mother)

"During counselling they said that I don't see myself as separate from my kids. They say my kids are me and I am me, but it's like one entity."[7] (Martinique Somers, Black mother in Brooklyn)

It is my position that "mother" is best understood as a verb, as something one does, a practice which creates one's identity as intertwined, interconnected and in-relation. Mothering is not a singular practice, and mother is not best understood as a monolithic identity. Even among the low-income queer moms individuated by a panoptic welfare system in East Vancouver in the 1990s, the practices vary significantly. Who a mother is and what it means to be one is context-specific. I in no way wish to universalize my discussion of mother as practice. The examples I use and my understanding of practice is currently limited by the urban, western, nonaffluent, predominantly white, feminist sphere I inhabit.

Judith Butler speaks of gender as "a kind of becoming or activity," and claims that as such "gender ought not to be conceived as a noun or a substantial thing or a static cultural marker, but rather as an incessant and repeated action of some sort."[8] To be a woman is to consistently re-enact femininity; it is an imitation, a theatrically produced effect.[9] To be a lesbian, as far as I can tell, is to repetitively deviate from the heterosexual matrix in such a specifically regimented way as to be accepted by other lesbians as one. To be a mother is to enact mothering. It is a multifaceted and everchanging yet painfully repetitive performance which although, like "woman," involves the way one walks, talks, postures, dresses and paints one's face, orients these activities directly and instrumentally in-relation to and with the walking, talking, posturing, dressing, undressing, dressing, undressing, dressing, undressing and painting of face (or, rather, the washing of paint off of face) of another who, due to a relation of near-complete interdependence, is not separate.

The ongoing in-relation of wiping up vomit and taking temperatures, rocking to sleep, being interrupted, taking a shower only when the baby is asleep and then doing so very quickly lest it wake up, the act of being so in-relation to and with that one wakes up as one's milk begins to let down a minute before the baby wakes up to nurse, constructs one as something both more and less than an individual. To mother is to clean, to mop, to sweep, to keep out of reach, to keep safe, to keep warm, to feed, to take small objects out of mouths, to answer impossible questions, to … It is everfailing imitations of socially constructed ideals. It is a series of responses to the fundamental needs of another who is so interconnected with the self that there exists no definitive line of differentiation.[10] When one mothers one is not one's own person.

This is most acute when mothering an infant. Although one is not one's own person, one is not someone else's person either, for the infant is both and neither "other" than the mother and the same thing. It is widely acknowledged that infants and young children do not differentiate themselves from their mother.[11] When mothering practice is such that the young child does not differentiate itself from the mother, the lines may also disintegrate for the mother. In cases where the practising mother has also carried and given birth to the child, lines of differentiation may never have formed.[12] In summation, "mother" is an identity formed through a repetition of practices which constitute one as so profoundly interconnected that one is not one, *but is simultaneously more and less than one.*

PRACTICES OF SUBJECTIVITY: "ONE" AND "I"

There "is no reason," writes Butler, "to divide up human bodies into male and female sexes except that such a division suits the economic needs of heterosexuality and lends a naturalistic gloss to the institution of heterosexuality."[13] I would like to suggest that there is no reason to divide up human bodies at all. Doing so suits the needs of western liberal capitalist democracies and lends a naturalistic gloss to the institution of individuality. Indeed, conceiving of the self as anything but divided, separated, individuated, problematizes the very foundations of our (if "we" are members of a western liberal democratic capitalist state) social, economic, political and judicial systems and disrupts the foundation of even the updated versions of the Social Contract.

Monique Wittig describes gender in language as stripping women of subjectivity, "the most precious thing for a human being".[14] In an effort to destroy gender Wittig goes further than simply dividing up bodies and individuating persons. She erases the possibility of a self defined in-relation. For Wittig, subjectivity in and of itself is an emancipatory goal exemplified in the linguistic use of "I":

> Gender is ontologically a total impossibility. For when one becomes a locutor, when one says "I" and, in so doing, reappropriates language as a whole, proceeding from oneself alone, with the tremendous power to use all language, it is then and there, according to linguists and philosophers, that the supreme act of subjectivity, the advent of subjectivity into consciousness, occurs. It is when starting to speak that one becomes "I". This act — the becoming of the subject through the exercise of language and through locution — in order to be real, implies that the locutor be an absolute subject. For a relative subject is inconceivable, a relative subject could not speak at all.[15]

A relative subject, that is, a subject in-relation, then, is not a subject. Mothers, if understood as necessarily in-relation, are not subjects.[16] A similar sentiment can be found in Descartes statement that "dependence is manifestly a defect."[17] Indeed, Wittig's construction of subjectivity can be understood as Cartesian in a number of senses. Descartes constructs the world upon his own existence as a self-reflexive thinking subject. Wittig claims that with the speech act "I," which designates one as a self-reflexive thinking subject, "I reorganised the world from my point of view and through abstraction I lay claim to universality."[18] Although Wittig's "I" differs at a basic level from the Cartesian "I" in that it is discursive, it is fundamentally Cartesian in its centrality, in its universality and in its singularity. It is upon his own existence as a thinking subject that Descartes constructs the rest of the world. It is the linguistic representation of the thinking subject through the use of "I" which acts, for Wittig, as a central axis for the reorganization of the world. It is this particular "I" that Wittig posits as emancipatory.

Wittig's lesbian is, materially, such an "I." Lesbians, as escapees from slavery, live as "I's." While women are relegated by heterosexuality to nonsubjectivity, lesbians claim subjectivity by separating from sociopolitical and economic relations of subordination to men.[19] This emancipation comes in the form of Cartesian selfhood; it comes in the form of an individual subject: ungendered, universal and whole.[20]

Although to abolish the two-gendered system altogether would effectively nullify both classes, slaves and masters, Wittig's approach is to create a world of masters, a world of "I's" and "one's." Slavery is to be abhorred, shunned and escaped from. The universalization of the universal subject, the master, the individual in the paradigm of the Social Contract, is what is to be aimed at. It is what lies beyond the two-gendered system of heterosexuality that enslaves the class "women." The challenge maternity poses to both the Cartesian self and Wittig's emancipated "I" is a self in relation. It is a self symbiotically connected and within a bond of dependence. Perhaps as such the maternal self cannot be said to be a self. Perhaps this is an area where we must search for modes of being beyond subjectivity.

My concern is that in destroying the categories of sex and gender, what is created is a separated autonomous subjectivity as the only acceptable conception of selfhood. If the individual subject is understood as the only type that can lay claim to credibility by proclaiming itself "free" and "emancipated," the self as in-relation will become further marginalized, reviled and driven deeper into the closet. My concern is that a process of forced individuated freedom, while it may untie persons from specific gender identities, ties them instead to a specifically privileged type of subjectivity, a subjectivity the pronoun "one" is indicative of:

> There is in French, as there is in English, a munificent pronoun that is called the indefinite, which means that it is not marked by gender, a pronoun that you are taught in school to systematically avoid. It is *on* in French — *one* in English ... here is a subject pronoun which is very tractable and accommodating since it can be bent in several directions at the same time. First, as already mentioned, it is indefinite as far as gender is concerned. It can represent a certain number of people successively or all at once —

everybody, we, they, I, you, people, a small or large number of persons — and still stay singular.[21]

Mothers cannot properly be referred to with the pronoun "one." One (language becomes difficult here) is not singular when one mothers: one's identity is both plural (inclusive of the self and the child/ren) and less than singular (one is not one's own self, but an extension of the child/ren). If "woman" can be understood as a repetitive imitation of an illusive heterosexual original,[22] and "mother" as a set of practices in-relation with and to children, perhaps "one" can also be understood in action terms: as an enactment. Perhaps the pronoun "one," whether singular (designating one particular person), or plural (designating one of any number of people in general), is better understood as a verb-pronoun. "One," to again import Butler's structure, is perhaps an imitation for which there is no essential origin, a multiplicity of discursive constructions dating back at least as far as Descartes. Perhaps the individual subject is the naturalistic effect produced by centuries of repetition. As such it would be perpetually at risk, each site of repetition holding the potential (or posing the danger, depending how one looks at it) for coming undone, or at least for shifting. The individual subject, then, to further build on Butler's armature, is perhaps constituted as an effect of its expression, a constitution which gives the illusion of essence.[23]

INDIVIDUATION AND EMANCIPATION

Michel Foucault is one of the theorists who takes seriously a rethinking of both emancipation and subjectivity. In "The Subject and Power," an essay concerning how human beings are made subjects, Foucault outlines three forms of struggle: struggles against domination, struggles against exploitation and struggles against prescriptions of individuation and identity. It is the latter I am most interested in, though I am dubious as to its divisibility from the first two. This third type of struggle is against a government of individuation that "separates the individual, breaks his links with others, splits up community life, forces the individual back on himself and ties him to his own identity in a constraining way."[24] The idea I wish to put forth is that liberation itself constitutes a constraint to which the individual is tied. This kind of constraint can be seen in lesbian and feminist antinatalism which at one and the same time unties the identity "woman" from the identity "mother" and reties "woman" to an ideal of emancipated subjectivity. This untying and retying can be seen in the work of Simone de Beauvoir, which has been instrumental in shaping both the emancipatory project of, and conceptions of, maternity and motherhood in more contemporary feminist and lesbian feminist theory.

Instead of levying the allegation of antinatalism against de Beauvoir, I wish to agree that mothering does mean a loss of individual agency and autonomy for mothers. Indeed, in confining this loss of agency to the processes of pregnancy and birth, de Beauvoir does not go far enough. The loss of agency is most acute *after* the birth of a child, as I hope my characterization of mother as practice has illustrated. The problematic lies not in the equation of motherhood with nonsubjectivity but in the privileging of an emancipated individuated subjectivity. The two are nicely played out in the following quote:

> Ensnared by nature, the pregnant woman is plant and animal, a stock-pile of celluloids, an incubator, an egg; she scares children proud of their young, straight bodies and makes young people titter contemptuously because she is a human being, *a conscious and free individual, who has become life's passive instrument.*[25]

The anitnatalism of de Beauvoir can be read as an attempt to extricate the category "woman" from the prescriptivity of motherhood. As Linda Zerilli so aptly puts it, de Beauvoir's antinatalism "is a sophisticated and underappreciated feminist discursive strategy of defamiliarisation: a highly charged, always provocative, and at times enraging restaging of the traditional drama of maternity."[26] By retelling the maternal narrative as horrific, parasitic and alien, de Beauvoir allows women to see maternity as separate from their identities as women.

The problematic arises not with positing mother as nonsubject in this process of extrication, but rather with the *depriviledging* of mother nonsubjectivity, with representing mother nonsubjectivity in such a way as to elicit scorn, contempt, pity and the charge of self-enslavement. That maternity "robs" one of subjectivity is not at issue; that the subjectivity one is "robbed" of through maternity is equated with an unquestioningly privileged emancipation is the more accurate site of mother-subordination. The problematic lies in the honouring of a view of the individual subject, which lends itself to a specific submission of subjectivity, which ties one to a specific type of emancipatory self-hood, the "master" subject, the "one":

> No subject will readily volunteer to become the object, the inessential; it is not the Other who, in defining himself as the Other, establishes the One. The Other is posed as such by the One in defining himself as the One. But if the Other is not to regain the status of being the One, he must be submissive enough to accept this alien point of view.[27]

Further, a "refusal to pose oneself as the Subject, unique and absolute, requires great self-denial."[28] While de Beauvoir does not tie *all* persons to an emancipated subjectivity, by denying legitimacy to any type of subjectivity, such as mothering, which does not partake of an emancipated master subjectivity, she ties the "liberated" woman to a prescriptive, individuated emancipation and the rest of us to submission and self-denial. "Woman" fails to "authentically assume a subjective attitude" because of sociopolitical and economic forced collusion with the (male) oppressors. Maternity constitutes such a collusion. The attainment of agency, of subjectivity, the claim of oneness, is the mark of liberation; it is what is to be fought for. While "woman," "a free and autonomous being like all human creatures,"[29] can overcome her otherness, her relegation to nonsubjectivity, and, while it may be argued that in many respects, and to some extent "woman" has indeed achieved such autonomy (if such an attainment can be called "achievement"), such a possibility is not open to mothers, whose autonomy, in their capacity as mothers, remains fundamentally impaired.

•

I would like here to make a small deviation from my main argument in order to consider the meaning and significance of autonomy. In political liberal theory autonomy designates, firstly, a unitary independence, and, secondly, a self-government that precludes external restraints.[30] The notion of autonomy is intimately linked to notions of freedom and liberty, the basic liberties (movement, speech, and so on) being based in a deontological notion of the self as autonomous. John Stuart Mill argues that one cannot autonomously choose to enslave oneself, for such an exercise of autonomy would preclude one's future autonomy.[31] If motherhood is understood in slavery terms, such a precludement positions motherhood as, deontologically speaking, ethically wrong.

In one sense, de Beauvoir and others are not mistaken in characterizing motherhood as enslavement. For nonaffluent mothers, mothering is extremely restrictive. When I first became a mother, my freedom, along with my individuality, vanished. Freedom of speech? I could not even carry on a ten-minute conversation uninterrupted. Freedom of movement? It took all morning to get out of the house, and then they don't allow strollers on the buses and frown when you change diapers on the bus seats — but where else is there? Freedom of association? My friends were still meeting in pubs, where babies aren't allowed. I got kicked out of the gym because they said it was no place for a baby. Movies scared the baby, who then would cry, disrupting the audience, and evening meetings didn't work because they interrupted the baby's bedtime routine.[32] The mistake lies not so much in equating motherhood with a loss of freedom and autonomy, but rather in adopting autonomy as an ideal.

The feminist preoccupation with winning autonomy for women must face what has been lost in the battle, who has been subjugated by it and what the costs have been. When I assert that a revaluing of motherhood is in order, I speak as a mother forced to put her child into daycare at too early an age. The cries of the child, clinging, torn limb by limb from my body, still reverberate in my ears. I speak as a mother forced by emancipation to wrench my child from me, to, day after day, compartmentalize my child away, so that I could pretend for eight hours that I was an individual. That is the price, for many mothers, of autonomy, of freedom, of movement, of speech; that is the price of this text (and now that I have finished it, I'm going to go and pick up my child), and that is a price which is too high to pay.

ON REFUSAL

The problematic arises when, in the name of liberation, untying "woman" from "mother" results in or leads to a delineation of liberation that precludes mothering. The question now becomes both how to liberate ourselves, mothers as mothers, from an all-pervasive nonmother liberation, and how to liberate the sign "lesbian" from designating a prescriptive emancipatory subjectivity. I have a small suggestion regarding the liberation of mother qua mother, regarding "lesbian"; however, I have, for now at least, reached an impasse.

Judith Butler speaks of the danger of being recolonized by the sign "lesbian," and asks: "If to become a lesbian is an *act*, a leave-taking of heterosexuality, a self-naming that contests the compulsory meanings of heterosexuality's *women* and *men*, what is to keep the name of lesbian from becoming an equally compulsory category?"[33] In Foucauldian terms, what Butler is speaking of is the danger of "lesbian" becoming an identity one is tied to (or outside of, or in the margins of) in a prescriptive way.

For the type of individuation which binds the individual to specific and prescriptive identities in a constraining way, Foucault suggests the refusal of identity as a tactic of insubordination.[34] It is this very tactic which Wittig employs in hailing "lesbian" as a refusal of heterosexual patriarchal enslavement, and which de Beauvoir engages in in alienating "woman" from "mother." Butler problematizes this refusal by pointing out that "lesbian" as a refusal of heterosexuality reinscribes the very heterosexual matrix which it disavows, but, interestingly enough, adopts a highly sophisticated version of the Foucauldian refusal tactic in an attempt to rescue "lesbian" from its (already realized but disruptable) potential as a prescriptive and exclusionary sign. The strategy Butler suggests is: "a thoroughgoing appropriation and redeployment of the categories of identity themselves, not merely to contest 'sex,' but to articulate the convergence of multiple sexual discourses at the site of 'identity' in order to render that category, in whatever form, permanently problematic."[35]

Identity is a dangerous game not only because, as Foucault explains it, the government of individuation ties one to a specific identity in a prescriptive way, or, as Butler puts it, one faces being recolonized by the very sign that holds the promise of liberation; danger lies not only in being tied to a specific identity through individuating processes, but in being tied to a specific subjectivity through identificatory processes. Within lesbian discourses, "lesbian" ties one to an (ideally) emancipated, individuated and separated subjectivity. Butler's suggestion of rendering the category "lesbian" permanently problematic does not alter the status of the sign as signifying an emancipated subjectivity, but instead seeks to preserve the emancipatory potentiality of the sign in a way which its solidification would prohibit.

To refuse is not enough not only because to refuse would be to be defined by one's refusal, categorized by it, which, within a binary system of meaning, simply results in the reinforcement of the identity one refuses, but also because the refusal of an identity does little to alter the basic tenants of subjectivity. Further, refusal, while it may be an appropriate tactic for white male intellectuals, is impractical for mothers. To refuse the identity "mother" would necessitate a refusal of practices of mothering, which, although some mothers have resorted to this, is too much to ask of any mother. To refuse mothering would not only have very real consequences for the lives of children, not to mention the state, economy and future of "society" itself, but would also be a refusal of the kind of self a mothering self becomes through mothering. To suggest a refusal of mothering is to suggest one tear out what one is as a mother, that one split one's own identity in the most painful way imaginable. While practices of sex and gender lend themselves well to the refusal tactic, to interchangeability, self-reflexivity and, ultimately, to emancipation, practices of mother do not.

Jean Baudrillard also suggests refusal, though of a slightly different sort:

> To a system whose argument is oppression and repression, the strategic resistance is the liberating claim of subjecthood. But this reflects rather the system's previous phase, and even if we are still confronted with it, it is no longer the strategic terrain: the system's current argument is the maximisation of the word and the maximal production of meaning. Thus the strategic resistance is that of *a refusal of meaning and a refusal of the word — or of the hyperconformist simulation of the very mechanisms of the system,* which is a form of refusal and of non-reception.[36]

As much as I respect and enjoy Baudrillard, I cannot help but think that mothering, to some limited extent, defies the production of meaning in late capitalist democracies, and thus defies both the possibility of a refusal of meaning and of hyperconformism. No matter how hard one tries to "hyperconform," to simulate the perfect mother, the baby will always disrupt the simulation. It will throw up all down your dress, refuse to nurse when it should, sleep through the night when it shouldn't, cry for hours when you've done everything right, and cause, out of shear frustration and fatigue, or from some love deeper than you knew could exist, a shattering of the simulation. Motherhood shatters simulations in much the same way I would imagine many larger catastrophes such as floods, earthquakes and wars do. One simply acts in panic and desperation.[37] Mothering, at least of infants, precludes a refusal of the word through obliterations of the word. The word is replaced by snorffles and milk and (lack of) sleep and smells and excretions. In making this claim I in no way wish to deny the discursive constructions of motherhood, nor do I wish to deny that mothering practices continue to serve western capitalist, patriarchal democracies well, but rather I wish to add that there is something about mothering practices that both underlie and go beyond the word, the construction, the institution and the image. This is not to say that mothering is anything other than practice, but rather that mothering practices at times preclude a refusal of meaning and make hyperconformism, at least sometimes, just plain impossible.

As a tactic, refusal is fraught with pragmatic and theoretical complications, and yet there is something very satisfying in the concept. *Hip Mama* is a zine put out and contributed to by mothers who are radical, poor, young, single, queer and angry.[38] It embraces motherhood while subverting prevalent conceptions of the "good" mother. For example, while featuring an article by a mother recounting her homeless pregnancy, *Hip Mama* proclaimed teenage pregnancy "hip" thereby validating and giving voice to the extreme difficulties faced by homeless teen moms, while simultaneously fostering motherpride, allowing the embracement of teen pregnancies. *Hip Mama* features legitimating articles by socially illigitimated mothers: stripper moms, queer moms and poor moms. And it endows mothering practices with value without shying from the profoundly interconnected and prohibitive nature of nonaffluent western mothering.

If refusal is the only tactic at our disposal, then perhaps a useful refusal for mothers is a refusal to conform to emancipatory subjectivities that subjugate mother practices. Perhaps a useful refusal for mothers is to refuse to refuse: to embrace motherselfhoods and to demand social, economic and political respect for mothering practices. But even here we must tread carefully, for "a mistake concerning strategy is a serious matter"[39] and identity is a dangerous game.

•

Mothers make my head turn. I want to kiss their tired eyes and lay them down — not in ecstasy, for small hands are ceaselessly tugging, small tongues licking and mouths groping — but to sleep, alone, in puke-free warmth. I'll take the babies to the park. And perhaps some day, after the house is clean and there is enough money to cover the rent, we will uncork the small filigree bottle, if we can still find it, and discover what remains of our passions.

Notes

1. More accurately, the rejection is not always total. There exists in much lesbian separatist literature from the 1970s and 1980s a glorification of raising daughters on womon-only land. Raising male children, however, is being a slave for the enemy. I have trouble with this genre of writing not only because of its sex and gender essentialism, but also, and especially, because it tends to posit solutions in self-righteous terms. I much prefer the Foucauldian practice of analyzing systems and making small suggestions toward tactics of insubordination to the practice of thrusting totalizing theories onto peoples lives.

2. Rosi Braidotti, *Nomadic Subjects: Embodiment and Sexual Difference in Contemporary Feminist Theory* (New York: Columbia University Press, 1994), 77. Emphasis in original.

3. Jeffner Allen, "Motherhood: The Annihilation of Women in Mothering," in Joyce Trebilcot, ed., *Mothering: Essays in Feminist Theory* (Totowa, NJ: Rowman and Allenheld, 1984), 317. Emphasis in original.

4. Margaret Dragu, Sarah Sheared, and Susan Swan, editors and interviewers, *Mothers Talk Back* (Toronto: Coach House Press, 1991), 141.

5. Lucia Valeska, "If All Else Fails, I'm Still a Mother," in Trebilcot, ed., *Mothering: Essays in Feminist Theory*, 75.

6. Sara Ruddick, "Maternal Thinking," in Trebilcot, ed., *Mothering: Essays in Feminist Theory*, 225.

7. Dragu, Sheard, and Swan, eds., *Mothers Talk Back*, 92.

8. Judith Butler, "Imitation and Gender Insubordination," in Henry Abelove, Michéle Aina Barale, and David Halperin, eds., *The Lesbian and Gay Studies Reader* (New York: Routledge, 1993), 112.

9. Ibid.

10. This is a common complaint among new mothers.

11. Nancy Chodorow, "Family Structure and Feminine Personality," in Nancy Tuana and Rosemarie Tong, eds., *Feminism and Philosophy: Essential Readings in Theory, Reinterpretation, and Application* (San Francisco: Westview Press, 1995), 201; Nancy Hartsock, "Feminist Standpoint," Tuana and Tong, eds., *Feminism and Philosophy*, 73.

12. Iris Marion Young, "Pregnant Embodiment: Subjectivity and Alienation," Tuana and Tong, eds., *Feminism and Philosophy*, 407.

13. Judith Butler, *Gender Trouble: Feminism and the Subversion of Identity* (London: Routledge, 1990), 112.

14. Monique Wittig, *The Straight Mind and Other Essays* (Boston: Beacon Press, 1992), 80, 81.

15. Ibid., 80.

16. This is not to say that persons who happen to mother can never be subjects, it is simply to say that, within this particular framework, in order to be subjects, mothers must leave their "mother" subjectivity and inhabit an "I" subjectivity.

17. René Descartes, "Discourse on the Method of Rightly Directing One's Reason and Seeking Truth in the Sciences," in Elizabeth Anscombe and Peter Geach, eds., *Descartes Philosophical Writings* (New York: Macmillan Publishing Co., 1971), 34.

18. Wittig, *The Straight Mind and Other Essays*, 81.

19. Cheshire Calhoun, in her essay "Separating Lesbian Theory from Feminist Theory," *Ethics: An International Journal of Social, Political, and Legal Philosophy* 10, no. 3 (April 1994), points out that "contrary to Wittig's claim, the lesbian may as a rule have *less* control over her productive and reproductive labour than her married heterosexual sister. Although the lesbian escapes whatever control *individual* men may exercise over their wives within marriage, she does not thereby escape control of her productive and reproductive labor either in her personal life with another women or in her public life. To refuse to be heterosexual is simply to leap out of the frying pan of individual patriarchal control into the fire of institutionalised heterosexual control ... The lesbian may be free from an individual man in her personal life, but she is not free" (564-565). Emphasis in original.

20. Wittig, *The Straight Mind and Other Essays*, 80.

21. Ibid., 83. Emphasis in original.

22. Butler speaks of gender as drag, that is as a performance, an imitation for which there is no original, which, through a repetition of the performance, constitute naturalistic effects.

23. This is the framework Judith Butler uses to discuss lesbianism in "Imitation and Gender Insubordination."

24. Michel Foucault, "The Subject and Power," in Hurbert L. Dreyfus and Paul Rabi-

now, eds., *Michel Foucault: Beyond Structuralism and Hermeneutics* (Brighton, UK: Harvester Press, 1982), 212.

25. Simone de Beauvoir *The Second Sex* (New York: Vintage Books, 1989), 495. Emphasis added.

26. Linda Zerilli, "A Process Without a Subject: Simone de Beauvoir and Julia Kristeva on Maternity," *Signs: Journal of Women and Culture in Society* 18, no. 1 (1992), 112.

27. de Beauvoir, *The Second Sex*, xxiv.

28. Ibid., xxxi.

29. Ibid., xxxv.

30. Gerald Dworkin, *The Theory and Practice of Autonomy* (New York: Cambridge University Press, 1988).

31. John Stuart Mill, *On Liberty* (London: Penguin Classics, 1985).

32. All this suggests that it is not mothering practices that need changing but rather the adult-centric "public" sphere that could use comprehensive revamping.

33. Butler, *Gender Trouble: Feminism and the Subversion of Identity*, 127. Emphasis in original.

34. Foucault, "The Subject and Power."

35. Butler, *Gender Trouble: Feminism and the Subversion of Identity*, 128.

36. Jean Baudrillard, *In the Shadow of the Silent Majorities or, The End of the Social and Other Essays* (New York: Semiotext(e), 1983), 108. Emphasis added.

37. A friend of mine, and early childhood educator, aptly characterizes mothers with children under the age of six as living in a constant state of crisis.

38. Ariel, ed., *Hip Mama: The Parenting Zine* (Oakland, CA: Hip Mama, California, 1997).

39. Baudrillard, *In the Shadow of the Silent Majorities*, 109.

Chapter 17

MOTHERING THE WELL-BORN:
CHOICE AS A SYSTEM OF GOVERNANCE

Fiona Alice Miller & Melanie Rock

"DOES A BIRTH MOTHER who has chosen to carry a fetus to full term owe a duty of care to that fetus?" In this chapter we consider the circumstances that made it possible for this question, put to the Supreme Court of Canada in 1997, to be asked. This question presupposes that the fetus has a moral, and potentially legal, status that governs women. How have women's choices become instruments of women's governance? How has the fetus achieved the "right" to be "well-born"?

This key question was considered by the Supreme Court in the "G" case. "G" is the name given to a pregnant woman in Manitoba forced, in the "interests" of her fetus, into "treatment" for substance abuse. Fortunately, a higher court overturned this lower court judgement, which the Supreme Court of Canada upheld in a ruling on October 31, 1997. Yet in the legal arguments, court decisions and public discussion of this case, the fetus emerged as a "subject" with "interests." The child welfare agency that initiated the action against "G," the lower court judge and two out of nine Supreme Court judges found that fetal "interests" can trump women's rights. Moreover, even some of those who argued against the use of force, explicitly argued that the fetus's interests ought to have moral authority. How could this happen?

Most feminist scholars who have considered this question find the answer in certain medical and cultural technologies that seem to portray the fetus as a "public actor." Most potent among these are the fetal visualization technologies such as ultrasound.[1] For example, Barbara Duden has argued that "the formation of the fetus is to a large extent the history of its visualization."[2] Antiabortion activists have used these technologies to present a vision of the fetus as an isolate — an encapsulated astronaut. Women do not usually figure in such images — suggesting that women have less moral or political significance than fetuses. Recent research suggests that nonvisualizing technologies have also played a role in the emergence of the fetus onto the public stage.[3] The common thread in the literature is the argument that post–WWII medical technologies have produced an innovation — the public fetus.

Recent historical research by Karen Newman provides a much needed corrective. She has argued, convincingly, that the fetus is not a new subject. Indeed she demonstrates that medical efforts to visualize the fetus can be dated from at least the ninth century. Newman suggests that the crucial question is not, "How has the fetus come to be a subject?" but rather, "How is the fetus made to 'mean' in different historical epochs?"[4]

In this chapter we take Newman's argument as a starting point and examine how the fetal subject has been invested with "meaning" in the latter half of the twentieth century. We argue that the fetus has been given meaning through narratives of health, and we situate some of the most potent of these narratives in the developing science and practice of medical genetics — what we call, a "genetic science of the unborn."[5] First, we examine the role medical genetics has played in constructing the fetal subject. We also look at the implications of developments in medical genetics for abortion rights activism in second-wave feminism. Next we examine the "G" case in some detail. We look at the contradictions that this case poses for feminists, seeing these as extensions of the historical developments. Finally, we recommend a politics to address the dilemmas presented by the "G" case.

In making these arguments we draw on the literature of governmentality and moral regulation. This literature provides alternative ways for thinking about power in liberal democracies, arguing that "power relations are not structured by traditional oppositions between the state and civil society and coercion and consent."[6] Power, as Nikolas Rose and Peter Miller have argued in an influential piece, "is not so much a matter of imposing constraints upon citizens as of 'making up' citizens capable of bearing a kind of regulated freedom."[7]

The concepts of governmentality and moral regulation point to the way that health and its absence can be used as instruments of power. As Monica Greco has argued, health is not "just" a biological state; it is a social and moral state that addresses the individual as a rational public actor. Disease can thus reflect failure of rational agency: "the event of illness ... become[s] a moment of truth about a subject's moral aptitude to form part of the society within which he or she lives."[8] Recent research by Gary Kinsman suggests that the self-governance of health can be enabled through the rhetoric of responsibility. As Kinsman notes, narratives of responsibility can be deployed in systems of self-regulation of the "responsible," and as instruments of coercive governance of the "irresponsible."[9] Thus "informed choice" functions as an instrument of governance.[10] It is a means of marshalling power.

Once internalized, the moral meanings of health motivate responsible action. The primary locus of action is the individual's own body.[11] In this light, the close connection between fetal interests and fetal health in popular culture as well as medical circles holds particularly troubling implications for women. Women are not only responsible for managing their own bodies and appetites,[12] they are also responsible for managing the "health" of fetuses and potential fetuses. This increases the likelihood that women will become subject to direct coercion and more subtle, but no less real, forms of governance in promoting these health "interests."

The cultural status of genetic knowledge reinforces the moral authority of health in constructing "interests." From the latter half of the nineteenth century and throughout the twentieth century, genetic science has had the cultural status of constitutive knowledge. That is, it can speak definitional truths about individuals and populations.[13] In Euro-American cultures, ascriptions of kin, gender or congenital disability cannot be dispensed with. Once defined as "diseased," "disabled" or "female," such "facts" constitute individuals in ways that resist challenge. Through such categories, and their justification in genetic science, types of people and types of fetuses are "made up."[14]

A GENETIC SCIENCE OF THE UNBORN/WELL-BORN

In the late twentieth century, in the context of the Human Genome Project, genetic tests, prenatal diagnosis and the prospect of "gene therapy," we take medical applications of genetic science for granted. But this has not always been the case. Medical genetics began to take form in the 1930s;[15] as it has developed, it has promoted a "genetic science of the unborn." Beginning with eugenics and concern with abstract future populations, refining this abstraction through genetic counselling and more predictive tests on the "family," and finally focusing directly on the fetus through prenatal diagnosis, medical genetics has contributed a particular understanding of the fetus. Typically, the fetus's "health" is what gives it meaning. Moreover, fetal "health" came to be understood primarily through genetic narratives of *ill*-health.

According to the conventional view, science and medicine develop through research unhampered by culture or politics. In fact, the genetic science of the unborn derived, as all science does, from a complex interplay between social, cultural and experimental phenomena.[16] Cultural assumptions about disease and disability, about women, men and families figure prominently in genetic science. Moreover, the development of the science and the attendant clinical practices depended on social changes to take root and flourish.

Genetic counselling has been the key clinical activity of the genetic science of the unborn, and the perceived needs of this clinical context have influenced the development of genetic science. Genetic counselling emerged in the 1930s out of a reform eugenics impulse that disavowed compulsion and turned its attention to "families" afflicted with hereditary ailments.[17] Despite some important differences between early-twentieth-century eugenics and medical genetics, the focus on the abstraction of "future children" remained.[18] The institutional structure of medical genetics — which grew up within pediatric departments of universities and hospitals throughout North America — reflected this orientation.

Norma Ford Walker at the Hospital for Sick Children in Toronto pioneered genetic counselling in Canada; she began her work as a heredity counsellor in the 1940s. She provided a picture of statistical risk based on patterns of hereditary disease in the family — a pedigree.

Equipped with this information, those counselled could decide to avoid marriage, avoid bearing children or have children through adoption or "artificial" insemination. Norma Ford Walker gave advice in order to help "people avoid the tragedy of a defective child."[19]

Genetic counselling grew slowly through the 1950s and 1960s. But by 1960, the developing science of human cytogenetics was advancing rapidly. Having identified the correct number of human chromosomes in 1956, researchers went on to identify a range of human congenital conditions as due to chromosomal anomalies, such as Trisomy 21, or "Down's syndrome." In contrast with earlier more fluid views of heredity,[20] chromosomal anomalies were now understood to prove the point that "Life begins, for the human being, at the instant a sperm from the father enters and fertilizes the egg in the mother," as a 1960 *Chatelaine* article declared. "At that moment of fertilization, the new baby's entire heredity is forged ... The new baby's physical and mental potentialities are decided, not at the moment of birth, but at this instant of conception."[21]

Genetic counselling reflected this sense that genetic status was fundamental. But there were still important limits in the extent to which genetic science could provide concrete information about the unborn. "Would it be possible for a geneticist to tell a pregnant woman what kind of physical and mental qualities her future child will possess?," the *Chatelaine* article continued. No, as it turned out, "The geneticists can't tell a pregnant woman *exactly* what kind of child she'll have since many of the details are still shrouded in mystery."[22]

That mystery began to recede as researchers pursued the science of cytogenetics in the prenatal period. In 1963, David Carr at the University of Western Ontario published his classic work on the higher than expected incidence of chromosomal anomalies among human spontaneous abortuses and stillbirths.[23] In 1966 researchers announced that they could detect certain fetal chromosomal anomalies in amniotic fluid.[24] These discoveries enabled the much anticipated shift in genetic counselling from abstract "future children" to the reified fetus. As one geneticist noted in 1973, "couples whose genes were not a good match might be educated to find another mate. But that would be more difficult than 'letting everybody marry whom they want' and monitoring pregnancies in couples who were carriers of genetic diseases so their abnormal fetuses could be aborted."[25]

At the end of the 1960s, despite these developments, the clinical and thus social impact of this science of the unborn remained very small. In the 1970s, Canada's Medical Research Council (MRC) sponsored a national research project that led to widespread clinical use of prenatal diagnosis. As a result the genetic science of the unborn, with its understandings of women, of disease and of the fetus became routine medical practice.

ROUTINIZING THE PREVENTION OF THE "ABNORMAL" FETUS

The mandate of the Medical Research Council (MRC) is to fund medical research. So the Working Group on Prenatal Diagnosis of Genetic Disease funded by MRC from 1971 through 1976 presented their project as research. In reality, members of the Working Group were far more interested in establishing prenatal diagnosis as a standard medical practice than in researching its efficacy and value. True, the Working Group conducted a large clinical trial of amniocentesis for genetic disease,[26] but this fell well short of the stated research objectives in the funding proposal. When defending their project against the charge of repetition, in light of similar national studies in the US and the UK, Working Group members made explicit their commitment to service. A brief to the MRC reads,

> The Canadian study has already had a profound influence on the development and delivery of amniocentesis services across the country. The study was started and the Working Group established at a time when Canadian labs were just beginning to consider establishing this service on a routine basis. The establishment of the collaborative study involving the majority of Canadian centres has ensured a certain uniform standard of recording and follow-up of patients and has thus raised the quality of service to be rendered to the Canadian public in these centres. In addition, the establishment of the study has led to the formation of collaborative groups in many centres consisting of obstetricians, geneticists and paediatricians with the prime purpose of co-ordinating and establishing local standards for the delivery of service in their areas.[27]

Of course, the MRC could not admit to this function of the Working Group. The president of the MRC recommended removing this section of the brief.[28]

This quote reveals a determination to make amniocentesis for genetic disease widely available, but according to certain standards of practice. Some of these standards were matters of technique, such as the recommendation that ultrasound be used alongside amniocentesis for greater accuracy and safety in inserting the needle. Other standards concerned indications for prenatal diagnosis — such as the ages at which women should be offered the tests, and under what conditions. These latter standards clearly reflected more than just technical issues. In deciding that all women pregnant over the age of forty should be offered the test, and that women in the age range of thirty-five to thirty-nine should be considered, the Working Group demanded a massive growth in the use of this technology, and identified the prenatal detection of Down's syndrome as a clear social priority. Soon, the Working Group formalized these assumptions, as members aided in the development of the "Canadian Guidelines for antenatal diagnosis of genetic disease."[29]

The MRC study played a crucial role, then, in making amniocentesis for genetic disease routine clinical practice. How it introduced this medical innovation reflects the cultural context enveloping the history of twentieth-century genetics. The Working Group members believed that aborting "defective" fetuses provided the rationale for prenatal diagnosis.[30] This assumption was written into the Canadian Guidelines, which stated that "[b]oth parents' views on therapeutic abortion should be ascertained before amniocentesis and the tests should not be undertaken where (in the face of serious genetic disease untreatable *in utero*) the parents are unalterably opposed to abortion."[31]

Prenatal diagnosis of genetic disease appeared as a technology that could define the value of prospective children. A genetic framing of health status constructed the fetus as a subject — with "interests." This genetic narrative also established the relative worth of fetal subjects. In doing so, the Working Group diverged considerably from a feminist approach to reproductive decision making.

This statement in the Canadian Guidelines also points to the single-most important reason for the growing routinization of prenatal diagnosis in the 1970s — the liberalization of abortion laws and practices.

Medical geneticists from across North America acknowledged this, as a review article on prenatal diagnosis from the early 1970s pointed out: "Until very recently the suggestion that a hereditary disorder might be detected prenatally would have drawn from most clinicians the equivalent of 'why bother?' Nothing could be done about such a diseased fetus is any case, so why should anyone undertake the presumably formidable task of diagnosis in utero." One reason, the author suggested, was the "almost explosive increase in understanding of hereditary disease."

> However, since most hereditary diseases are still not treatable even when diagnosed, these developments might not have sufficed to swing the balance had it not been for the changes in attitudes toward early interruption of pregnancy. In recent years the feeling has grown among both physicians and the general public that we must be concerned not simply with ensuring the birth of a baby, but of one who will not be a liability to society, to its parents and to itself. The "right to be born" is becoming qualified by another right: to have a reasonable chance of a happy and useful life. This shift in attitude is shown by, among other things, the widespread movement for the reform or even the abolition of abortion laws.[32]

ABORTION AND SECOND-WAVE FEMINISM

By the late 1960s there was an increased medical and social willingness to see abortion legalized under some conditions.[33] Abortion was most commonly defended at this time for three reasons: "maternal" health and life; rape or incest of the "mother"; and fetal "defect." Second-wave feminists identified access to abortion as a women's rights issue, but they too adopted this triad of justifications.[34]

Two of these three arguments identified women's interests as the central defining factor in the justification for abortion. But the eugenic argument about fetal "defect" gave space to an argument favouring access to abortion that was decidedly not about freedom for women.[35] The eugenic argument provided a forum for public discussion about the fetus as a subject with increasingly articulate, genetically defined, health interests. While feminists have for the most part demanded that attention focus on the pregnant woman, they have conceded the argument that attention be paid to a fetus defined through its health status. The "G" case clearly reflects some consequences of this concession.

THE "G" CASE

In the summer of 1996, a young pregnant Aboriginal woman living in Winnipeg became forged into the form of a case eventually heard by the Supreme Court. This woman was addicted to sniffing solvents, and the justification for judicial intervention was clear — the health "interests" of the fetus demanded it. We have reviewed the circumstances of "G," the woman in question, as written up in legal decisions and the facta presented to the Supreme Court for "G" and the child welfare agency, which initiated the case against "G."[36] We also singled out three interveners' facta for particular attention because they explicitly regard the case as one of women's rights.[37] We refer to them collectively as the "feminist facta."

The law informs these documents in explicit and implicit ways. How Canadian law has historically engaged pregnant women is very important. In 1969, the Criminal Code was amended to clarify the legality of "therapeutic abortion" under strictly delineated circumstances.[38] Ultimately in 1987, the Supreme Court ruled that these provisions infringed the "right to life, liberty and security of the person."[39] Madam Justice Wilson, the sole woman member of the Court at the time, asserted that access to abortion was fundamental to women's status in society.

Madam Justice Wilson also found, however, that the state has an accruing interest in the fetus as it develops, such that "reasonable limits" could be placed on pregnant women's rights.[40] While there have been no restrictions placed on abortion in Canada under criminal law since the 1987 judgement,[41] this statement by Madam Justice Wilson points to the direction that newer challenges to women's reproductive rights have taken. This is reflected in the questions put to the Supreme Court in the "G" case:

1) Does a birth mother who has chosen to carry a fetus to full term owe a duty of care to that fetus?

2) If the answer to Question 1 is "yes," in what circumstances, if any, should a Court intervene to enforce compliance with the duty to care?[42]

The extent to which these questions and the facta all rely on the fetus's "interests," and the rubric of choice in defending these interests, is striking. Accordingly, "G" appears as a woman who has made a choice about her pregnancy: she has chosen not to abort. This decision is subsequently subjected to a "rationality test." In the appeal to the Supreme Court, Winnipeg Child and Family Services insisted that a mother's professed intention to carry a pregnancy to term obliges her to serve the interests of fetal health. The child welfare organization used the medical consensus on health effects of chemical substances to suggest that "choices" made by "G" lacked rationality. On this basis, it argued that the state cannot rely on her or others like her to behave in the best interests of the fetus for the duration of the pregnancy. Fortunately, in the majority decision, the Supreme Court found that legally, "[a]ny right or interest the fetus may have remains inchoate and incomplete until the child's birth."[43]

Through the case-making process,[44] "G" has been made into a "typical" example of those pregnant women who, atypically we are told, do not "strive to make positive choices during pregnancy to ensure the health of their child."[45] The series of contingent and contested circumstances that enmeshed "G" in the web of the law back in June 1996 have become distilled into a "duty to care." In light of the Supreme Court's decision, it would seem that this duty is not legally enforceable during pregnancy.[46] But as we have argued, the fetus's "interest" in its health, once granted moral authority, does govern women.

Each factum examined presents the fetus as a subject in pursuit of health. All three feminist facta contend that forced confinement or medical treatment is counterproductive in achieving the objectives of maternal and fetal health. Arguably, such measures inhibit women — specifically women with addictions or other problems that place the fetus "at risk" — from obtaining needed professional services.[47] These facta, while arguing vigorously against direct state coercion, advocate "positive" state intervention. For example, the Women's Legal Education Action Fund (LEAF) maintains that Winnipeg Child and Family Services "should not be able to argue that coercion against individual women is now necessary because the government of Manitoba has failed in its duty to provide adequate services."[48]

In summary, "G" appears in the documents presented to the

Supreme Court as an agent who chooses. While she may have impulses that conflict with her health and that of the health of her fetus, her capacity for motherhood — biological and social — will be evaluated in terms of the risks to which she exposes the fetus. The biological father, it must be noted, is invisible in these accounts. Historically and still today, the Canadian state strives to ensure children's well-being through maternal responsibility.[49] The facta and the previous judgements invoke this history in arguing for or against state coercion during pregnancy. In these arguments, the healthy body consistently appears as a product of rational choice.[50]

CONCLUSION

The cultural authority of genetic knowledge, together with the social practices of medical genetics, have given particular meanings to the fetus over the last half of the twentieth century. This "genetic science of the unborn" has given the fetus a status and corollary set of interests in its health. The legacy of eugenics influenced the emergence of medical genetics as an area of research and, in turn, the application of this research in medical practice. However, the emphasis on preventing fetal pathology — producing the "well-born" — permeates our society. The perceived obligation to produce "healthy babies" and later "healthy children" mandates a series of actions in and out of the clinic. To become a mother in Canada — to reproduce society biologically and socially — carries a heavy weight of responsibility.

In the late twentieth century a pregnant woman in Canada who has not opted for abortion seems obliged to serve the health interests of her fetus. Though the Supreme Court has decided against making this obligation legally enforceable during pregnancy, a woman's moral obligation remains. In this chapter, we have argued that this moral obligation is a form of governance which operates through self-management and social suasion in the pursuit of health.

This form of governance relies on the expectation of rational choice making by women in dealing with their reproductive capacity. Ironically for feminists, "self-governance" in accordance with perceived moral obligations may exert at least as much influence as regulations or legislation that clearly delimit available options during pregnancy. Notably, "self-regulation" turns upon standardizing women's comportment, especially during pregnancy. Regulating prenatal medical services contributes to this standardization. However, much depends on conformity among women's desires and expectations.

Defending reproductive freedom and women's rights through "choice," that is "self-governance," leaves considerable space for coercion when a woman's actions do not appear rational. The possibilities for intervening coercively in women's lives increase when a fetus has health "interests" of its own. However, coercion is rarely necessary to achieve governance. The "G" case and others like it are exceptions that prove the rule. Furthermore, the impact of a fetal subject invested with health interests is not restricted to pregnant women. All women are subject to many practices that govern mothering and pregnancy. Nevertheless, the least subtle forms of social control mostly target women who have been most marginalized.

We find, therefore, that blanket approval of all interventions relying on the "positive" powers of the state to ensure the best interests of the fetus by promoting maternal health rest on an inadequate analysis of how power operates. By examining how the fetus became commonly portrayed as a subject invested with health interests, we have developed a more complex account of how pregnancy and women generally are governed in Canada today.

This account has many implications for feminist scholarship and activism. Feminists must contest rather than rely on rhetoric granting women reproductive autonomy through rational decision making. Feminists must also resist the notion that the fetus has transparent health interests. Such goals are shot through with troubling views of disability, health and identity.

Notes

Fiona Alice Miller and Melanie Rock both wish to acknowledge support from the Social Science and Humanities Research Council of Canada in the form of doctoral fellowships. In addition, the Hannah Institute for the History of Medicine and the Scottish Rite Charitable Foundation have supported Fiona Miller's doctoral research.

1. Rosalind Petchesky, "Foetal Images: The Power of Visual Culture in the Politics of Reproduction," in Michelle Stanworth, ed., *Reproductive Technologies: Gender, Motherhood and Medicine* (Minneapolis: University of Minnesota Press, 1987); Janelle Taylor, "The Public Fetus and the Family Car: From Abortion Politics to a Volvo Advertisement," *Public Culture* 4, no. 2 (Spring 1992); Sarah Franklin, "Fetal Fascinations: New Dimensions to the Medical-Scientific Construction of Fetal Personhood," in Sarah Franklin, Celia Lury, and Jackie Stacey, eds., *Off-Centre: Feminism and Cultural Studies* (London: Harper Collins Academic, 1991).

2. Barbara Duden, *Disembodying Women: Perspectives on Pregnancy and the Unborn* (Cambridge, MA: Harvard University Press, 1993), 92.

3. Lorna Weir, for example, argues that "the fetus [can be understood] as a co-patterning of lingual and visual distinctions across a variety of biomedical textual genres, ranging from the experimental article to the 'results' of standardized blood tests that confer upon the fetal body a range of physiological and pathological properties." "Recent Developments in the Government of Pregnancy," *Economy and Society* 25, no. 3 (August 1996), 374.

4. Karen Newman, *Fetal Positions: Individualism, Science, Visuality* (Stanford,CA: Stanford University Press, 1996), 2.

5. A comprehensive history of the science and practice of perinatal medicine has yet to be written. When it is, we will be better able to see how medical genetics fits into the total developing "science of the unborn."

6. Deborah Lupton, *The Imperative of Health: Public Health and the Regulated Body* (London: Sage Publications, 1995), 3.

7. Nikolas Rose and Peter Miller, "Political Power Beyond the State: Problematics of Government," *British Journal of Sociology* 43, no. 2 (1992), 174. See also, Mariana Valverde, ed., *Studies in Moral Regulation* (Toronto: Centre of Criminology, 1994).

8. Monica Greco, "Psychosomatic Subjects and the Duty to be Well: Personal Agency Within Medical Rationality," *Economy and Society* 22, no. 3 (1993), 362.

9. Gary Kinsman, "Responsibility as a Strategy of Governance: Regulating People Living with AIDS and Lesbians and Gay Men in Ontario," *Economy and Society* 25, no. 3 (1996), 393.

10. Margaret Lock, *Encounters with Aging: Myths of Menopause in Japan and North America* (Berkeley: University of California Press), 1993.

11. For a helpful discussion of the governmentality literature and the way that discourses of health situate power see, Deborah Lupton, "Introduction," *The Imperative of Health*.

12. Carla Rice, "Out From Under Occupation: Transforming Our Relationships with Our Bodies," *Canadian Woman Studies/les cahiers de la femme* 14, no. 3 (1994), 136.

13. Marilyn Strathern, "Kinship Knowledge," in Lorna Weir, ed., *Governing Medically Assisted Human Reproduction: Report of an International Symposium* (Toronto: Centre of Criminology, 1997). Strathern points out that there are two kinds of knowledge, constitutive and regulative knowledge. Regulative knowledge is the kind that can be subject to the action of personal choice — you can choose to dispense with the information provided in your morning paper for example. Constitutive knowledge, however, cannot be subject to your choosing — because it makes you. In different cultures, different kinds of knowledge have constitutive status.

14. Ian Hacking, *The Taming of Chance* (Cambridge: Cambridge University Press, 1990).

15. The term "medical genetics" was coined by Canadian geneticist Madge Thurlow Macklin. See, M. T. Macklin, "'Medical Genetics': A Necessity in the Up-to-date Medical Curriculum," *Journal of Heredity* 23 (1932).

16. There is an extensive literature in the social studies of science. For example, see the journal *Social Studies of Science;* see also Adele Clarke and Joan Fujimura, eds., *The Right Tools for the Job: At Work in Twentieth-Century Life Sciences* (Princeton, NJ: Princeton University Press, 1992). For an early and compelling account of this process, see Ludwik Fleck, *Genesis and Development of a Scientific Fact*, trans. Fred Bradley and Thaddeus J. Trenn (Chicago: University of Chicago Press, 1979).

17. Early-twentieth-century eugenics encouraged births among the "fitter" classes and sought to intervene coercively in the sexual and reproductive capacities of individuals deemed "unfit." It was a method of reproductive control with limited predictive power; it focused attention on individuals who fulfilled the characteristics of a class of persons — the "better sorts," or the "feebleminded." Specialized heredity counselling clinics started to open during the 1940s in North America. For the earliest North American medical book on genetic counselling, see, Sheldon Reed, *Counseling in Medical Genetics* (London: W.B. Saunders Company, 1955).

18. For the major text on eugenics in Canada, see, Angus McLaren, *Our Own Master Race: Eugenics in Canada, 1885-1945* (Toronto: McClelland and Stewart, 1990).

19. While Ford Walker disavowed compulsion, she retained "a deep interest in eugenics — improving the vigor of the human race." Sidney Katz, "She Knows the Kind of Children You'll Have," *Maclean's Magazine* (December 1, 1954), 32, 84.

20. Charles E. Rosenberg, "The Bitter Fruit: Heredity, Disease and Social Thought," *No Other Gods: On Science and American Social Thought* (Baltimore: The Johns Hopkins University Press, 1976).

21. Christina McNall Newman, "How Close Are We to Test-tube Babies?," *Chatelaine* (September 1960), 62.

22. Ibid. Emphasis in original.

23. David H. Carr, "Chromosome Studies in Abortuses and Stillborn Infants," *Lancet* (September 21, 1963), 605.

24. M. W. Steele and W. R. Breg, Jr., "Chromosome Analysis of Human Amniotic-Fluid Cells," *Lancet* (February 19, 1966), 383–385. Later confirmations that these cells could be cultured and thus reveal biochemical and other defects contributed to this technological capacity.

25. Marilyn Dunlop, "Doctor Suggests Lifetime Gene-Defect Card," *The Toronto Star*, 25 January 1973.

26. Nancy Simpson et al., "Prenatal Diagnosis of a Genetic Disease in Canada: Report of a Collaborative Study," *Canadian Medical Association Journal* 115 (October 23, 1976), 739–748.

27. Draft, "Brief to Executive," Feb. 1974, submitted to Dr. M. Brown, President of the MRC (National Archives, RG128, V 191, File 1250-2 pt. 2).

28. Dr. M. Brown, letter to Dr. J. Hamerton, Feb. 15, 1974 (National Archives, RG128, V 191, File 1250-2 pt. 2).

29. "Canadian Guidelines for Antenatal Diagnosis of Genetic Disease: A Joint Statement," *Canadian Medical Association Journal* 111 (July 20, 1974), 180–183.

30. See also, Leone Kirkwood, "If An Abnormal Fetus Not Aborted, Lab Technicians Upset," *The Globe and Mail*, 16 November 1973.

31. "Canadian Guidelines," 183.

32. Joseph Dancis, "The Prenatal Detection of Hereditary Defects," in Victor McKusick and Robert Clairborne, eds., *Medical Genetics* (New York: HP Publishing Co., Inc.: 1973), 247.

33. Jane Jenson, "Getting to Morgentaler: From One Representation to Another," in Janine Brodie, Shelley Gavigan, and Jane Jenson, eds., *The Politics of Abortion* (Toronto: Oxford University Press, 1992), Chapter 2.

34. See for example, the Royal Commission on the Status of Women's statement on abortion; the statements in *Chatelaine* magazine, including the firebrand feminist editorials written by Doris Anderson; and the policy documents from Canada's first national abortion rights organization — the Association for the Modernization of Canadian Abortion Laws (AMCAL): Canada, *Report of the Royal Commission on the Status of Women* (Ottawa, 1970), 287; Mollie Gillen, "Our New Abortion Law: Already Outdated," *Chatelaine* (November 1969); Doris Anderson, "Change the Abortion Law Now," *Chatelaine* 43 (September 1970); Mollie Gillen, "Why Women Are *Still* Angry Over Abortion," *Chatelaine* (October 1970); "Canadian Conference on Abortion, sponsored by the Association for the Modernization for Canadian Abortion Laws," November 7 and 8, 1967, Ottawa (National Archives, MG 281350, File 2-15).

35. It is likely that some women would have considered abortion on these grounds liberatory; our point is that the argument for abortion on these grounds was not articulated as serving the interests of women, unlike the arguments for abortion on the grounds of women's health or rape. Rayna Rapp's research on women's experience of prenatal diagnosis suggests that some women do see amniocentesis as a way of minimizing the chances of increased burden that might attend the birth of a child with a disability. See, "Accounting for Amniocentesis," in S. Lindenbaum and

M. Lock, eds., *Knowledge, Power and Practice: The Anthropology of Medicine and Everyday Life* (Berkeley: University of California Press, 1993); "The Power of 'Positive' Diagnosis: Medical and Maternal Discourses on Amniocentesis," in D. Bassin, M. Honey, and M. Mahrer Kaplan, eds., *Representations of Motherhood* (New Haven: Yale University Press, 1994). Rapp has also acknowledged that these understandings of "burden" take place in the context of few social and health services for people with disabilities. See, "Risky Business: Genetic Counseling in a Shifting World," in J. Schneider and R. Rapp, eds., *Articulating Hidden Histories: Exploring the Influence of Eric R. Wolf* (Berkeley: University of California Press, 1995).

36. G. (D.F.), "Factum of the respondent," Winnipeg Child and Family Services (Northwest Area) v. G.(D.F.) in the Supreme Court of Canada (on appeal from the Court of Appeal in the Province of Manitoba), 1997; Winnipeg Child and Family Services (Northwest Area) v. G. (D.F.), Court of Appeal of Manitoba, 12 September 1996; Winnipeg Child and Family Services (Northwest Area) v. G. (D.F.), Court of Queen's Bench of Manitoba, 13 August 1996; Winnipeg Child and Family Services (Northwest Area) v. G. (D.F.), Supreme Court of Canada, 31 October 1997; Winnipeg Child and Family Services (Northwest Area) v. G. (D.F.), "Factum of the appellant," Winnipeg Child and Family Services (Northwest Area) v. G. (D.F.) in the Supreme Court of Canada (on appeal from the Court of Appeal in the Province of Manitoba), 1997.

37. Canadian Abortion Rights Action League, "Factum of the intervener, Canadian Abortion Rights Action League," Winnipeg Child and Family Services (Northwest Area) v. G.(D.F.) in the Supreme Court of Canada (on appeal from the Court of Appeal in the Province of Manitoba), 1997; Women's Health Rights Coalition, "Factum of the intervener, Women's Health Rights Coalition," Winnipeg Child and Family Services (Northwest Area) v. G.(D.F.) in the Supreme Court of Canada (on appeal from the Court of Appeal in the Province of Manitoba), 1997; Women's Legal Education and Action Fund, "Factum of the intervener, Women's Legal Education and Action Fund," Winnipeg Child and Family Services (Northwest Area) v. G.(D.F.) in the Supreme Court of Canada (on appeal from the Court of Appeal in the Province of Manitoba), 1997.

38. Alison Prentice, Paula Bourne, Gail Cuthbert Brandt, Beth Light, Wendy Mitchinson, and Naomi Black, *Canadian Women: A History* (Toronto: Harcourt, Brace, Jovanovich, 1988), 354.

39. Canada, "Canadian Charter of Rights and Freedoms" (Ottawa, 1982); "R v. Morgentaler in the Supreme Court of Canada," in Eike-Henner W. Kluge, ed., *Readings in Biomedical Ethics: A Canadian Focus* (Scarborough, ON: Prentice Hall Canada, 1993), 338–352.

40. Ibid.

41. There have, however, been efforts to restrict legal abortions and to restrict abortion access, and feminists cannot be sanguine. See, Brodie, Gavigan and Jenson, eds., *The Politics of Abortion.*

42. "Factum of the appellant," 6.

43. Kirk Makin, "Court Puts Mothers Before Fetuses," *The Globe and Mail*, 1 November 1997, A1.

44. In analyzing this material, we are assisted by Dorothy Smith's reading of the case-making process. Smith contends that an ideological circle "structures how individual circumstances appear as cases. This structure gives the case its 'facticity.' By entering the information according to relations that govern the case-making process, and ultimately, society, the professionals can claim that what they write is a true and accurate depiction of all relevant information." Dorothy Smith, *The Conceptual Practices of Power: A Feminist Sociology* (Toronto: University of Toronto Press, 1987), 89–100.

45. "Factum of the appellant," 7.

46. The majority decision was in line with Canadian law that recognizes the fetus as having personhood only if and when born alive. Any changes to this fundamental precept of Canadian law would have to be undertaken by the federal legislature, the judges argued. Tort law actions that grant the fetus legal interests in its health are actionable, however, if the fetus is born alive, and this may well be an important site for further legal challenges to women's reproductive rights. (Many thanks to Lorna Weir for this insight.)

47. "Factum of the intervener, Canadian Abortion Rights Action League," 15; "Factum of the intervener, Women's Health Rights Coalition," 30; "Factum of the intervener, Women's Legal Education and Action Fund," 21.

48. "Factum of the intervener, Women's Legal Education and Action Fund," 22.

49. Karen Swift, *Manufacturing "Bad Mothers": A Critical Perspective on Child Neglect* (Toronto: University of Toronto Press, 1995).

50. Nevertheless, the interveners do vary in the extent to which the embodied person, rather than a particular set of social relations such as the state, serves as the locus of moral responsibility: Compare Alan Young, "Moral Conflicts in a Psychiatric Hospital Treating Combat-Related Posttraumatic Stress Disorder," in George Weisz, ed., *Social Science Perspectives on Medical Ethics* (Dordrecht, The Netherlands: Kluwer Academic Publishers, 1990), 65–82. Young found that while workers recognized the possibility of multiple selves for the purposes of treatment, ex-soldiers were made morally accountable for their actions during their tour of duty in Vietnam. The political actors and social forces involved in the war all but disappeared from view in the clinical setting.

Chapter 18

MOTHERS FOR "HIRE": WHY DO WOMEN FOSTER?

Baukje (Bo) Miedema

MOLLY DELARONDE, born to a methadone-addicted mother, was taken to hospital with critical head injuries. Her foster mother was charged with assault.[1] Stories like this one are common in the popular media. Many problems with child welfare services in Ontario, British Columbia, Manitoba and New Brunswick have been reported. All of these provinces have initiated inquiries into these problems in their child welfare services. Although not all children in care of child welfare services end up in foster care, the majority do. In general, there is a sense in Canada that child welfare services, particularly foster care services, are in crisis. Some of the factors that deepen the sense of crisis are that today more children are coming into care than was the case ten years ago, the children entering care tend to have multiple problems and fewer families are willing to foster.[2] Furthermore, many reports about abusive foster care placements appear in the media and do not give foster care a positive image. But what really goes on in a foster family? What type of work is involved in caring for a foster child? Child welfare agencies and media reports use the term "foster and family" to acknowledge that foster care is considered a family responsibility. However, in reality it is the foster mother who does the day-to-day caring.[3] This is referred to as "gendered care." How do foster mothers feel about what they do?

This chapter is based on a study I conducted between 1993 and 1994 to find out foster mothers' views of fostering. Voices of other players such as biological mothers, social workers and foster children are not included. The fact that these voices are not included does not indicate that they are not important. The study focused solely on foster mothers because they are a group of women whose voices are seldom heard. Even though they are the backbone of the child welfare system in Canada, their work is almost completely invisible.

The study consisted of two phases: a survey sent to all 635 foster families in New Brunswick (return rate of 275 surveys or 45 percent) and twenty interviews with foster mothers. The survey package contained a blue card which could be returned if a foster mother was interested in being interviewed. Ninety-three percent of the returned surveys were answered by foster mothers. Of the 174 women who indicated that they were willing to be interviewed, twenty were randomly selected. Because the foster family community in New Brunswick is small, I will not indicate the location of the interview and the identities of the foster mothers in order to protect them.

THEORETICAL DEFINTIONS OF MOTHERING

The theoretical definition on mothering is somewhat bifurcated: it relies on either a social construction or a biological explanation of mothering. Neoconservative feminism and liberal feminism both argue that women's mothering is inevitable and that society should strive to make mothering as rewarding as possible without changing the patriarchal structures in society.[4] On the other hand, feminists grounded in psychoanalysis and radical feminist thought argue that mothering is socially constructed. Nancy Chodorow[5] states that mothering is a culturally learned activity, not the result of biology alone. Chodorow sees mothering as the outcome of a psychological process. She argues that mothering is a role model that is conveyed differently to sons and daughters. Radical feminists see motherhood as being exclusively socially constructed and the inevitable ultimate outcome of patriarchy.[6] The goal for women, according to radical feminists, should be to abolish "motherhood as an institution and the domestic responsibility of women."[7] Radical feminists reject the notion that women's experiences should be viewed as being different from men's. They focus their inquiry on the various social aspects of exploitation, originating in the relations between biological and social reproduction, and on the subjective division of public and private domains. Regardless of the theoretical framework explaining mothering, they all deal almost exclusively with biological mothering[8] and ignore women who mother other women's children. Nevertheless, a theoretical understanding of (biological) mothering is important and imperative in analyzing women's roles in society, including the role of foster mothers. What is equally important is to listen to and understand how a group of women, in this case foster mothers, construct and make sense of their own caring practices.

PROFILE OF FOSTER MOTHERS
IN NEW BRUNSWICK

Based on the survey data, it is possible to sketch a profile of foster mothers in New Brunswick. The foster mothers in my study lived throughout the province and the number of French- and English-speaking foster mothers parallels the province's linguistic makeup — roughly one-third of the foster mothers spoke French as their first language, and roughly two-thirds spoke English. Because New Brunswick has a rather homogenous ethnic population and the Aboriginal communities have jurisdiction over their own child welfare system, the vast majority of foster children and parents belonged to the white dominant racial group. Therefore issues around ethnicity did not surface.

All but 13 percent of foster mothers were married with the rest being single, widowed, divorced, separated or living in a common-law relationship. These numbers reflect the unstated assumption of the New Brunswick Department of Health and Community Services that foster mothers should be married. The average age of the foster mothers was forty-three years. Most of them still had some or all of their own children living at home. In general, the foster mothers' own children were teenagers with an average age of nineteen years. Foster mothers and their families lived predominantly in rural areas (81 percent) and the vast majority (88.9 percent) were actively involved in a variety of religions, including Roman Catholic and Pentecostal.

More than half of the foster mothers were "stay-at-home" women (54.8 percent). One-quarter of the foster mothers worked outside the home full time and a further 20 percent worked outside the home part time. The occupations they practised ranged from hairdresser to short-order cook to manager. On an educational level, almost half of the foster mothers had finished high school (47.6 percent), while nearly one-quarter (23 percent) had some postsecondary education, ranging from community college to university.

Of the spouses of the foster mothers, the majority worked outside the home (63.9 percent), one-sixth (17 percent) worked part time and the rest were unemployed or retired. The spouses' occupations or professions ranged from labourer to university professor. On average, however, the educational level of the spouses was lower than that of the foster mothers. Almost half of the foster mothers had finished high school compared with 36 percent of their spouses.

Finally, fostering was a long-term commitment for these foster mothers, who had volunteered to care for children apprehended by the state. They received only financial compensation for the cost incurred by caring for a child, and that was often not enough. The women who responded to the survey had been fostering for seven years on average, and had cared for an average of thirteen foster children during their individual fostering careers. Thus, once committed to fostering, foster mothers in New Brunswick tended to stay with it.

WHAT KIND OF CARE DO THEY PROVIDE?

The role of the foster mother and other foster family members is to provide the apprehended child with "the stability of a substitute family."[9] Foster mothers in New Brunswick occupy a unique and central role in the delivery of foster care services. This role is shaped by their belief in mothering and carried out within a framework of provincial rules and regulations. Foster mothers are often sandwiched by the demands of the foster child, the demands of their own family members and the demands of the state. These demands not only bring conflict, but are characterized by paradoxes and contradictions. For example, for a foster mother to spend time with her troubled teenage foster child, she may have to devote less time to her own children.

In New Brunswick, foster mothers provide twenty-four hour care to troubled children for the cost of the child's room and board in the foster family's home. As part of their contractual relationship with the state, as well as the taken-for-granted notions concerning the role of parenting, foster families agree to accept children on short notice (often only two to three hours before the placement); receive little information on the child's present problems or past difficulties with the law or education system; transport and accompany the child to medical and therapeutic services; provide ongoing academic support to the child, including daily assistance with school work; offer physical care including the provision of meals, lunches, laundry and a clean living space; and provide emotional support and counsel to multiproblem children in a frequently tense environment.

The most frequent descriptions foster mothers offered about the type of caring they provided to foster children was rooted in mother care and not in professional care. One foster mother stated that "I treat them like my own" and "I make them part of the family." This sentiment was repeated by almost all of the foster mothers. A fifty-five-year-old foster mother, who had five children of her own, explained it this way:

> We just do as a family would do, as we always do. I'm a mom. I make sure that they are out of bed in the morning, I make sure that they are clean, I make sure that they have plenty to eat, I make sure that they are happy. If they're down, I do things, that's it. There is nothing more, there is just family. There is no other way to say it, that's it. I just take care of them ... That is what I mean by family; it is based on an everyday routine thing. The love and care and all the things that go with it and they are no different than my own kids.

Another foster mother, who was thirty-four years old, working full time as a counsellor and raising her own two children, described how she cared for her foster children:

> ... you make them a part of your family. Don't make them an outcast. Don't treat them as the outsider. You try and integrate them into your family activities, into things that they like to do. You do it as a family and ... every day you go on as a family. This is how you do it ... They need protection, they need to be loved, they need to be accepted, they need to know that they are okay. They need their self-confidence and their self-esteem back and you treat them as family. They are family and you treat them as family.

The foster mothers felt that they provided care to other children from within the family unit, drawing upon their experiences as a mother, and they did this without any special expertise — they were not family counsellors, they were not therapists, they were not teachers. They were mothers and they mothered their foster children. The care they provided encompassed a multitude of different tasks, including physical care (cooking, laundry, and so on) for the child, representing the child's interests and protecting the child from others. The foster mothers wanted to take care of other women's children because they wanted to mother them. They felt that mothering was not a learned activity and that mothering skills come naturally when women bear children.

This view created difficulties for foster mothers when they had to interact or were confronted with the foster children's biological family. As a result, they wanted little contact with the children's biological mothers, choosing instead to regard her as a failed mother, for whom there was little hope of change.[10] Foster mothers clung rather tightly to their attitudes about the biological parents of foster children because these views were so often reinforced by unsuccessful home visits.

FOSTER MOTHERS AND THE BIOLOGICAL FAMILY

Because the foster mothers saw fostering as an extension of mothering, they were reluctant to engage with the biological parents of the foster child. All foster mothers interviewed, except for one, reported ambivalent feelings toward their relationship with the foster child's natural parents. By and large, the women would rather not have any contact with the foster child's parents or other family members of the foster child. On the other hand, many foster mothers recognized that if the reunification of the biological family was to have any chance of being successful, the foster children had to have contact with their parents or their family. However, as a group, the foster mothers were very skeptical about family reunification, particularly when the foster child's family was not offered any assistance to solve their own family problems. As one foster mother expressed her frustration, "I was trying to explain [that] to social services — how can you fix a problem just by removing the children and putting the children back six months later without those parents having been helped?" The foster mothers endured the contact with the biological family of their foster child because they felt that they had no choice — the courts or the social worker had ordered the visits.

Besides seeing the biological parents as "failed" parents, there were a number of other reasons foster mothers did not like contact with the foster child's family. Sometimes the foster mothers felt unsafe when they had to interact with a parent who was perceived to be violent. However, in many cases the foster mothers did not like contact with the foster child's parents because they felt strongly that their role was to protect the foster child. They seemed to feel that they failed the child when they had any extended contact with the foster child's family. The reasons for these sentiments were rooted in the fact that many foster children were distressed when they returned from a visit with their family. In some cases, for a couple of days after the visit the foster children were difficult to handle, but above all, the children were sad, depressed or angry because the visit did not work out the way they had anticipated. As a result, foster mothers viewed the foster child's parents in rather negative ways. This feeling was exacerbated when foster mothers knew that the foster child had been abused by the biological parents.[11] A thirty-four-year-old woman who cared for foster children along with her own two children explained her feelings and actions about the foster children's parents.

> ... these people have lost their right to parent. They lost that right, they proved themselves unfit. I don't want any contact with them; it only will make my job worse because the child is not going to respect me and listen to my rules if they can keep going back to the natural parents. It won't work.

Another foster mother who worked on her farm and cared for her biological and foster children agreed that the children come first: "We are here for the children not for the parents. I feel that it is not my problem but the social worker or something like that. I am here for the children."

Foster mothers also sensed that sometimes the foster child's parents considered the foster parent as the "enemy," as someone who had taken their child away. At best, the relationship between the foster mothers and the foster child's parents was uncomfortable, emotional and rocky; at worst, it was hostile.

THEORIZING FOSTER MOTHERING

Foster mothers view on mothering seem to correspond to the neoconservative feminist and liberal feminist view of mothering: women's mothering is inevitable and society should endeavour to make mothering as rewarding as possible. Foster mothers see their primary role toward the foster children as being the mothering role, and this role has given them a sense of worth. The state, however, has encouraged and exploited this because it has been completely dependent on this ideology for providing a pool of women who are willing to care for other women's children without receiving any wages for their demanding labour. Foster mothers are scrutinized and investigated by the official representatives of the state to be certified "good" mothers, while the foster child is "rescued" by the same agency from a "failed" mother. Karen Swift argues that:

> When children are removed from the care of their mothers, the proposed remedy is the "rescue" of the child(ren) from the mother, usually leading to the substitution of another mother for the original deficient mother. That the work and responsibility is passed on to another woman is seldom questioned.[12]

The fact that foster mothers see their caring as an extension of their mothering experiences explains why they are willing to foster without getting any financial rewards for their work: "mothering is a labour of love." Ironically, the ideology of mothering held by foster mothers, and encouraged by the state, may appear to challenge emerging social work notions about the importance of family reunification. Much of the difficulty a foster mother experiences from contact with the child's biological family is linked to her perception of her own role as foster mother. As long as these women see themselves as the mother who "rescues" the foster child and provides that child with mother love and mother care, family reunification will appear to undermine both their role and purpose. Because many foster mothers see their own care deeply rooted in their mothering experiences and skills, which are believed to be within the repertoire of every woman who bears a child, it is not an accident that these women are very reluctant to interact with the "other" mother. Undoubtedly, the reluctance of the foster mothers to have contact with the foster child's biological mother is in large measure a result of the conflict of the two mothering roles.

The foster mothers interviewed for this research had enjoyed their own mothering experiences and wanted to recreate that part of their lives, even though most of these women still had children living at home.[13] For many of the women interviewed, fostering gave them a sense of self-worth and increased ther self-esteem. They were appreciated and admired for the difficult job of fostering.

The state encourages women in their views of foster mothering. It wants women to feel good about themselves and to believe that what they do is "good," but not hard. In one pamphlet used to recruit foster families, the phrase "no skills required" reveals how the state interprets foster mothers' caring. The state is reluctant to view foster mothers' care as anything other than this because, in the short term, this is economically beneficial to it. The majority of children in the care of the Department of Health and Community Services in New Brunswick are cared for at little cost to the state.

These women's love for mothering, however, disadvantaged the state because deeply rooted caring and biological understanding of mothering made it difficult for foster mothers to interact with the biological mothers. Furthermore, the foster mothers' views hindered some innovative programs designed to make fostering a joint venture between social workers, foster mothers and biological mothers so as to perhaps provide the best possible care and outcome for a child in foster care.

Despite these hindrances, foster mothers continue to be the backbone of the child welfare service and continue to be exploited by the state because they are women who derive their identity and satisfaction from their love for mothering.

Notes

1. Robert Matas, "Foster Parent Hard Job to Fill," *The Globe and Mail*, 19 May 1997, A1.

2. Provincial Government of New Brunswick, *Playing for Keeps!* (Fredericton: Office for Childhood Services, 1991).

3. Karen Swift, *Manufacturing "Bad Mothers": A Critical Perspective on Child Neglect* (Toronto: University of Toronto Press, 1995); Martin Kendrick, *Nobody's Children* (Toronto: McMillan of Canada, 1990).

4. Francine Descaries-Belanger and Shirely Roy, *The Women's Movement and Its Currents of Thought: A Typological Essay* (Ottawa: CRIAW/ICREF, 1994).

5. Nancy Chodorow, *The Reproduction of Mothering: Psychoanalysis and the Sociology of Gender* (Berkeley, CA: University of California Press, 1978).

6. Rosemarie Tong, *Feminist Thought* (San Francisco: Westview Press, 1989).

7. Descarries-Belanger and Roy, *The Women's Movement and Its Currents of Thought*, 16.

8. Chodorow, *The Reproduction of Mothering*; Christine Everingham, *Motherhood and Modernity* (Philadelphia: Open University Press, 1994); Meryle Mahrer Kaplan, *Mother's Images of Motherhood* (London: Routledge, 1992); Amy Rossiter, *From Private to Public* (Toronto: The Women's Press, 1988); Joyce Trebilcot, ed., *Mothering: Essays in Feminist Theory* (Totowa, NJ: Rowman and Allanheld, 1983); and Betsy Wearing, *The Ideology of Motherhood* (London: George Allen and Unwin, 1984).

9. Foster Care Pamphlet (Fredericton, NB: Health and Community Services, n.d.).

10. It is no surprise that foster mothers often saw the biological mothers as failed mothers because it justified their own jobs as foster mothers. But more importantly, foster mothers saw mothering very much as a biological issue and not as a social construction. Therefore, many foster mothers did not see that, sometimes, socioeconomic issues such as poverty and other issues such as past abuse can result in difficulties in caring for children. Perhaps one reason foster mothers may not easily link poverty to difficulties with mothering is because many foster mothers themselves have low incomes.

11. The majority of children in care of the state are apprehended because of neglect. A smaller group of children have been physically or sexually abused.

12. Karen Swift, "Contradiction in Child Welfare: Neglect and Responsibility," in Carol T. Baines, Patricia M. Evans, and Sheila Neysmith, eds., *Perspectives on Social Welfare* (Toronto: McCelland and Stewart, 1991), 161.

13. Only one of the twenty foster mothers interviewed had entered fostering with a view to adoption. This woman had no biological children. She had adopted one of her foster children and was in the process of finalizing the adoption of her second foster child.

STUDY NOTES

ONE OF THE intentions of this book is to provide a broad perspective of interpretations of motherhood which might be useful for students of women studies, sociology, history and courses on Canadian culture. In this final section we offer suggestions to deepen the reflective reading of this book as well as to extend research and discussion possibilities based on our own experiences as course instructors. Specifically, we have selected three currently favoured methodologies to consider: Reflective Journal Writing, Case Studies and Thematic Research Projects. In each methodology, chapters that might lend themselves to each approach will be identified along with a brief example of how each process could evolve. Since topics and themes overlap throughout the book, there is no linear order that needs to be followed.

REFLECTIVE JOURNAL WRITING

In order to truly understand any phenomenon, students need to do more than simply acquire facts. They need to engage in a conscious inner dialogue that promotes the expression of one's own beliefs, ideas and strong feelings. We believe that developing such beliefs and ideas is not a solitary event, but that it occurs in an ongoing conversation with peers and with text. Journals address these learning needs by promoting critical reflective thinking of problematic, ambiguous and mulitdimensional issues. They offer open-ended possibilities for students to extend and broaden their conceptual frameworks and to consider opposing ideas by standing back from their own perspectives and moving beyond a dualistic absolute stance. According to Elaine Surbeck, Eunhye Han and Joan Moyer, journal writing addresses "the important function of integrating course content, self-knowledge, and practical experiences."[1] In addition, Chris Anson and Richard Beach point out that a "journal serves as a forum for grappling with a host of voices representing a host of others' beliefs and attitudes" in which students "learn to connect the inner dialogue with the outer dialogue."[2] By sharing journal entries in class, students oscillate between self and a community of selves and begin to appreciate that their interpretations of knowledge and text vary from person to person. Journal writing prior to class discussions also helps students formulate their thoughts and provokes more substantive dialogue.

When introducing journal assignments, it is important to encourage students to describe their prior experiences with journal writing. Many students often find journal writing to be time-consuming or intimidating. They may be reluctant to put their heart-felt thoughts on paper, feeling that this invades their privacy. Reflective journal writing is spontaneous, exploratory and subjective, which might make some students feel uncomfortable and resistant at first. By showing actual samples of academic journals, students are made aware that these journal entries are not personal diary disclosures or a series of mini-essays, but that the focus is kept on an academic (rather than a confessional) level instead. In order to ease students into this less scholarly academic genre, guidelines can be provided to help them structure entries that encourage fluency and confidence. Samples of guidelines we have found to be useful in our own classes are listed below.[3]

STRUCTURING JOURNAL RESPONSES

1. A simple framework of questions or headings such as "reaction, elaboration and contemplation" offers students categories for writing in their journals as well as provoking progressively deeper levels of thinking: (1) to "recall" the main points of the essay (factual information only), (2) to indicate something they "resonate" with (draws on feelings, attitudes, opinions and relates to personal experience), (3) to "resist" or argue with the author (involving a theoretical stance or principles grounded in research), and(4) to ask probing questions, point out gaps or biases, or offer new insights or opinions (a critical stance).

2. Using Venn diagrams (intersecting cirles), tree maps or concept webs might also encourage comparisons of key issues raised.

3. A list of generic topics to focus freewriting might include a fond memory of my mother, a difficult dilemma as a mother, my advice

as a mother, things I admire about other mothers, my biggest regret as a mother, something I wish I had told my mother, by biggest disappointment as a mother, how I have changed as a mother/daughter over time, mothers I remember from TV, film or literature.

4. Open-ended questions that progressively broaden the scope of understanding might include "What does it say, what does it mean, what does it mean to me, and what does it mean to the world?"

5. Prompts that encourage reactions to readings and classes as well as personal recollections might also engage students in journal writing: Write about why this class is enjoyable, frustrating, challenging. What do you spend the most time on or avoid doing? What are you discovering about yourself? Write about doubts and how you cover them up. How do your own biases and stereotypes come into play? What aspects of this issue do you resist or critically oppose? How would you handle this situation in a different way? I was impressed by ... I wonder about ... I disagree with ... This reading makes me feel ... It was interesting that ... An alternative solution might be ...

6. Students can create a dialogue of different voices that offers different perspectives on a topic. For example, in response to Baukje Miedema's report on foster mothering in Chapter 18, students might create a fictitious dialogue between the foster mother, the biological mother, the child taken into foster care and the social worker. Another example could be a dialogue developed from Chapter 15 in which Yeoman's daugher and her great-grandmother discuss their notions of race and gender. Conversations between famous people, celebrities or historical characters such as Virginia Woolf, Audre Lorde, Margaret Atwood, Alice Walker or Madonna could also be created.

7. Two-way conversations can also be developed between the "self" and the "alterego" to create a confrontational inner dialogue with the self. A line is drawn down the centre of the page and reflective notes are written on the left side. After a period of time these notes are read again and response notes are juxtaposed on the right side that challenge, question, analyze or probe more deeply into the initial responses and personal life events that are brought to mind.

Students can also use the right-hand column to formulate reasons for their initial responses, consider underlying assumptions, confront personal biases and social norms and reflect on dissonance in their own perceptions.

8. Peer dialogue journals whereby entries are exchanged with an instructor or peer might also appeal to some students who prefer more social interaction and reciprocity from an immediate, trusted audience. E-mail entries could be considered as well. In some cases, students may be more open and uninhibited with other students than with the course instructor. Journal entries can be used to create a classroom community and to build positive relationships between class participants by asking students to pair up at their own discretion or by assigning response partners (considering gender, culture and theoretical orientation). Specific guidelines for offering positive, encouraging feedback as well as how often and when to exchange entries are recommended. A sample of a typical exchange might be helpful to provide as well.

9. If time permits, in-class journals can eliminate the time-consuming process of writing journals at home and avoid the tendency for some students to reluctantly fill the page to beat the deadline without putting much thought into the responses. During class discussions, the class is stopped and students are asked to write their thoughts about the topic.

10. Students may be encouraged to clip articles from newspapers or magazines that relate to chapter readings and write critical responses to these current events in their journals.

11. Course instructors are also encouraged to keep journals that record reactions to their own teaching.

GUIDELINES FOR EVALUATING JOURNALS

It is difficult to evaluate journal entries without interfering with honest, authentic responses especially if students' thoughts reflect personal experiences, negative reactions to the course or opinions that differ from the instructor's or the readings. Standardized criteria for evaluation are unrealistic and students often feel these are intrusive, unfair or extremely biased. Evaluations of this nature will even encourage some students to write to please the evaluator, which defeats the whole purpose of journal writing. It is important to keep in mind that journals reflect ongoing knowledge construction rather than final outcomes and, as such, it is more beneficial for instructors to *respond* to work in progress rather than *evaluate* completed products. With this in mind, journal readers (instructors or peers) should offer *descriptive* rather than *judgemental* comments and provide feedback on entries that represent changes in the writer's thinking or struggles to confront limitations imposed by their personal beliefs, knowledge and biases. Four indicators of transformation that should be evident in effective journal writing are: (1) identifying one's own emerging doubts or self-contradictions when comparing earlier entries to current understanding, (2) acknowledging that former views have been challenged by some external theory or event, (3) re-examining the evidence that supports former beliefs, and (4) constructing a new alternative perspective or set of beliefs.[4]

The most essential component of journal writing, however, involves the critical re-reading of one's own entries at a later point in time (for example, mid-term or end of term) in order to reassess and analyze the relevant implications that emerge. If journals are to be used for evaluation or grading purposes by the instructor with some degree of standardization and satisfaction, then the focus of this evaluation can only be the students' own critical reflections on their own journal work. Therefore, instructors should periodically require students to submit two-page written critical self-analyses of their journal writing. Providing guidelines for this critical self-analysis will help students look for the major themes and prevailing ideologies in their own thinking as well as changing patterns or shifting perspectives that evolve as their knowledge broadens and expands. Here are some suggested criteria and guidelines for students to use in evaluating their own work:

1. In preparing a written critical analysis of your journal, you will first need to ask yourself, "What does this journal material mean to me *now* and how have my concepts changed?"

2. Assess your ability to write descriptively: kind of language used, is

it detailed? does it bring back the moment? a sense of how processes unfolded?

3. Categorize topics that you address throughout your journal (jot these in the margins or use a highlight marker to identify significant issues and patterns throughout the text). What do you write about the most? the least? or tend to avoid? It is important to dig deeply into issues you find unsettling.

4. Re-read previous entries and identify significant settings, people, events, processes and rules/norms that you repeatedly make reference to, or compare your reactions to the text based on references to external authorities versus those based on your own personal experiences and beliefs. For example, you may find it revealing to note that most of your entries focus on mothering at home or in the private milieu rather than in public or institutionalized settings. You might conclude that this focus represents personal tensions in you own home environment, adding new dimensions to chapters that discuss lesbian motherhood, pressures to have children and give up careers, or abilities to negotiate egalitarian domestic divisions of labour. Conversely, you might decide that you have never been consciously aware of the influence of public authority on ideologies and stereotypes of motherhood and that you now realize that you have the option of examining, questioning and resisting these restrictions.

5. As part of the evaluation process, you might include your own self-evaluation by assessing the level of your own metacognition. In re-reading your journal, assess your ability to move beyond a simple "retelling or recalling" of main points of the chapters to more indepth levels of inquiry. For example:

   • "engaging" with the text and characters to identify personal feelings and concerns;
   • "inferring, explaining, and elaborating on" issues with reference to theory comparisons, peer dialogues or class discussions;
   • reflecting on different "voices" in your entries;
   • "identifying" relevant subcultures and norms;
   • "connecting and cross-referencing" different chapters, issues and previous entries;

- "interpreting" meanings based on larger issues or populations as well as your own experiences;
- formulating "critical judgements and opinions" in which you draw on personal feelings and attitudes to resist, argue, agree or offer resolutions to problems; and
- asking deeper "probing questions" of the text.

CASE STUDIES

Many of the essays in this book are based on complex personal problem-centred stories or autobiographies that are situated in both physical and emotional contexts that involve specific intention, time and place. Mothering acts often preclude tacit understandings, resulting in vague assumptions and a great deal of unexamined thinking. Using case analysis to problematize and write about one maternal issue may encourage a greater level of precision and articulation. As ethnographic phenomenological studies, the following chapters are particularly suitable for use as case studies because they represent underlying taxonomies of broader categories or multiple representations of actual experiences that merit more serious consideration and reinterpretation:

Chapter 1 (mothers' influences on children's schooling);
Chapter 2 (lesbian parenting);
Chapter 5 (splitting the self/body as mother and scholar);
Chapter 10 (deciding to remain child free);
Chapter 12 (mother loss),
Chapter 15 (constructing racial identity through oral
    family history).

Cases are "complex educational instruments that appear in the form of narratives"[5] and are drawn around interdisciplinary real-life problems concerning real people. According to Lee Shulman, "Cases engage our attention, lodge in our memory, and capture our commitment"[6] and play a valuable role in connecting theory to the wisdom of practice. The case method is a relatively new pedagogical technique. It utilizes an active learning process that encourages students to identify universal themes, apply theory, generate their own analysis, modify generalizations and debate all sides of an issue in a class discussion.[7] As students are challenged to consider alternative readings and multiple layers of meanings, these compelling and persuasive multidimensional stories can be transformed into more propositional forms of knowledge. As cases, these stories can become catalysts for reflective inquiry and dialogue and also be used for a variety of purposes:

(1) to draw out and reflect on underlying themes and related issues (such as guilt, mother blame, control, oppression, choice, boundaries and transcendence);

(2) to identify problems, analyze situations and consider alternative solutions by carefully confronting the principles involved (for example, health treatments and support, legal policies, prejudice, matrophopia);

(3) to consider alternative perspectives (such as biological mothers, foster mothers, daughters or outside agents).

In an assignment suggested by Anna Richert,[8] students can be challenged to find a problem, issue or dilemma in one of the narrative essays and write a clear and precise two-page analysis about it. It is important that students be instructed *not* to read the discussion or conclusion section of the chapter until they have developed their own analysis. Each piece of writing must include a description of the specific context, the problem or universal issue and a variety of possible solutions. Copies of this writing are shared among groups of three or four students who are asked to provide written commentaries on both its content and its quality before discussing each issue as a group. Final revisions of each case analysis and related commentaries are then provided to all members of the class. Student versions of the cases can be used to stimulate larger class discussions by comparing these with the actual discussion and conclusions of the author.

A SAMPLE CASE STUDY APPROACH

Before reading Chapter 1, "Comparing How Mothers Influence the Education of Daughters and Sons," as a case study, invite students to think of how their own education during elementary, secondary and postsecondary levels was influenced by their mother or significant care-giver. Once they have identified these processes, encourage them to highlight the unexamined assumptions inherent in their recollections and problematize one issue or conflict that is brought to light by these reflections (for example, sibling rivalry, role-modelling, high expectations or controlling influences of mothers). Students can share these issues in a whole-class debriefing session in order to define universal themes that are repeatedly mentioned and to encourage students to make their own meanings and develop ongoing conceptual awareness. Students might even be encouraged to write their own case studies based on their personal family experiences. Next, students should read the chapter up to the conclusion and compare the universal themes raised by the class with those the authors selected to address (living up to mother's expectations, coping with school's limitations at various levels, uses of language to silence or control others and gendered standpoints at home and school).

Ask students to select one of the themes identified in the chapter and write a two-page in-depth analysis that includes (1) a description of the specific context (small, white, middle-class, well-educated families in urban Ontario — either traditional nuclear family or single-parent structure); (2) a significant problem or issue (sex-role stereotyping, inequitable divisions of labour and unexamined patterns of conformity and language use; self-esteem, silencing and reluctance to take action; contrasting self-images of males and females; disillusionment and frustration with mediocre and biased teaching and alternative ways of coping or resisting; assertive, controlling mothers with perfectionist ideals and guilt complexes; doubts, regrets and cultural pressures mothers experience about splitting attention between graduate studies, career advancement and home; economic and "insider" advantages; and diverse hegemonic assumptions about masculinity and femininity), and (3) the student's own thoughtful resolution to the problem chosen. This resolution must take into account various perspectives and relevant theory (for example, if the problem of patriarchal standards was selected, the student would justify their resolution to this problem by referencing current scholarly readings in this area).

One might argue, for instance, that patriarchal standards raise different dilemmas for (1) daughters (role-modelling the silence patterns of their mothers and resigning themselves the disempowering structures of school), (2) sons (caught between peer pressures of male culture and their mothers' commitment to feminism), and (3) feminist mothers (criticizing patriarchal norms that undoubtedly privilege their own sons, recognizing the impossible task of being ideal feminist models for their daughters, and imposing unrealistic expectations on themselves as "good" mothers and conscientious professionals). Resolutions to these perceived problems of patriarchal structures might include designing awareness workshops for teachers and gender equity curriculum for student teachers; deconstructing the images of daughters, sons and mothers in popular culture (for example, media and advertising) and suggested action plans (for example, activist letter writing to newspapers and magazines); and encouraging open and honest discussions at home and school about the realities of being a mother, son or daughter.

Foreshadowing questions can also be developed as an alternative pedagogical strategy for case studies. These can be assigned by the course instructor to raise the dilemma or universal themes in the case, to identify cause and effect relationships, to honour multiple realities and opposing perspectives, to encourage progressive focusing and problematizing and to consider alternative interpretations and resolutions.[9] Good case study questions do not lead students to isolate facts, but rather "encourage the application of knowledge in the examination of ideas ... in analyzing data and in proposing solutions ... to enable students to bring sharper analysis to bear on the issues and work toward deeper insights."[10] Opportunities should be provided for students to discuss their responses to these study questions. For example, questions for Chapter 1 might include, What are the key issues raised in this case? Is the point of view and the intention (or bias) of the author(s) readily apparent? What needs, feelings and problems were most strongly expressed by these mothers, sons and daughters? Whose behaviour here is problematic? What contradictions or tensions are evident? What alternative decisions or actions might have improved these situations? How do these mothers define the ideal image of the "good" mother? How do you think this image is influenced by socioeconomic standards, race or sexual orientation? How have these mothers advantaged or disadvantaged their children as academic "insiders" and as feminists? What specific challenges face the single mother in this case? Contrast the reactions of sons and daughters to their schooling and discuss possible reasons for the distinct patterns that emerged at various ages and levels. Compare how these mothers have influenced their sons and daughters. How could these mothers have provided more egalitarian structures for their sons and daughters? How do your own memories of maternal influences relate to the experiences of these families? Whose position do you relate with (agree with, disagree with) in this case?

An evaluation checklist of a case analysis might include the following: Are significant themes and problems identified? Are alternative perspectives addressed? Are the issues developed in a serious and scholarly way? Have sound assertions been made? Has adequate attention been paid to various contexts? Has current theory been applied to a persuasive discussion and resolution? Are personal biases examined?

THEMATIC RESEARCH PROJECTS

There are multiple perspectives and concepts to address throughout the book. Students might choose one of the following themes for an extensive research project. By comparing how these complex themes connect and overlap in the relevant chapters, an argument can be defined and substantiated with current theory. Here is a sampling of possible topics to examine:

body wisdom (Chapters 5, 7, 13, 16)

boundaries, barriers and categories (Chapters 1, 2, 3, 4, 5, 10, 11, 15, 16)

choices, rights, control/empower, oppression (Chapters 2, 3, 6, 7, 8, 10, 11, 14, 15, 17)

diverse and alternative structures of mothering (Chapters 1, 2, 7, 10, 11, 18)

domesticity, school and wage-earning conflicts (Chapters 1, 4, 5, 6, 8, 16)

equality and divisions of labour (Chapters 1, 5, 6, 8, 16)

loss: abortion, custody, illness and death (Chapters 7, 12, 13, 17)

guilt and self-doubt (Chapters 1, 2, 3, 7, 9, 10, 12, 13)

health and safety issues (Chapters 7, 13, 17),

ideals, stereotypes and myths (Chapters 1, 2, 3, 6, 9, 10, 11, 15)

influence of culture, religion or race (Chapters 10, 11, 13, 14, 15)

intergenerational relations (Chapters 1, 3, 7, 8, 9, 10, 11, 12, 13, 14) lesbian discourses (Chapters 2, 16)

mother-blame (Chapters 1, 3, 5, 9, 13, 18)

mothers of adolescents (Chapters 1, 2, 7, 9, 15)

multiple identities or roles (Chapters 1, 4, 5, 13, 15, 16, 18)

silences (Chapters 1, 2, 3, 5, 10, 11, 13, 14, 15)

socializing mothers and daughters (Chapters 1, 2, 3, 4, 5, 6,7, 8, 9, 15)

transitions, transformations and change (Chapters 6, 7, 8, 9)

Notes

1. Elaine Surbeck, Eunhye Park Hue, and Joan E. Moyer, "Assessing Reflective Responses in Journals," *Educational Leadership* 48, no. 6 (1991), 25.

2. Chris Anson and Richard Beach, *Journals in the Classroom: Writing to Learn* (Norwood, MA: Christopher Gordon Publishers, 1995), 40.

3. Many of these ideas are based on suggestions from Chris Anson and Richard Beach, *Journals in the Classroom: Writing to Learn.*

4. Richard Haswell, *Gaining Ground in College Writing: Tales of Development and Interpretation* (Dallas, TX: Southern Methodist University Press, 1991).

5. Selma Wassermann, *Introduction to Case Methods Teaching: A Guide to the Galaxy* (New York: Teachers College Press, 1994), 3.

6. Lee Shulman, "Toward a Pedagogy of Cases," in J. Shulman, ed., *Case Methods in Teacher Education* (New York: Teachers College Press, 1992), 23.

7. Rita Silverman, William Welty, and Sally Lyon, *Case Studies for Teacher Problem Solving* (Toronto: McGraw-Hill Companies, Inc., 1996).

8. Anna Richert, "Writing Cases: A Vehicle for Inquiry into Teaching Process," in Shulman, ed., *Case Methods in Teacher Education* , 155–174.

9. Robert Stake, *The Art of Case Study Research* (Thousand Oaks, CA: Sage Publications, Inc., 1995), 9.

10. Wassermann, *Introduction to Case Methods Teaching: A Guide to the Galaxy*, 4.

GLOSSARY

Amniocentesis: A procedure performed on pregnant women that involves removing a small amount of fluid from the amniotic sac for laboratory analysis. It is usually undertaken between the sixteenth and twentieth weeks of gestation to aid in the diagnosis of fetal anomalies. The procedure induces abortion in approximately 1 percent of women who undergo it.

Antinatalism: A feminist discursive strategy that resists notions of motherhood as enslavement that serve to oppress women and are directly opposed to emancipation and autonomy.

Binary: A simplified and often distorted mode of theory construction that recognizes only two opposing or dichotomous polarities without considering other complexities, variables, combinations or possibilities.

Biological/natural parent(s): May mean two biological parents but can also include one biological parent with a partner who is not biologically related to the child.

Biography: A feminist research methodology that utilizes narratives and life histories to uncover the reality and myths of women's lives and work by collapsing the traditional dissociations between women's private and public experiences. When the researcher discloses and analyzes her own life story, the term autobiography is used.

Body-subject: Maurice Merleau-Ponty's concept that all the elements of historical, social and political influences are brought together into the body, which represents a country or place or life-text where we live in felt experience and construct knowledge.

Cartesian: A descriptive term used to define Descartes' theoretical model of constructing a universal and singular world view based on his own existence as a self-reflexive thinking subject.

Child welfare agencies: In Canada, these are agencies that fall under provincial jurisdiction and therefore differ from province to province. Guided by the *Family Service Act,* their mandate is to protect children from being harmed in the home environment.

Constitutive outside: Describes an excluded realm that forms a determined "inside." Since what is "inside" is dependent on the "outside" for its definition, the binary between the two cannot hold: the inside is always part of what it is not. For example, the construction of heterosexuality is dependent on the "constitutive outside" of homosexuality which always threatens to return and disrupt heterosexuality's self-identity.

Cultural feminism: A theoretical perspective that attempts to revalue female experiences such as mothering by celebrating them as feminine traits.

Daughter-centricity: A subjectivity that is daughter-centred; viewing the mother solely from the perspective of the daughter.

Disablism: A point of view that assumes that biology which falls within average norms determines humanity, and that anyone whose physiology, biochemistry or appearance falls outside those norms is naturally incapable of conceiving, bearing or parenting children, forming an adult partnership, participating in paid employment, utilizing housing or transportation in an independent manner, attaining an education or participating fully as a citizen.

Discourse: A set of stories, texts, versions of events, people and places which generate social phenomena and, in circulating in the social field, can attach to strategies of domination as well as to those of resistance, resulting in important implications for social change. Meanings are negotiated through competing discourses.

Emancipatory research: A collaborative process of self-analysis in which the researcher joins the participants in the act of self-disclosure and the data is generated from people within relationships. The goals of this research are to encourage self-reflection and to create new ways of viewing or unravelling a situation or relationship that frees the person to consider options that were previously unimagined.

Equality: Being treated as equal.

Equity: Deliberately constructed practices that attempt to eliminate stereotypical bias and provide for inclusiveness and fairness for all involved parties.

Essentialism: A theoretical standpoint that privileges and universalizes women's social and biological experiences as a position from which to critique all human relations and as a consequence of this perspective reproduces a gendered and cultural power hierarchy similar to the patriarchal power structure that is being critiqued.

Eugenics: Science and policies that aim to improve the genetic composition of the human population. Compare with euthenics, the identification of means to improve the physical and social environment such that the quality of the population improves.

Familialism: A widespread and deeply imbedded ideology about how people ought to live. It argues that the best way for adults to live is in nuclear families as socially and legally recognized heterosexual couples who normally expect to have children.

Feminist pedagogy: A teaching philosophy and practice that acknowledges difference and positionality in students' experiences as a way of empowering and validating them as the unique creators of their own knowledge.

Feminist sociology: A field of study that allows the experiences and voices of women to be heard, thereby creating a place for their narratives within the academic discourse.

Feminist theory: A theoretical perspective that challenges traditional race-class-sexuality-power arrangements that favour men over women, whites over non-whites, adults over children, able-bodiedness over non-able-bodiedness, residents over nonresidents, and the employed over the unemployed. This viewpoint generally encompasses four concerns: (1) to understand the gendered nature of all social and institutional relations; (2) to problematize all gendered constructions and relate these to other inequities and contradictions in social life; (3) to view gender relations as historical and sociocultural productions which are subject to reconstitution; and (4) to advocate politically for social change.

Foster families: The main intent of foster families is to function as a substitute family for the foster child to help the child heal and pursue healthy life goals. Although the entire family is involved in caring for a foster child, it is the mother who does most of the day-to-day caring.

Gender: A culturally specific, relational domain through which differences in values, behaviours, attributes and practices are socially constructed, usually on the basis of normalized and presumed sexual differences.

Governmentality: Processes of governing, usually that operate only in part through the state. Government, by contrast, typically refers to control exercised by the state.

Gynocentric mothering: Characteristics and experiences of mothers defined by women.

Hybridity: The idea that cultures and ethnicities, rather than being pure and polarized categories, are intricately interwoven and overlapping.

Inauthentic mothering: A repudiation of one's own maternal perceptions and values by relinquishing authority to the dominant male culture.

Individualism: A set of prescriptions and ideals regarding the self, dominant in the "western" modern world, in which individual persons are understood to be transcendental, autonomous and self-directed subjects, whose source of identity, intention and agency is considered to lie inside the self.

Individuation: The development of separate but mutually interdependent lives.

Institution of motherhood: Characteristics of mothering roles defined and controlled by male universal authority.

Intersubjectivity: An egalitarian, reciprocal research relationship that acknowledges the mutual and two-way nature of the research relationship in which the researcher and the researched are both active participants in the social construction of knowledge.

L'écriture féminine: A mode of writing that seeks to voice and celebrate the repressed feminine of the pre-Oedipal and pre-linguistic maternal space. Often termed "writing from the body," l'écriture féminine challenges the binarisms of phallocentrism and relishes in a textual play of difference, heterogencity, and plurality.

Liberal feminism: This viewpoint takes women's equality with men as its major political goal and focuses on learned gendered roles and the denial of opportunities as the primary causes of women's oppression. This standpoint argues for fairness and seeks to improve women's status by advocating equity and equal rights for men and women that includes: ending women's legal, economic, and social dependence on men; obtaining the freedom and equal opportunity to acquire training and education; promoting open and unbiased competition; and enacting laws and policies that guarantee equality of choice and opportunity for all. Second-wave feminists also seek married women's access to waged labour, parental sharing of childcare, protection of maternity and special treatment for disadvantaged groups of women.

Marxist feminism: This perspective views women's oppression and economic dependence as originating with the introduction of private property, class systems and the division of labour by sex. This viewpoint emphasizes that childcare and housework have no exchange value and relegates women's public work to a secondary status.

Maternal epistemology: To know, understand or claim a particular authority and knowledge based on experiences of mothering.

Matrophopia: The fear not of one's mother or of motherhood but of becoming one's mother.

Metanarrative: An overarching narrative that explains a central aspect of life or the world.

Mother-blaming: A psychodynamic tradition that attributes fault to mothers for the range of their children's problems and is based on an acceptance of absolute maternal responsibility.

Motherline: Reclaiming knowledge of female ancestral roots and uncovering the archetypal mother's wisdom of the ancient worldview that connects body and soul of all life forms. By encountering female ancestors who struggled with similar difficulties in different historical times, a woman gains carnal knowledge of her own body, becomes grounded in her feminine nature and acquires a life-cycle perspective that softens her immediate situation. The motherline provides a way for women to understand their life stories and gain female authority.

Narrative: Knowledge or experience communicated in story form.

Neoconservative feminism: This stance argues that women's mothering is inevitable and that society should strive to make mothering as rewarding as possible without changing the patriarchal structures of society.

Nuclear family: A family composed of two heterosexual parents and their offspring living in the same household, typically with the male as the major (or only) breadwinner. A model of family that is generally assumed, in western societies, to be the "natural" or the best family form.

Oral history: Individual stories of lived experience, often the stories of people neglected by traditional historians.

Other: The idea that we give ourselves an identity in opposition to someone different, an "other" (for instance, male/female, black/white, and so on).

Othermothers: Women who assist bloodmothers by sharing mothering responsibilities.

Perfect mother: Idealized, sentimentalized or trivialized images of motherhood and assumptions about how "good" mothers should think and behave. These mythical notions are usually unattainable and unrealistic expectations of a selfless, available care-giver that tend to limit the full potential of women and girls, especially their ability to have a realistic and meaningful relationship with each other.

Phallogocentric: A merging of the words "phallocentric" and "logocentric," signifies a discourse founded on the concepts of transcendent unity and authority represented by both the phallus and the logos. A phallogocentric discourse aligns "man" with reason, truth and origin, thus positing a secure place of departure for all definitions of experience.

Phenomenology: A human science that studies persons and begins with the world as they immediately experience it. It attempts to investigate layers of experience as it is lived, rather than as it is conceived. As well, it seeks to describe people's orientations to their lived experience as well as to bring a reflective awareness to the nature of the events in their lives. It invites a personal engagement and a dialogical response from readers and challenges them to compare or contrast their own experiences with the phenomena described.

Postcolonialism: The study of formerly colonized regions, nations or peoples that usually includes an emanicpatory agenda.

Postmodernist feminism: This position seeks to establish egalitarian and nonexploitive modes of research. It resists taking a position that presumes a unitary, static self or that assumes we could ever come to know a self and seeks to interrogate the exclusionary operations by which positions are established in the first place. It questions the idea that individuals comprise stable, coherent and rational subjects which are unattainable and lead to various forms of oppression.

Postmodern lesbianism: An eclectic feminist stance also known as "queer theory" that connects the analysis of sexism with heterosexism. While foregrounding the marginalization of lesbians from women's studies this theoretical perspective also refuses to centre or naturalize earlier feminist discourses. It attempts to deconstruct binary models of female sexuality in order to develop a more complex way of imagining sexual differences by repositioning the relevance of lesbianism and feminism in a variety of ways. Some theorists reject the preoccupation with boundary-keeping and favour universalizing the minority category of lesbianism thereby making queerness a theoretical perspective that is open to anyone regardless of sexual experience or identity. Other theorists advocate that essentialist notions of identity are a politically disastrous reverse discourse and argue instead for "denaturalizing" gendered identities and encouraging them to be seen as performances.

Poststructuralism: An umbrella term to refer to the range of theoretical positions developed from the works of Derrida, Lacan, Kristeva, Althusser and Foucault that share fundamental assumptions about language, meaning and subjectivity. Poststructuralists argue that language constructs reality rather than merely reflecting it and that meaning is constituted through language and not inherent in things themselves or created from the subject who speaks it. Consequently, subjectivity is a site of change and conflict as opposed to a stable and unified identity.

Pre-Oedipal: The Freudian term for the first two to four years of life where the child is not aware of sexual difference. The pre-Oedipal stage ends at the moment of the Oedipal crisis where the girl child, upon seeing her brother's penis, turns away and against the mother, blaming her for her own absence of a penis (a response Freud called "penis envy"). The boy, in turn, upon realizing his sister does not have a penis, renounces his love for his mother fearing castration by the father (a response Freud called "the castration complex").

Privatized mothering: Mothering organized in such a way that individual mothers (rather than the community) bear responsibility for meeting their children's needs.

Qualitative methodology: An approach to research that values personal voice, life histories, collaboration and transformation. It emphasizes understanding subjective everyday experience and meaning-making as a multilayered construction of multiple and partial realities rather than seeking proof of universal truths. Participants in these studies are acknowledged as experts of their own contextual experience and holistic meanings are shared and negotiated between researcher and participants. In this framework, the knower and the known cannot be separated.

Queer theory: See postmodern lesbianism.

Radical feminism: This point of view advocates that women's oppression is the most significant form of human oppression and results from culturally learned roles and patriarchal positioning of autonomous power. One of the goals of this position is to reject or abolish motherhood as an institution and with it the domestic responsibility of women.

Reductionism: The limited assumption that significant characteristics of the social order are those derived from individuals who live within its constraints.

Reflexivity: To be reflective and sensitive to all forms of communication, as a researcher, in order to understand both the knower and the known.

Relational development theory: The idea proposed by Nancy Chodorow that well-adjusted sons separate from their mothers while daughters identify with their mothers.

Self-governance: The legal position that defends reproductive freedom/autonomy and women's rights through choice, assuming a certain level of moral obligation, rational decisionmaking, self-management and social suasion in the pursuit of health.

Semiotics: A philosophical theory of signs and symbol meanings that stand for and represent something else. Semiotics teaches how to read and interpret signs.

Situated knowing: The idea that what we know, believe and value is always relative to our time and place in history and to our own experience.

Socially constructed knowledge: The idea that knowledge is not fixed, objective and permanent but, rather, is produced through discourse and discursive practices in relation to others.

Social feminism: This perspective views women's relationship to the economy as the origin of women's oppression and seeks to dismantle barriers of class, gender, sexuality and race in public and private spheres. Gender is viewed as a social, political, ideological and economic category that is shaped by capitalism, exploits women in the work force and devalues unpaid labour, reproductive work and domestic roles.

Subjectivity: The description or interpretation of an experience from the perspective or position of the person engaged within the experience.

Subjugated knowledge: Trivialized, marginalized or discredited knowledge that is lost or silenced as a result of circulating outside of the accepted boundaries of the master narrative or universal discourse (patriarchal).

The Semiotic: A term coined by the French feminist theorist Julia Kristeva that is linked with the pre-Oedipal of Freudian theory. The Semiotic refers to the prediscursive "language" of the prelinguistic and pre-Oedipal mother-child space. This "language" is characterized by fluidity, heterogeneity, plurality and excess, the original primordial language of the body. The Semiotic is opposed to the Symbolic, the phallocentric language of patriarchy. The Semiotic continually re-emerges in language to interrupt and disturb the symbolic. Kristeva defines melody, laughter, word play and rhythm as semiotic interruptions.

Universalization: A limited, naive or distorted world construction that imposes a singular interpretation, significance and authority based on the viewer's biased and privileged standpoint.

CONTRIBUTORS

SHARON ABBEY has an Ed.D. in curriculum studies (OISE/FEUT) and is an Assistant Professor of Education at Brock University as well as a founding member of the Centre on Collaborative Research. Previous to this, she worked for twenty years as an Ontario elementary teacher, program consultant and school principal. Sharon Abbey serves on the Board of Directors for the National Foundation of Body Image and Eating Disorders and recently received the FWTAO Ruby Kinkaid Doctoral Studies Award and the President's Grant to co-ordinate a Speaker's Series on Body Image and Eating Disorders. She currently teaches social studies curriculum courses in the Faculty of Education as well as a course on mothers and motherhood in the Women's Studies Department.

KATHERINE ARNUP is the Director of the Pauline Jewett Institute of Women's Studies and an Associate Professor of Canadian Studies at Carleton University. She is the editor of *Lesbian Parenting: Living with Pride and Prejudice* (Charlottetown, PEI: gynergy, 1995; 1997), and the author of *Education for Motherhood: Advice for Mothers in Twentieth-Century Canada* (Toronto: University of Toronto Press, 1994), as well as numerous articles on lesbian mothers and legal issues.

KAREN A. BLACKFORD is a sole-support mother, a disabled woman, a Northern Ontario resident and a former tenant in public and then co-operative housing. Her research, writing, organizing and advocacy have focused on areas related to these personal experiences. She is Associate Professor of Nursing and Human Development at Laurentian University and a board member of the Canadian Research Institute for the Advancement of Women (CRIAW).

JOYCE CASTLE is currently an Associate Professor in the Faculty of Education at Brock University where she teaches reading and language arts courses and works with student teachers and teachers in the field to promote professional development, teacher thinking, school-university collaboration and gender issues within these contexts.

MIELLE CHANDLER is a usually single, definitely queer, ex-welfare mom living in a closet-sized apartment in Toronto. She is a graduate student in social and political thought at York University where she pursues her fascination with maternity and political philosophy when not washing the dishes.

ALICE COLLINS is Professor of Education, Memorial University of Newfoundland. She teaches courses on legal and moral issues in education and school reform and governance. Her research interests include women in education and school councils.

ELIZABETH DIEM, RN, PhD has practised or taught nursing since 1963. She taught in the School of Nursing at Lakehead University in Thunder Bay, Ontario, for ten years and in 1997 moved to Ottawa to teach at the University of Ottawa. Her research interests include the study of the welfare of adolescent girls.

RISHMA DUNLOP teaches in the Department of Language Education at the University of British Columbia. Her poetry, prose and scholarly essays have been published in numerous books and journals including *Literator, Journal of Educational Thought, Educational Insights, Room of One's Own, Inkshed, Whetstone* and *English Quarterly.*

CATHERINE FOOTE is a feminist social worker who specializes in grief research and therapy. She is currently writing her doctoral dissertation for the Faculty of Social Work, University of Toronto, on the experiences of parents who have had a child die.

BONNIE FOX has been teaching sociology since 1976 when she was also a member of the Toronto Women's Press collective. She has published a number of articles on feminist theory and women's position in the labour force and the home. She now teaches sociology at the University of Toronto. Since 1989, when she became a mother, she has been working on the study of first-time parents.

SYLVIA HAMILTON is a filmmaker and writer who lives in Halifax, Nova Scotia. Her films have won awards and have been screened in festivals in Canada, the United States, Europe and the Caribbean. She was the co-founder of the New Initiatives in Film (NIF) program at the National Film Board's Studio D. Her literary and nonfiction writing has appeared in a variety of Canadian journals. She was a contributor to and co-editor of *We're Rooted Here and They Can't Pull Us Up: Essays in African-Canadian Women's History*, published by the University of Toronto Press in 1993. She is a graduate student in education at Dalhousie University in Halifax, where the focus of her work is African Baptist women and community activism.

NINA LYON JENKINS is currently a PhD graduate student at the University of Georgia in the Department of Child and Family Development. Her areas of concentration include ethnic minority families, specifically Black families and Black motherhood, and identity issues for women of colour. She has completed a graduate certificate in Women's Studies at the University of Georgia and plans to finish her degree program in December. Her dissertation research is a qualitative study of the subjective experiences of Black middle-class, middle-aged mothers. Nina and her husband, Kevin, have three children, Simone (13), Sierra (8) and Stephan (6).

MARTHA MCMAHON is an Associate Professor of Sociology at the University of Victoria where she teaches in the areas of gender, women and the environment, and qualitative methods. She has worked in a variety of government-sponsored programs for immigrant women, sole-support mothers and women on social assistance. She is the author of *Engendering Motherhood: Motherhood and Self-Transformation in Women's Lives* for which she won the American Sociological Association's Sex and Gender Section Book Award for 1996.

BAUKJE (BO) MIEDEMA was born in Friesland, Holland. She trained and worked as a psychiatric and a general nurse in Groningen and Utrecht, The Netherlands, until she moved to Canada in 1981. In 1984 she moved to Fredericton, NB, where she completed her bachelor's degree at the University of New Brunswick in 1987. In 1986 she became involved with Women Working with Immigrant Women and has been involved ever since. In 1990 Baukje completed her MA and in 1995 her PhD at the University of New Brunswick. Since 1993 she has been on the board of CRIAW (Canadian Research Institute for the Advancement of Women). Baukje is also the co-ordinator of a research team affiliated with the Muriel McQueen Fergusson Centre for Family

Violence Research. The research team is examining family violence in immigrant communities in New Brunswick. Baukje is the author of numerous scholarly research papers. As of January 1998 she will be a SSHRC post-doc with the Muriel McQueen Fergusson Centre for Family Violence in Fredericton, New Brunswick.

FIONA ALICE MILLER is a PhD candidate in history at York University. Her dissertation is entitled "A Blueprint for Defining Health: Research in Medical Genetics, 1949–1979."

ANDREA O'REILLY is an Assistant Professor in the School of Women's Studies at York University where she teaches a course on Toni Morrison and on motherhood and mothers and daughters. She has presented her research at numerous international conferences and is the author of more than a dozen articles and chapters on these topics. She was the co-ordinator of the first international conferences on Mothers and Daughters, 1997, and Mothers and Sons, 1998, sponsored by the Centre for Feminist Research at York University. In 1998 she was the recipient of the "University-Wide" Teaching Award for Contract Faculty. She is the author of *Toni Morrison on Motherhood,* forthcoming from Ohio State University Press. Andrea and her common-law partner of sixteen years are the parents of a thirteen-year-old son and two daughters, ages eight and eleven.

CECILIA REYNOLDS is an Associate Professor in the Faculty of Education at Brock University and the Chair of the Department of Graduate Studies, as well as the founding Director of the Women's Studies Program. Since receiving her doctorate in education from the University of Toronto, she has continued to conduct research and publish work on gender equity concerns in education, including cross-generational and cross-cultural perspectives. She is the co-editor of *Women and Leadership in Canadian Education.*

MELANIE ROCK is pursuing a PhD in anthropology at McGill University. The working title of her thesis is "Uncertain Futures: Genetic Research on and Testing for Breast Cancer, Spina bifida and Down Syndrome."

ERIN SOROS is completing her Master of Arts in English at the University of British Columbia. Her work has appeared in the journals *Fireweed* and *Tessera* and in the anthology *Eye Wuz Here* (Douglas & McIntyre).

ARLENE TIGAR MCLAREN is Associate Professor of Sociology in the Department of Sociology and Anthropology at Simon Fraser University. Her publications include studies on women in adult education, the history of birth control and abortion, feminist sociology, feminist analysis of schooling and girls' and boys' accounts of their schooling. Her recent research focuses on traditional schools in BC and on immigrant family settlement in the Vancouver area.

MARY VALENTICH, PhD, is a Professor in the Faculty of Social Work at the University of Calgary, recently "early retired." She is a Registered Social Worker with the Alberta Association of Registered Social Workers, and a Certified Sex Educator, Counselor and Therapist with the American Association of Sex Educators, Counselors and Therapists. Her scholarly and practice interests are feminist social work practice, human sexuality and career management.

ANN VANDERBIJL received her MA in the Department of Sociology and Anthropology at Simon Fraser University. She has taught at Kwantlen University College. She has a particular interest in critical medical anthropology and her areas of research have included ethnicity and conceptualizations of health; chronic illness; immigration; sexual abuse and embodiment; elder abuse; women and tobacco; and the effects of housing on the health of disadvantaged women.

ELIZABETH YEOMAN, PhD, is an Associate Professor in the Faculty of Education at Memorial University of Newfoundland where she teaches courses in second language teaching and curriculum and critical educational theory. She also teaches in Memorial's interdisciplinary Women's Studies program. Prior to this appointment she taught French, English and Spanish in New Brunswick, Quebec, Ontario and Bolivia. Her current research interests are teachers' narratives and social justice, teacher education, and issues of race, culture and identity.